ARM

REPORT

OF THE

WAR OFFICE COMMITTEE

OF

ENQUIRY INTO "SHELL-SHOCK."

Presented to Parliament by Command of His Majesty.

The Naval & Military Press Ltd

in association with

The Imperial War Museum
Department of Printed Books

Published jointly by
The Naval & Military Press Ltd
Unit 10 Ridgewood Industrial Park,
Uckfield, East Sussex,
TN22 5QE England
Tel: +44 (0) 1825 749494
Fax: +44 (0) 1825 765701
www.naval–military-press.com
www.military–genealogy.com

and

The Imperial War Museum, London
Department of Printed Books
www.iwm.org.uk

ARMY.

REPORT

OF THE

WAR OFFICE COMMITTEE

OF

ENQUIRY INTO "SHELL-SHOCK."

Presented to Parliament by Command of His Majesty.

LONDON:

PRINTED & PUBLISHED BY HIS MAJESTY'S STATIONERY OFFICE

To be purchased through any Bookseller or directly from H.M. STATIONERY OFFICE
at the following addresses: Imperial House, Kingsway, London, W.C.2, and
28 Abingdon Street, London, S.W.1; 37 Peter Street, Manchester;
1 St. Andrew's Crescent, Cardiff; or 23 Forth Street, Edinburgh.

1922

Price 6s. 0d. net.

Cmd. 1734.

TABLE OF CONTENTS.

CONSTITUTION OF THE COMMITTEE.

Chairman :

    The Right Honourable Lord SOUTHBOROUGH, G.C.B., G.C.M.G., G.C.V.O., K.C.S.I.

Members :

    T. BEATON, Esq., O.B.E., M.D., M.R.C.P. (Admiralty).

    J. L. BIRLEY, Esq., C.B.E., M.D., F.R.C.P. (Air Ministry).

    C. HUBERT BOND, Esq., C.BE., F.R.C.P., M.D., D.Sc. (Board of Control).

    Sir MAURICE CRAIG, Kt., C.B.E., M.D., F.R.C.P. (Ministry of Pensions).

    Wing-Commander MARTIN FLACK, C.B.E., M.B. (Air Ministry).

    H. W. KAYE, Esq., M.D. (Ministry of Pensions).

    HAMILTON C. MARR, Esq., M.D., F.R.F.P.S. (Board of Control for Scotland).

    Surgeon-Captain E. T. MEAGHER, R.N. (Admiralty).

    Colonel (Hon. Brigadier-General) J. G. S. MELLOR, C.B., C.M.G., K.C.

    Sir FREDERICK W. MOTT, K.B.E., F.R.S., M.D., F.R.C.P.

    Major A. D. STIRLING, D.S.O., M.B., R.A.M.C. (A.M.D.2, War Office).

    W. ALDREN TURNER, Esq., C.B., M.D., F.R.C.P.

    STEPHEN WALSH, Esq., M.P.

    Major W. WARING, C.B.E., M.P.

Secretary :

    Major W. R. GALWEY, O.B.E., M.C., M.B., R.A.M.C.

Cost of the Committee :

	£	s.	d.
Travelling expenses of Members and Witnesses	929	12	1
Extra duty pay to Military Members	35	5	0
Cost of printing and presentation to Parliament	149	0	0
	£1,113	17	1

The Committee have taken into full consideration the terms of reference submitted to them by the Army Council on the 12th day of August, 1920. The reference is as follows :—

" To consider the different types of hysteria and traumatic " neurosis, commonly called ' shell-shock '; to collate the " expert knowledge derived by the service medical autho- " rities and the medical profession from the experience of " the war, with a view to recording for future use the " ascertained facts as to its origin, nature, and remedial " treatment, and to advise whether by military training or " education, some scientific method of guarding against its " occurrence can be devised."

This reference was the outcome of a debate initiated by Lord Southborough in the House of Lords on the 28th April, 1920, when he moved for a committee to investigate the subject of what is commonly called " shell-shock." The motion was accepted by Viscount Peel, then Under-Secretary of State for War, on behalf of the Government, and the speeches delivered in the House of Lords upon the motion should be referred to in order fully to understand the genesis of the Inquiry.*

Work of the Committee.

We met for the first time on the 7th day of September, 1920. We have held 41 sittings and examined 59 witnesses The Committee have had the advantage of hearing evidence from a number of distinguished men representing opinion on the military, medical and legal aspects of the case. We have also received the evidence of officers who have suffered from " shell-shock," and of men who have been the victims of one form or another of war neurosis. We have also had the opportunity of hearing the evidence of General Lord Horne, G.C.B. ; of Lieutenant-General Sir John Goodwin, K.C.B. ; of Air Vice-Marshal Sir John Salmond, K.C.M.G., and of many combatant and medical officers of great experience, men who served in France and elsewhere through the storm and stress of the most vigorous fighting of the war. Further, we had the advantage of listening to evidence from several well-known naval officers, who recorded that " shell-shock " as a disorder was of infrequent occurrence in the Navy. It should also be noted that members of the Committee had themselves a large professional experience of " shell-shock," and they were, therefore, in a position to approach the investigation with a foundation of knowledge, and with sufficient experience of the disorder in its various forms, to enable them to

---

* Hansard Parliamentary Debates, House of Lords, Vol. 39, No. 29, p. 1094, dated 28.4.20.

lay down the lines of investigation in such a way as to secure a full answer to the Terms of Reference. The Committee were, in fact, in a position, as a result of their expert knowledge, to hold from the outset of the inquiry that " shell-shock " is a grievous misnomer for the disorder or disorders grouped under that head; we recognised, however, that as " shell-shock " appears in the Reference and is the popular or vulgar term in general use we were constrained to retain it for the purposes of this report, and we have been content to print the term throughout in inverted commas and to use it as governed by the definition hereinafter referred to.

Delimitation of term " Shell-Shock."

At our first meeting we decided that for the purposes of the enquiry we would treat " Shell-shock " as falling under the following heads :—

(1) (*a*) Commotional disturbance ;
    (*b*) and/or Emotional disturbance.
(2) Mental disorders.

It will be convenient to state in general terms the reasons why the Committee unanimously agreed to work on this basis.

Use and Abuse of the Term.

We were charged with the duty of collating the expert knowledge derived by the Service medical authorities and the medical profession from the experience of the war, with a view to recording for future use the ascertained facts as to the origin, nature, and remedial treatment of " shell-shock." For this purpose we had to decide what " shell-shock " is and what it is not. Without going too deeply into the history of the origin of the term, we conclude that it was born of the necessity for finding at the moment some designation thought to be suitable for the number of cases of functional nervous incapacity which were continually occurring among the fighting units. Undoubtedly " shell-shock " signified in the popular mind that the patient had been exposed to, and had suffered from, the physical effects of explosion of projectiles. Had this explanation of the various conditions held good, no fundamental fault could have been found with the term. But with the extension of voluntary enlistment, and afterwards the introduction of conscription, it was discovered that nervous disorders, neurosis and hysteria, which had appeared to a small degree in the Regular Army, were becoming astoundingly numerous from causes other than shock caused by the bursting of high explosives. It was observed in fact that these conditions were perpetually occurring although the patient had not suffered from commotional disturbance of the nervous system caused by bursting shells. It even became apparent that numerous cases of " shell-shock " were coming under the notice of the medical authorities where the evidence indicated that the patients had not even been within hearing of a shell-burst. On the other hand, it became abundantly plain to the medical profession that in very many cases the change from civil life brought about by enlistment and physical training was sufficient to cause neurasthenic and hysterical symptoms, and that the wear and tear of a prolonged campaign of trench warfare with its terrible hardships and anxieties, and of attack and perhaps repulse, produced a condition of mind and body properly falling under the term "war neurosis," practically indistinguishable from the forms of neurosis known to every doctor under ordinary conditions of civil life.

The Committee recognised, therefore, from the outset of the inquiry that the term "shell-shock" was wholly misleading, but unfortunately its use had been established and the harm was already done. The alliteration and dramatic significance of the term had caught the public imagination, and thenceforward there was no escape from its use.

A combination of factors had led to a loose and indiscriminate use of the term "shell-shock," and a reconsideration of all the factors became imperative. From the technical point of view, as our colleague Sir Frederick Mott states in his valuable work on the subject of war neurosis, the conditions of functional nervous incapacity were in reality no new developments. Once their nature had been determined it was possible for the medical man who was previously familiar with the handling of cases of nervous and mental diseases to place each case under its proper caption. But, as Sir Frederick pointed out, only a comparatively few medical men prior to the war had had an opportunity of becoming thoroughly familiar with this very distinct branch of medicine, and it frequently occurred that a medical officer who was not so happily placed found himself in the position of having to deal with large numbers of such cases. Under the circumstances, therefore, with the official adoption of "shell-shock" as a technical term, with the feeling of not being justified in making a more definite diagnosis, with the desire to avoid the stigma to the patient of describing his condition as a mental disorder, the medical officer preferred, or was driven, to include any particular case under the more general but less implicating heading of "shell-shock."

Further, cases could be cited from experience of serious organic disease of the nervous system with mental symptoms, passing through medical establishments and emerging still labelled as "shell shock." Again it was not an uncommon event in work connected with the Ministry of Pensions to meet with cases of marked insanity which had been diagnosed from the time of their invaliding as "shell-shock," but in which there was no room for any question that the real nature of the trouble had been one of a developing insanity from the commencement.

Popular Use of the term " Shell-shock."

Bearing in mind the difficulties of the medical profession in dealing with these matters, it is no surprise to find that the general lay conception of the term was so very loose and ill-informed, and in this connection other important considerations had also to be weighed. The general sentiment of the public during the war found its expression in the statement that every man apparently physically capable should be sent to the Front, but at the same time there was much anxious solicitude as to the incapacitated, and such was the appeal of the term " shell-shock " that this class of case excited more general interest, attention, and sympathy than any other, so much so that it became a most desirable complaint from which to suffer. Moreover, to the relatives of a soldier who had broken down mentally, or who by reason of an inherently timorous disposition could not face the military life, or whose natural tendencies had led to his getting into trouble, the use of the term " shell-shock " came as a great relief. It may be said that to the public mind any condition which arose during the war and which gave rise to the assumption of irresponsibility of conduct by the individual concerned was to be ascribed to " shell-shock."

As regards the officially recorded cases of " shell-shock," there could be little doubt that included under this heading there were cases of many and various conditions. For instance disorders such as hysteria, anxiety neurosis, and mental troubles of many kinds ; and, the Committee are in agreement with the bulk of opinion in saying that all these conditions can be regarded as reactions of the individual under stress of environmental circumstances, that they are bound together by their dependence upon fundamental psychological laws, and that any one case may be found to exhibit the characteristics of two or more types of reaction. Thus a hysteric may show signs of anxiety neurosis and may also exhibit evidence of congenital mental defect, while his irresponsibility in any specific conduct may be due more to his degree of mental defect than to his hysteria.

Questions asked by the Committee.

The Committee having decided upon the definition of " shell-shock " undertook the preparation of a series of Questions for the guidance and consideration of witnesses. The object aimed at was the marshalling of evidence and the production of facts. These Questions indicate clearly the line and scope of our inquiry. We were glad to find that the witnesses concurred in our definition of " shell-shock " and that they were materially assisted in their evidence by following the Questions submitted to them. These will be found at length in Appendix No. 1.

Following on the circulation of these questions to witnesses we appointed three sub-committees to consider and advise upon several subjects germane to the general inquiry, namely :—

(a) Treatment of patients.

(b) Enlistment and observation of the recruit.

(c) Training and courts-martial.

The advice of these sub-committees presided over by Dr. Aldren Turner, C.B.; Dr. H. W. Kaye; and Brigadier-General Gilbert Mellor, C.B., C.M.G., respectively, has been accepted by, and is incorporated in, this Report, and the Committee are deeply indebted to the members of the sub-committees for their valuable work.

Before we make detailed reference to the précis of evidence there are several other matters of general importance to which the Committee desire to draw attention.

Absence of Statistics.

Unfortunately we have been unable to obtain any reliable statistics covering cases of " shell-shock." It would have been desirable to record the number of cases of the disorder under the general term " shell-shock," and to supply tables giving figures of the varieties of disorder classified under that head. The Committee have failed to obtain this information. Much statistical matter was unavoidably lost during the progress of the war, and other material of a statistical kind, buried in the archives of the War Office and other Departments is at present inaccessible. The Committee were advised by Lieutenant-General Sir J. Goodwin, that it could not, in fact, be obtained without a pro-hibitive amount of labour and expense and an expiration of time which would have postponed our Report until the Official History of the War is published; that publication which must be of supreme interest and importance will no doubt contain exhaustive information as to the casualties of the war.

On the other hand, we are satisfied that we can cover the terms of our Reference without this statistical evidence. We should have desired to quote statistics as a matter of general interest; but after a careful examination of some tables and figures put before us by unofficial witnesses, the Com-mittee is doubtful whether any statistics would be reliable having regard to the general conclusions at which we have arrived. The Committee have no doubt that the thousands of cases falling under the loose term " shell-shock " have in fact been returned on no uniform statistical basis and that the result at this date would be wholly misleading if an attempt were made to sift and sort them into sound and reliable categories. The want of statistics may be the subject of adverse criticism but the Committee find consolation in knowing that the term " shell-shock " is such a serious misnomer that any general statistics based upon that name must be of little practical value. The Committee have, however, considered here and there some statistical matter put before them upon adequate authority; this was found useful when illustrating certain specific points but we are conscious that even these figures were not compiled on approved statistical principles and must be treated as nothing more than an aid or illustration to make certain points with which the particular figures treat.

"Shell-Shock" and Neurosis in Former Wars.

Another question of interest is that of any history of "shell-shock" or war neurosis in earlier wars. The only direct evidence we have been able to find is the account of nervous injuries produced at a distance by the projectiles of war given by Professor Octave Laurent in his book, "La Guerre en Bulgarie et en Turquie," published in 1914. An extract from his work will be found in another place in this report. (*Vide* page 109.) As regards earlier wars our search for direct evidence was of no avail, and we suspect that in former wars a soldier who lost self-control was usually court-martialled and frequently suffered the penalty for the military crime of cowardice or of desertion. That we have no evidence of "shell-shock" in previous campaigns is not extraordinary, when it is borne in mind that the use of high explosives, of the violence and intensity developed in the recent War, was wholly unknown in the conflicts of the past. It is true that if we turn from the term "shell-shock" to that of neurosis or hysteria, we find, as may well be imagined, that there are references in history and in literature to the nervous symptoms and troubles among soldiers, which probably arose from anxiety and the wear and tear of battle and which may in certain cases have led to breakdown, producing some form of war neurosis.

In reply to an enquiry, the Honourable John Fortescue, the historian of the British Army, communicated to Lord Southborough the following interesting memorandum on the subject:—

"I am afraid that I find it quite impossible to contribute "anything of scientific value to the researches of the Com- "mittee upon 'shell-shock,' with its subsidiary manifesta- "tions denominated 'commotional-shock' and 'emotional- "'shock.'"

"The writers upon the wars of the past do, indeed, men- "tion occasionally details which bear upon the question; but "their narratives, generally composed some time after the "event, are not too trustworthy, and those of private "soldiers in particular are always to be regarded with "suspicion."

"That 'shell-shock' proper—that is to say, the shock of "an explosion—was not unknown is certain. For instance, "one of the engineer officers who blew open the Gate of "Ghuznee, in 1839, was so close to the petard when it "exploded that he was seriously shaken, and, while suffering

" from the shock, gave false information which imperilled
" the success of the assault. No one, in the circumstances,
" blamed him. On the contrary, everyone made excuses for
" him. He was unwounded."

" On the other hand, a drunken Irish soldier who was
" accidentally left inside the fort of Muchee Bhawn, outside
" Lucknow, when that fort was blown up in 1857, presented
" himself a few hours later before one of the gates of Lucknow
" with the words, ' Arrah, be Jasus, open your gates.' He
" had been blown up with the fort, but was none the worse,
" apparently not even quite sobered."

" No doubt there were men who, from one cause or
" another, broke down in every campaign; and I have little
" doubt that this was one of the causes that led to desertion.
" But such breaks down, when they are recorded, are not
" very sympathetically treated, and unless a man had proved
" himself of good courage earlier in action, are dismissed as
" not differing greatly from cowardice. Of course, numbers
" of men went out of their minds in the old campaigns, as
" they still do."

" The worst lot of men that we ever sent out to war
" were the reinforcements that went to Flanders in the
" middle of 1794 and to the West Indies in 1795-96. Both
" behaved infamously, as was to be expected from the scum
" of England gathered together by crimps; and I have no
" doubt that there was a good deal of emotional shock
" among them. But the men in Flanders had only canvas
" clothing in which to face a very hard winter, and those
" in the West Indies had to go through an arduous campaign
" in the tropics—the latter died almost to a man of yellow
" fever; the former melted away with cold and starvation.
" They notoriously included many boys of feeble intellect;
" but there are no details about them individually. Con-
" sidering the hardship to which they were exposed, it
" would not be safe to draw inferences from such details
" even if we possessed them."

" It is, I believe, a fact that even the bravest man cannot
" endure to be under fire for more than a certain number
" of consecutive days, even if the fire be not very heavy.
" Lord Byng, I am pretty sure, found this out in South
" Africa, after 80 or 90 days. My brother, Brigadier-
" General Charles Fortescue, had, in his column in South
" Africa, a Canadian officer who was a proverb for daring;
" but even this officer broke down for the time after every
" enterprise of any continuance and needed a fortnight's
" rest from fire to restore him. To this fact I attribute
" the occasional notices of the mysterious disappearance of
" tried old soldiers in former wars."

" Finally, can emotional or commotional shock, induced
" by battle, be differentiated from the like shock induced
" by other forms of catastrophe?"

" I saw the kit of one of the two survivors of the *Eurydice*
" sold on board H.M.S. *Dido* in 1882 or 1883. The man
" had deserted, and, as he was utterly unnerved and useless,
" the Captain (Compton Domvile) made no attempt to
" recover him. The Captain of the *Victoria*, I believe,
" never recovered the sinking of his ship, and certainly died
" soon after. I knew a lady who had gone through the
" siege of Lucknow, lost her husband and children there
" and married one of the relieving force. She was a happy
" wife and mother when I knew her, but she turned white
" and trembled at the word ' Lucknow.' Similarly, I knew
" a man who had survived the great volcanic explosion in
" New Zealand in 1886. He was a light-hearted person,
" but the word ' Tarawhera ' sufficed to unnerve him com-
" pletely. All of us can recall the like experience."

" It is curious that Marryat in his novels gives no instance
" that I can remember of men being permanently, or even
" temporarily, upset by an incident in a naval action.
" But he draws (in ' The King's Own,' I think) a very
" vivid picture of an officer going mad under the stress of
" shipwreck. Shell was not used in naval actions in
" Marryat's day (unless ships engaging land batteries) but
" the crash of falling top hamper and the flying of splinters
" after a broadside must have been very trying."

" Of course in old days noise played a less important part
" than at present, and men could *see* their enemies, which
" undoubtedly reduced the strain. The agony of terror
" caused by the missiles of an unseen enemy in old days
" can be measured by the accounts of Braddock's disastrous
" action on the *Monongahela* in 1755. On the other hand,
" the supreme trial of old days has no parallel in the present.
" This was ricochet round-shot, which men could see
" bounding towards them like cricket balls and could easily
" have avoided by stepping aside. But such stepping aside
" was, of course, forbidden, as it would have disordered the
" ranks, so the victim had to watch death or mutilation
" coming straight upon him, and not move an inch to
" escape it. Few troops could stand this ordeal. The British
" could and did, but they didn't like it ; and the trial must
" have been too much for the nerves of many."

References in Classical Literature.

Again, Sir Frederick Mott, in his book to which reference
has already been made, touches upon the psychology of terrifying
" soldiers' dreams "—a general and very distressing symptom
of war neurosis, which bars recovery until they disappear—and
gives several interesting quotations which have reference to such
dreams and their significance so true to recent experience.

Sir Frederick quotes Lucretius* :—

" And generally to whatever pursuit a man is closely tied
" down and strongly attached, and on whatsoever subject we
" have previously much dwelt, the mind having been put
" to a more than usual strain in it, during sleep we for the
" most part fancy that we are engaged in the same; lawyers
" think that they plead causes and even draw up covenants
" of sale, generals that they fight and engage in battle,
" sailors that they wage and carry on war with the winds.
" We think that we pursue our task and consign it when
" discovered to writings in our own native tongue. So all
" other arts and pursuits are seen for the most part during
" sleep to occupy and mock the minds of men."

And again, Lucretius* calls attention to the evidence of dreams
in animals :—

" And often during soft repose the dogs of hunters do yet
" all at once throw about their legs and suddenly utter cries
" and repeatedly sniff the air with their nostrils as though
" they had found, and were on the track of wild beasts."

And also in another passage :—

" Again the minds of men which pursue great aims under
" great emotions often during sleep pursue and carry on
" the same in like manner; Kings take by storm, are taken,
" join battle, raise a loud cry as if stabbed on the spot."

And apt reference is made by Sir Frederick to two passages in
Shakespeare which may have had their inspiration in the
quotations from Lucretius given above; one is the speech on
Queen Mab by Mercutio and the other that of Lady Percy to
Hotspur.

A man dreams of whatever pursuit he is closely tied down to;
in recent days the soldier dreamt that he was in the trenches
fighting Germans, he hears and sees the shells bursting, shouts
in his sleep and wakes with a start. How truly Shakespeare
describes this† :—

" Sometimes she (Queen Mab) driveth o'er a soldier's
" neck,
" And then dreams he of cutting foreign throats,
" Of breaches, ambuscadoes, Spanish blades,
" Of healths five fathoms deep; and then anon
" Drums in his ear, at which he starts and wakes,
" And being thus frighted swears a prayer or two
" And sleeps again."

(In the quarto 1597 the text had " countermines " instead of
" Spanish blades," which seems singularly appropriate now.)

---

* De Rerum Naturae.
† Romeo and Juliet. Act I, Scene 4.

In Lady Percy's speech to Hotspur there is the following passage* :—

" Why hast thou lost the fresh blood in thy cheeks;
" And given my treasures and my rights of thee
" To thick eyed musing and curs'd melancholy?
" In thy faint slumbers I by thee have watch'd,
" And heard thee murmur tales of iron wars;
" Speak terms of manage to thy bounding steed;
" Cry ' Courage ! to the field ! ' and thou has talk'd
" Of sallies and retires, of trenches, tents,
" Of palisadoes, frontiers, parapets,
" Of basilisks, of cannon, culverin,
" Of prisoners' ransom and of soldiers slain,
" And all the currents of a heady fight.
" Thy spirit within thee hath been so at war
" And thus hath so bestirr'd thee in thy sleep,
" That beads of sweat have stood upon thy brow,
" Like bubbles in a late-disturbed stream ;
" And in thy face strange motions have appear'd,
" Such as we see when men restrain their breath
" On some great sudden haste. O what portents are
  " these? "

These quotations so well known and hackneyed as some may think may be found to assume a new interest when considered in the light of the evidence on recent war neurosis.

The Committee will now turn to the all-important questions what " shell-shock " is and what it is not.

Without exception our witnesses condemned the term " shell-shock " and held that it should be totally eliminated from medical nomenclature.

Summary of the Evidence given by Witnesses.

Amongst the large number of distinguished witnesses who have given evidence before us there has been practical unanimity both in evidence and opinion on the subject of " shell-shock."

Their evidence has been of such weight and authority that we have determined to set out even at considerable length the opinions to which we have listened with close interest.

We have decided to print the summary of evidence of witnesses in the order which, in our opinion, gives the best connected story. For this reason no attempt has been made to establish an order of precedence ; nor have we separated witnesses who served with combatant formations from those who served with Medical units, or in an administrative capacity.

By so doing we feel that we shall best follow the terms of our Reference and " collate the expert knowledge derived by the " Service medical authorities and the medical profession from

---

* 1st Part Henry IV, Act II, Scene 3.

'' the experience of the war, with a view to recording for future
" use the ascertained facts as to its origin, nature and remedial
" treatment."

The evidence of these distinguished witnesses should remove
from the public mind any doubt of the true nature of " shell-
shock."

*Lieut.-General Sir John Goodwin, K.C.B., C.M.G., D.S.O.,
F.R.C.S., Director-General Army Medical Service.*

Lieutenant-General Sir John Goodwin said that he thought
everyone was agreed that " shell-shock " was an unfortunate
misnomer. It has covered a multitude of imperfections and, as
he understood the term, it included—

    (a) Shell concussion and,

    (b) War neurosis.

That was really the same as " Commotional " and " Emotional "
" shell-shock " and included neurosis and emotional conditions
occurring both in peace and war.

Shell concussion is very uncommon as compared with neurosis.
" This," Sir John added, " I satisfied myself about from my
" own experience."

On the question of the desirability of enlisting nervously
unstable men the witness said that nervous unstability was very
difficult to define; but that, from the point of view of the
examining medical officer, he took it to mean the man who is
nervous in his manner, apparently highly strung, and lacking
in self-confidence. Actual war is, in his opinion, the really final
and crucial test of nervous instability in a soldier, and he considered it very difficult to say at a recruit's examination whether
he would eventually become a good soldier or not. In the case
of officers, especially young officers, and more especially the first
time they are in action, he repeatedly noted that the fear
of being afraid amounted to an obsession. The more highly
strung a man is the more he feels that; but many men who are
apparently nervously unstable gain self-confidence and after
training become excellent soldiers.

The witness went on to say that he could not sufficiently
emphasise the importance of gradual sympathetic and really
efficient and thorough training as the best suggestion to offer
towards lessening or preventing " shell shock " in the future.
He was certain that troops who had been rushed through a short
period of training would be much more liable to break down
than those whose training had been more gradual and more
thorough.

He had been out in France with the original Army. With
the cavalry in the first place, then the Guards Division, and he
said that he really saw very little " shell shock " actually at
the front. He was certain that well trained and well disciplined
troops were less liable to suffer from these troubles, and by no

means the least important part of a soldier's training is the inculcation of *esprit de corps*, loyalty, pride in himself and his unit, and the old history of the regiment to which he belongs. That was very important indeed. It was very marked in the Guards Division. If we could have an ideal army in which every officer and every man was firmly convinced (and was proud of the fact) that he himself was one of those who formed the best company or squadron of the best regiment of the finest army of the best nation of the earth, we should see very little of " shell shock." Pride and prestige have a tremendous lot to do with it. He saw a great deal of that, and it was astonishing the pride taken in their regiment by men of the Guards.

" I am certain," said Sir John, " that troops which have been " well trained and disciplined have a tremendous advantage in " every way over those who have not been so well trained. I " shall never forget the original Expeditionary Force in the " retreat and the way they behaved. It was absolutely " magnificent and beyond all words. Those men were utterly " exhausted, wearied to the point of hardly being able to walk " and hardly able to keep awake. You could not put a man on " to a horse—I often tried to give a man a lift on a horse, but " he fell off from sheer exhaustion unless you held him on. " And yet those men were ready and not only ready, but eager, " to stop and fight at any moment. They were absolutely " splendid. I can never forget them or say enough for them. " I must frankly say that, in my opinion, they had an immense " advantage in that they were thoroughly well trained and were " proud of the units of the arm to which they belonged."

" In the field, of course, you must consider troops that have " had a thorough training and discipline and also the newly " joined troops. I am afraid here I am simply going to make " a lot of statements which are probably well known already. " The first is that the men should be very carefully looked after " in every possible way. As regards their comfort; attention " should be given to their cleanliness, baths, feeding, clothing, " recreation, the cooking of their meals, the serving of their " meals; in fact, everything which tends to make men comfort- " able, healthy, contented, and satisfied, as far as they can be, " with their surroundings. When troops are at rest, when they " are brought out for those comparatively short periods of rest, " as was done in the recent war, I think an immense amount " can be done in the way of making that period a period of real " rest, both physical and mental. I do not mean to say that " the men ought to be loafing about and doing nothing, but they " ought to be given change of occupation, games, dancing and " everything that will cheer them up, change of exercises, change " of environment and atmosphere altogether

" The third point that I have put down is that, if possible, " troops should not be left too long in one sector of the line. " While it is impossible to legislate for military exigencies, and " military exigencies are always arising, I think that if a unit

" has had a very bad time in one particular sector, it is a mistake
" to send it back to that part of the line if it can be avoided,
" but, of course, one has got to look at that from every point of
" view. On the other hand one particular sector of the line
" gets a bad name, for instance the Ypres salient. The troops
" naturally, although they did their best, did not like going there.
" I do not want to say anything against their gallantry; they
" were splendid; but no one loved the Ypres salient. I think if
" troops are going to a sector like that it would be almost better,
" after the unit had had a real bad doing, not to send them back
" there if it could be avoided, and that if another regiment or
" battalion were sent there, it would be more or less understood
" that they would have to take their turn there, but that after
" they had had a good bit of fighting they would be taken out.
" But again, military exigencies come in. It is not always pos-
" sible to do it and I realise that."

" On one point I do feel very strongly and that is that men
" should not be left too long in any lonely position or in a lonely
" nature of employment. It is very trying indeed for them."

" There is another point which I have left to the last, not
" because I consider it of least importance, and that is the ques-
" tion of Regimental Medical Officers. These officers can exert
" an influence on the regiment to which they belong, or to which
" they are attached, which is of incalculable benefit. I can never
" say enough for the medical officers I had under me both in the
" Cavalry Division and in the Guards Division. No words can
" show what I think of them; they were splendid; the pains and
" trouble they took with the men, the way they knew and worked
" with the men, was simply splendid; and even when a young
" officer was put to a regiment straight away it was astonishing
" how quickly he got to know the tone of the regiment and the
" different companies in the regiment and how hard he worked
" for them and the extraordinarily good influence he had with
" them."

Upon the question as to how emotional breakdown should be
regarded in a regiment from the military standpoint, Sir John
Goodwin thought that if a very large number of men break down,
without a very obvious cause, and are sent back, it would be
viewed with apprehension, possibly with suspicion. He had
never seen it happen, but held that opinion because one knows
that in a really good, well-trained, well-disciplined regiment, no
matter what the stress is, there is comparatively little in the
way of breaking down.

If, in the case of two regiments under similar conditions in the
line, one showed a considerable amount of so-called " shell-
" shock " and the other comparatively little, he thought it would
be evident that the former regiment was not as efficient as the
latter, and he personally would look to the officers to see what
their influence was with the men and how they were looking
after them; how close they were to their men and how much
they were believed in by their men. He would look to the

medical officers as to how they knew and understood their men. He thought it was inevitable that such a state would be detrimental to the honour of the regiment concerned.

He felt it quite possible that, if so regarded, " shell-shock " would be less likely to occur ; though the disorder itself must be looked upon as a genuine affliction.

General Lord Horne, G.C.B., K.C.M.G.

General Lord Horne told the Committee that when he first became acquainted with the term " shell-shock " he understood it to apply to " the immediate result of concussion caused by " close proximity to a violent explosion." He then found that it was afterwards applied—

" (1) to cases of loss of control of the mind or nervous " system, as the result of battle, and
" (2) later on to nervous breakdown due to strain."

He thought it probable that " miners and agricultural labourers, " and men who lived open-air lives, such as shepherds and game- " keepers, were less liable to the disorder than the clerk or arti- " san." He was of opinion that " shell-shock " was more likely to occur in troops which had not had experience of the line and that they became subject to it " during an engagement, or during " and after an engagement in somewhat different form."

He would put aside commotional " shell shock " which might come to anyone. It was the result of a blow, or whatever the medical term might be. He would put it entirely on one side. No man could avoid it. Also, " shell shock " in the nature of a wound he would put on one side. He agreed with the regimental opinion that a large number of " shell shock " cases in a battalion may be taken as a sign of poor morale. He did not state it in stronger terms and say that it was a disgrace. As an Army Commander he looked with disfavour on a unit in which there was much " shell shock." He placed it in the same category as a unit in which there were many little fingers missing on the left hand, viz., poor morale. He was in favour of doing everything possible to improve the morale of a regiment. A large number of cases of " shell shock " may result from poor morale, and poor morale may be due to failure in training to the proper state of efficiency. In addition to the ordinary sources of morale, such as justice of cause, pride in regiment, and supremacy in the use of weapons, etc., there is one thing that assists morale very highly—good food and good care taken of the men. It is not only bad morale but physical condition as well that influences " shell shock."

The General further said that he considered that " shell shock " became a serious factor in this war owing to the peculiar character of the war. The high explosives and bombardments had never been known before. He thought that in moving warfare we should not experience anything like it.

Major W. J. Adie, M.D., M.R.C.P., R.A.M.C. (Special Reserve); Physician Great Northern Central Hospital; Neurologist Min. of Pensions.

Another witness (Major Adie), who was asked to tell the Committee what he thought " shell shock " was, answered in these terms :—

" It seemed to me to cover all the various conditions which " have been described as ' shell shock ' in the late war.; I " should say any state of the mind or body engendered or " perpetuated by fear, which renders the soldier less efficient " or enables him to evade his duty with impunity. I have " thought about that, and I think we must admit that all these " conditions are either engendered by fear, or having been " engendered by something else, such as concussion, are per- " petuated by fear. I say ' renders the soldier less efficient ' " as many of us were suffering more or less from ' shell shock,' " which made us not so efficient, and yet we remained in the " line ; ' or enabled him to evade his duty with impunity '—I " mean by that that all sorts of people got out of the line with " so-called ' shell shock,' and the result was that they evaded " their full duty and yet were not punished."

When the witness was asked whether he considered that " shell shock " would arise not only in the individual from some strong commotion or emotion, but also in a body of men, he answered that that was certainly so. He instanced two battalions side by side in a well-known salient in France. In one the morale was good—it had a good colonel and officers and a good medical officer —and they had practically no men going down with " shell shock." The other battalion was sending ten men away at a time. " You could have foretold that it would be so by looking " to the men's appearance. In the good battalion the men were " always smart, but the others were bad soldiers with bad officers. " That is the crux of the matter. Keep up the morale of the " troops and you will not have emotional ' shell shock,' at least " you will reduce it tremendously."

This witness, following up Lord Horne's statement that the result of a blow might cause to any one commotional " shell shock," described his own experience of that form of the disorder. He added

" My opinion is that no man who has simply broken down " mentally should be given a wound stripe, but the man with " an obvious commotional shock who has been buried or blown " up deserves one. I distinguish rather sharply between the " two conditions."

" Large numbers of men suffered from hysteria during con- " valescence from the various diseases for which they had been " admitted to hospital. They all received the same sort of treat- " ment by rapid—what I might call Queen Square methods. The " most frequent symptom was aphonia. During one period I used

" to collect these cases once or twice a week and parade them in a
" surgical theatre in a tented portion of the hospital. I have had
" as many as a dozen men on one day. My method was to place
" the first patient on an operating table, and after explaining that
" his voice would certainly come back I gave him a whiff or two
" of ether. (I had no suitable electrical apparatus or I should
" have used it.) After a few whiffs the man would attempt to
" remove the mask I then said to him ' I shall remove the mask
" ' when you say " take it away." ' At the same time I pricked
" the skin over the larynx rather vigorously with a pin. Very
" soon the patient said in a tone of disgust : " Oh ! take it away."
" I then asked him for his name, number, regiment, etc., and
" after a short conversation sent him off.

" This was repeated on the second patient and perhaps on the
" third. By this time the rest of the men, who had heard every-
" thing, although they could not see what was going on, were
" easily caused to speak without the use of ether.

" There was no doubt in my own mind that these cures were
" permanent. The patients worked well about the hospital with
" the other convalescents and I never saw a recurrence.

" I think I can say truthfully that no patient was ever sent
" down the line from No. 7 General Hospital during my time as
" O/C Med. Div. for any functional nervous disorder."

*Lieut.-Colonel E. Hewlett, C.M.G., D.S.O., late Inspector of
Infantry Training.*

Lieut.-Colonel Hewlett observed that, " Ability to stand
" modern war depended almost as much on mental and nervous
" condition as upon physical condition. The term ' shell shock '
" has been wrongly used," he said, " and has popularly become
" accepted to include any man suffering from nerves. It really
" means the effect of the explosion of a shell so near as to ' knock
" ' a man silly.' I have seen cases of men who were apparently
" killed only by the shock of a large shell. That is, they bore
" no visible outward trace of wounds, but had been killed by
" ' shell shock.' Unfortunately, the term came to be applied to
" forms of nervous breakdown owing to stress, mental or physical,
" or both, and not necessarily to those who had actually received
" the ' shock ' of ' shells ' bursting close at hand. A battalion
" of real countrymen (less intelligence) will stick out a situation
" which a battalion of townsmen (greater intelligence) will not "

*Commander N. D. Holbrook, V.C., R.N. (late Submarine
Commander).*

Commander Holbrook, V.C., gave evidence before us and said
that he had " no experience of ' shell shock ' in the submarine
" service. There were cases of nerves, but under my command
" never anyone suffering from ' shell shock.' " He said he
could not distinguish " shell shock " from nerves. That was so

in the Navy. '' If you are a captain of a submarine and you have
'' nerves, you have no right to be a captain. All the men's lives
'' depend on you. They can do nothing, especially in a sub-
'' marine.'' There was nothing, as far as he knew, of the instinct of self-preservation being very omnipresent in the sailor
and the repression of the instinct of running away to avoid
danger did not show itself in morbid manifestations. He added :
'' I used to feel in an awful funk at times. It is absurd to say
'' you do not. I have yet to meet the fellow who will lie in his
'' ship at the bottom of the sea and be depth-charged and not
'' suffer from cold feet. I felt the strain, but did not realise it
'' at the time ; but when you go back to harbour you must have
'' rest. You feel like a washed-out rag. With all these mines
'' around you you do not want a depth charge too close to send
'' you to glory.''

*Professor G. Roussy, Faculté de Médecine de Paris, late
Consultant in Neurology to the French Army.*

The Committee also took evidence from Professor G. Roussy,
the eminent French doctor. He said : '' I shall include under the
'' name ' shell-shock,' the disorders caused by the bursting of a
'' shell or bomb at a certain distance, and not determining any
'' visible lesion or injury.'' He held that '' the part played by
'' emotion in determining psycho-neuropathic disorders and also
'' commotional troubles remains predominant. Like commotion,
'' emotion is sufficient to develop neurosis or to fix psychological
'' disorder, which is at the base of all neuropathic accidents ; but
'' it must be admitted that very often commotion is added to
'' emotion, and to discern when the one ends and the other
'' begins is exceedingly difficult.''
He believed that '' of the patients exhibiting psycho-neuro-
'' pathic affections, the vast majority are predisposed. This pre-
'' disposition may be hereditary or constitutional, or date from
'' childhood as the result of lack of the necessary education.
'' Constitution is not the sole pre-disposing factor. The
'' depressant action of physical or of mental fatigue, the
'' temporary shortness of food, and the various intoxications, in
'' which alcohol takes first place, play a very important part.
'' Previous occupation and social status do not militate for or
'' against these complaints.'' He had observed neuropathic disorders in men in almost every walk of life. '' Nevertheless, the
'' professions which require the exercise of judgment and
'' criticism, and which demand a sustained effort, both physical
'' and mental, not only do not favour the occurrence of neuro-
'' pathic affections, but clearly militate against them. In the
'' case of an officer, it is not only his critical faculties and powers
'' of judgment that are at work in holding the emotional re-
'' actions in check, but also the knowledge of his responsibility
'' and the good example he must always show. The officer is
'' not a unit which may be lost in a large group, but he has an

"individuality upon which all eyes are focussed, and his own
"'amour propre' prevents him from flinching under any pretext
"whatever. This mental steadiness of the officer has a bearing
"not only on the individual himself, but also acts as a stimulus
"to the soldiers under his command. Thus, as several officials
"in the medical service have pointed out, the infrequency of
"such affections in the 'troupes d'élite' is accounted for by the
"stimulant influence of the high morale of the Commanding
"Officers. During the war, as many of our French Army doctors
"have remarked, the morale of troops had played a very im-
"portant part in the frequence of 'shell-shock' incidence, as
"also in the development of all so-called hysterical manifesta-
"tions. Well-trained troops whose morale was well maintained
"by the officers gave the minimum of neuropathic cases. On
"the contrary, in undisciplined troops, neuropathic or hysterical
"troubles were frequently met with and became contagious in
"the units."

He did not think there was much real malingering, but agreed
there was a great deal of—

"(a) voluntary and intentional exaggeration of a real dis-
"order ; and

"(b) voluntary and intentional prolongation of a real
"disorder."

The witness discussed the question of men who were apparently hypnotised—an important matter with regard to desertion.
He did not believe that it is correct to speak of "battle hypnosis."
Patients described as in this condition were, he thought, in reality
suffering from mental confusion.

Sir Frederick Mott gave one case, and the witness said : " I
"have seen many such cases. I saw a case of a soldier who
"found himself some miles from the front who did not know in
"the least how he had got there. He was mentally confused.
"There was nothing to indicate that he was simulating, and
"gradually he came round. Other observers have found similar
"cases, and the point is absolutely indisputable that such cases
"of epileptic fugue exist."

Professor Roussy did not think that, although it was not possible during the war to send men back often for a rest, that the
incidence of " shell-shock " was greater in the French Army
than in other Armies ; but, on the other hand, he said that as
regards individual regiments he thought there were statistics
to show that " shell shock " was less in divisions who had a good
deal of rest. Troops fresh in the battle line had not acquired the
battle spirit. They are not used to the dangers of war, the noise
of the shells bursting, the terrible sights, and all the phenomena
of the front line. Their emotive states became excited. When
a certain regiment was found to have a greater number of " shell
shock " cases than another it was considered that they were
inferior troops. He came across " shell shock " in the French

Army as early as August, 1914. He thought the mental defectives were very commonly found among the hysterical cases, but that it was impossible to eliminate them during the war, although he agreed that there would be certainly less emotional " shell shock " if they were excluded. But it would be an unfortunate thing for the nation if one kept behind all the mental defectives. and sent all the men of higher mental capacity to the front.

Asked whether he could define cowardice, Professor Roussy said : " Cowardice, I consider is lack of self-control of the indivi- " dual in the presence of a situation in which there is an element " of danger and in which there is an element likely to cause fear. " Any man who can control himself is a courageous man, but the " man who runs away, or who does certain other actions not " esteemed worthy, is defined as a coward. A courageous man " is a man who can exert his self-control." That condition may be habitual or it may be created by training. The man who flees. the battle-field as the result of not exercising sufficient self-control is a coward. The French used the word " lâcheté." You can distinguish sometimes the difference between the man who loses his self-control and flees the battle-field and the man who suffers from psycho-neurosis. It was difficult to distinguish between cowardice and emotional " shell shock," but in the one case the man was suffering from a genuine illness, and in the other case simply from lack of self-control. A definite pension was never given in France except for a fixed and definite disability.

Again, in regard to the cause of these " shell shock " manifestations, Professor Roussy said mental contagion plays a big part in their production, and if it were known that a fixed pension was given for such cases there would be a large increase in the number.

C. Stanford Read, Esq., M.D., late Officer i/c " D " Block, Royal Victoria Hospital, Netley, and Neurological and Mental Specialist, Ministry of Pensions.

Dr. Read defined " shell shock " as " a mental abnor- " mality brought about by emotional shock, of which a shell " explosion is only a frequent type. Mental dissociation is the " main mechanism involved, and the symptoms may be mani- " fold, and either mental or physical or a combination of the " two. A previous mental conflict usually can be traced which " mainly involves the impulses towards self-preservation and " duty." " When the Armistice came," said the witness, " the " neurosis stopped, and psychoses went on, showing that they " were different conflicts. Of the latter, the probability is that " the men have drifted into various asylums." Those service patients, who were still in asylums and whose histories Dr. Read had been able to follow, were nearly all suffering from dementia præcox. The witness thought that they would probably have broken down with any comparatively small strain under any circumstances. The great stress of war produced psychosis, or expedited its development.

F. Burton Fanning, Esq., M.D., F.R.C.P., M.R.C.S.

Doctor F. Burton Fanning was asked whether when a man stated he suffered from " a commotional disturbance " it was generally true. He said that the patients nearly always accounted for their condition by alleging " commotional " disturbance. He thought it was " emotional " in reality ; and in nearly all cases, whether real or unreal, it was exaggerated. " When we cross-" questioned the man we usually found that he had not been " blown up at all, but had been under heavy fire, that was all. " We came to the conclusion that it was mostly emotional dis-" turbance with which we were dealing." He had only one case in which there was any question of its being commotional with organic lesion. " In fact," he added, " there was only " one case of all the ' shell-shocks ' I saw in which there was " any question of its being more than emotional." As early as 1915 he came to the conclusion that one-third of the people admitted to the ordinary medical ward were really only nerve cases. He was speaking of Home Forces. These were the men who had fallen sick after being called up for training, and that sort of thing. He and his colleagues had agreed that they did not see any Expeditionary Force men amongst the cases of neurasthenia. " If the neurotic element had been kept out " instead of forced in there would have been very much less " ' shell-shock.' A tremendous number of neurotics resented " having been passed, and they had never the slightest intention " of trying to make soldiers of themselves. An enormous pro-" portion amongst the men who broke down had been neurotics " previously. He had seen the emotional condition arise from " every one of the causes quoted in Question 15, after severe " mental stress, from the stress of battle, and from gassing. A " large number of fellows broke down long before they had " finished their training. The patient's attitude of mind was " wrong prior to service. They had never taken exercise, they " had not been prepared for muscular exercise, they had always " lived a sedentary life. They knew they could not stand the " long marches, and they never intended to." He used to have a hundred to two hundred of these neurotic men at Cambridge. " They were marched out with non-commissioned " officers, and before they had gone one hundred yards some of " them would begin to turn giddy and faint, and I am sure " it was only from auto-suggestion. A large proportion of his " people gave as a cause of nervous break down, horses. They " had never had anything to do with horses in civil life. They " did not know one end of a horse from another, and they were " put to attend them and to ride them."

" At present patients are not very keen to believe that they " are fit to work, knowing they will drop their pensions, and any " advice and persuasion one gives them has evaporated before " they reach home." He had seen exactly similar cases and symptoms in civil life. He had recently had the case of a man who fell down a pit and had developed what we should call typical " shell-shock." The term " shell-shock " had done a great deal of harm. The men, themselves, would have hated being branded as mental cases. There is a vulgar stigma attached to it. A great many men who had been classified for base work would have been quite well if they had known they were going to be kept there. They were in such fear from travelling boards sending their pals to battalions at the front that they were in perpetual fear of being sent up themselves. They did not have any sort of assurance that the category they were in would be the category they would remain in, and that was a great grievance to them.

A. F. Hurst, Esq., M.D., F.R.C.P., Physician, Nervous Diseases, Guy's Hospital, late Officer-in-Charge, Special Neurological Hospital, Seale Hayne.

Dr. A. F. Hurst said that " the term ' shell-shock ' " was first employed to denote the results of exposure " to the effects of violent explosions in the immediate neighbour- " hood of the patient. These effects are now known to be due to " the combined action of concussion and emotion in varying " proportions and differ in no way from the results of concussion " and emotion in civil life. Concussion of the brain and spinal " cord result in structural changes which are, for the most part, " evanescent, so that the symptoms they produce are only " temporary, but they may be perpetuated as hysterical symp- " toms owing to suggestive influence. The immediate physical " results of emotions are even more temporary. They are very " frequently perpetuated as hysterical symptoms owing to " similar suggestive influences and may also lead to psychasthenia " and neurasthenia. The condition commonly described as " ' shell-shock ' is a syndrome in varying proportions of " hysteria, psychasthenia, and neurasthenia, to which may " occasionally be added cerebral or spinal concussion, or both. " The term ' shell-shock ' should be discarded."

" Emotional, highly-strung men are most likely to be affected " by war neurosis. The degree of intelligence seemed to have " no influence. No general characteristic was common to all " individuals affected, as with a sufficiently powerful provoca- " tion no man, however normal he may be at first, is likely to " be immune to ' shell-shock ' "; but " The only men I saw," said the witness, " who had broken down during training were " the true ' martial misfits ' who were constitutionally unfit, " physically or mentally, or both, to undergo training. It should " be possible to eliminate such men by an efficient medical " examination before their enlistment." Breakdown was very rare after severe physical stress without other factors. " I never " saw it from marching alone, but occasionally from exposure

" alone." The normal physical reaction, to severe mental stress
was often perpetuated " in the form of hysterical symptoms,
" such as tremor mutism and paraplegia (popularly called ' shell-
" shock ') and the mental reaction might show itself in amnesia
" and various psychasthenic symptoms. My experience in the
" East, during the Gallipoli campaign and in Salonika, and
" later in England, showed that infections such as dysentery,
" malaria, infective jaundice, and much less frequently trench
" fever, were liable to produce a condition of true neurasthenia,
" and also to predispose to the development of other neuroses."

" Exposure to the bursting of high explosives led to the
" ordinary sequelæ of concussion seen in civil life, such as head-
" ache. In addition, hysterical deafness frequently resulted from
" the perpetuation of the temporary deafness caused by the noise
" and concussion ; hysterical fits, hemiplegia, hemianopia or
" complete blindness, from the evanescent organic changes caused
" by cerebral concussion, and hysterical paraplegia from the
" evanescent organic paraplegia caused by spinal concussion."

" Prolonged responsibility was a common cause of breakdown,
" with the development of psychasthenic symptoms, in officers.
" The fatigue, strain and responsibility of long service eventually
" led to breakdown in many men who appeared to be constitu-
" tionally absolutely normal, and who stood the stress of battle
" and responsibility without any difficulty at first."

In the witnesses' opinion the most potent cause of " shell
" shock " and mental breakdown was severe mental stress in men
who were physically fatigued, especially if they were also unfit
from any other cause such as exposure, fever, or great heat.

" Shell shock " due to emotional disturbance was infinitely
more common than " shell shock " due to commotional disturbance. He knew of no tests by which neuroses from commotional
and emotional causes could be distinguished from each other, but
a complete neurological examination, especially in the early stages
frequently showed some slight evidence of organic change which
proved that commotional disturbance had taken place. Thus one
or both drums of the ears might be ruptured and extensor plantar
reflexes might be present ; and in a few cases the knee jerks and
ankle jerks were abolished.

After much investigation of the subject he had come to the conclusion that signs of genuine neurosis and simulation are identical
and that simulation can only be diagnosed with certainty in the
very few cases in which a malingerer has been detected
" flagrante delicto " or when he confesses that he is shamming.

In the course of his evidence Doctor Hurst said that in his
experience there is no question that emotion was far and away the
more important factor. In the majority of cases there was no
element of concussion at all, and in those in which concussion did
bear a part the patient improved very rapidly and would get well
completely or almost completely within a very short time unless
there was the emotional element there at the same time.

The emotion of fear—fear under normal conditions at home—would be likely to be followed by such physical results as shaking and giving way of the legs. If a man had become abnormally emotional and suggestible, these physical results, the normal results of fear, would tend to become perpetuated. He thought that so far as the hysterical symptoms, tremor, mutism and paraplegia, popularly called " shell shock," are concerned, in a great many cases they were independent of amnesia, but in regard to the development of the amnesia it seemed to him that a man who was in a condition of prolonged extreme mental stress passed into a condition of stupor. He hardly knew what he was doing. In many cases that might disappear quickly if he got into more favourable surroundings, and the medical officers under whom he came knew how to deal with him. In those conditions he might recover rapidly. In other conditions this stupor might pass into a condition of perfect amnesia which might last for years or which might disappear after lasting two or three years. The worst case of amnesia he saw which got well was a man who knew nothing of himself. He did not even know what his arms and legs were for, and had to be re-educated as you would teach a small baby. That continued for $3\frac{1}{2}$ years, by which time he developed a childish mind, and then suddenly his memory came back. It was an entirely emotional strain. He had been exposed to no shell explosion at all.

His experience was that the term " shell shock " was an unfortunate expression, because the vast majority of cases had nothing to do with what one should regard as " shell shock," that is, the result of commotion. The effect of being actually blown up is very much the same as being thrown on one's head from a horse. One may get concussion which may lead to amnesia and a prolonged condition of unconsciousness, but which does not lead to the type of symptom which one understands by " shell shock," which is due to emotion.

Doctor Hurst said that his experience in November and December, 1915, in Lemnos, was that practically every man coming out of the Peninsula was neurasthenic, whether he was supposed to be fit or not. Very few could hold their hands out without shaking, and they were all in a condition of profound neurasthenia. The vast majority of the men at that time were suffering from dysentery, and a great number of them had jaundice as well. Asked whether he would ascribe that to a physical cause or an emotional one, or to the two causes combined, Doctor Hurst said : " I think the two causes were " combined. The man never got away from the strain of shell " fire, but I think in that particular campaign infection was " probably the most important thing, because there was an " extreme degree of physical weakness, and very few men could " carry their packs on the march. They arrived at Lemnos after " the evacuation, and their power of marching had entirely dis- " appeared. They had to rest every hundred yards or so. It " was a condition of absolute exhaustion."

Asked as to cases of simulation, Doctor Hurst replied : " 1
" think that simulation was extremely rare among soldiers.
" I think, among recruits, it was probably not uncommon, but
" among men who had been to the front it was rare ; but what
" was extremely common was exaggeration and a tendency to
" prolong the condition. When the man was ready to get up he
" was unwilling to do so." He agreed that anxiety neurosis
was much more common in officers. He further said that the
type of man most liable to breakdown is the man who is probably
called " neurotic " ; a man who has the artistic temperament ;
a man who is more emotional than the average type of man.
Speaking of a pensioner invalid, he thought that if a job could
be found automatically for the man when he was cured, he would
get well at once. It was his opinion that if the Army have the
best regimental officers and medical officers and high morale,
they ought to have very few cases of " shell shock." There
might have been a more or less rapid cure for the majority of the
emotional cases at the front. They were the most easy to cure,
but as they went from hospital to hospital they became less
curable, and after being in hospital for two or three years they
often become absolutely incurable.

Asked whether we should have had anything like so many
cases if the problem had been tackled in the right way from the
first, Doctor Hurst said that the almost incurable types he saw
occasionally at the end of the war had already been in hospital
literally for years, and in a great many of the hospitals they had
had very imperfect treatment or none at all. In his view, even
the most normal man, if he were to spend all the time these men
have spent in one hospital or another, under one treatment or
another, would have become " hospitalised." It is almost a
disease in itself. Such men are not insane, they are suffering
from a complaint of official creation. " I think," said Dr.
Hurst, " the greatest cause of their production is the absence
" of sufficient occupation for the men in the hospital, and also
" having sent that type of man to V.A.D. hospitals, where they
" were petted and given nothing to do. In the early days, when
" I first came back to England and was sent to Oxford, I started
" a special V.A.D. hospital for these men in the country. I gave
" it up because I found they got worse. What they required
" was to remain under strict discipline, and that was the only
" way to get them well quickly. If they had been kept behind
" the firing line in rest hospitals we should have had little of this
" class of man now permanently invalided."

*E. Mapother, Esq., M.D., F.R.C.S., M.R.C.P., Medical
Superintendent, Maudsley Neurological Hospital.*

Dr. E. Mapother said " shell shock " is a misnomer for a
" mixture of conditions including :—
  " (1) Results of concussion of the nervous system without
      " visible external lesion. This was rare.
  " (2) Conditions of heightened emotionalism due to mental
      " strain or shock too prolonged or too intense for the

" particular individual to endure without the emotion
" becoming persistent. In some cases the strain or
" shock was quite inadequate to cause the resulting
" symptoms in a normal man, but was adequate for
" that individual on account of constitutional
" predisposition or acquired predisposition due to
" bodily causes, such as infection. In the great
" majority of cases this state of heightened
" emotionalism was one of fear. With it were
" associated the bodily accompaniments of fear, one
" or other of these being often disproportionately
" permanent in the particular case. In smaller
" numbers of cases the state of heightened
" emotionalism was one of remorse, horror, or grief,
" rather than fear.

" (3) A group slightly distinguished from the above in which
" the condition was rather one of exhaustion than
" heightened emotionalism.

" (4) A large group of cases with apparently physical lesions,
" in no way resembling the physical concomitants
" of emotion and, as a rule, not even associated
" with the latter. These simulated roughly organic
" lesions and the simulation was conscious in varying
" degree in different cases.

" In the ' shell shock ' hospitals were also seen examples of
" various organic nervous diseases and cases of ordinary peace-
" time psychoses, generally of minor severity and with symptoms
" coloured by war experiences. These, however, were generally
" recognised as not properly belonging to ' shell shock.' There
" was no characteristic common to all the individuals affected.
" There were, in fact, two different main groups of cases
" distinguishable in practice as well as in theory. These showed
" concurrent differences in respect of pre-war history, service
" before admission to hospital and sometimes in hospital. In
" one main group the individuals were constitutionally at least
" up to normal in respect of intelligence, self-reliance and
" commonsense. In the other group were individuals defective
" in one or more of these qualities and these could be divided
" into :—

" (1) Those defective in respect of intelligence—
" (a) The intellectually defective is incapable of
" endurable patriotism ; in fact, of attach-
" ment to any ideal so abstract as his
" country.
" (b) Far from receiving help in times of trouble,
" which others did from comradeship, he
" usually suffered continuously from his
" sense of the contempt of others. The
" result was frequently a psychosis with de-
" lusions of persecution.

" (2) Constitutional neurotics of the psychasthenic and
" hypochondriac types, that is, those who had
" habitually regarded themselves as weaklings of one
" kind or another, and started military service with
" a conviction of unfitness.

" (3) Those defective in social or moral sense. The im-
" portance of the latter factor in the genesis of
" admissions to ' shell shock ' hospitals has been
" greatly under-estimated, at least in published
" writings on the subject. The most important docu-
" ment received with the patient was generally the
" conduct sheet.

" Mental stress was by far the most potent cause of ' shell
" shock.' The general effect of prolonged stress was much
" more important than the effect of specific incidents often
" emphasised. ' Shell shock ' due to emotional disturbance was
" vastly commoner than that due to commotional. There is
" evidence by those who saw much of these cases during the
" early stages that commotional disturbance had been distin-
" guished by dullness and confusion rather than excitement.
" Tendon jerks diminished rather than increased, there was
" slight inequality of pupils and rupture of tympanum. In the
" later stages commotional disturbance could only be diagnosed
" where with history of explosion and in absence of visible
" lesions there were signs of undoubted organic nervous disease
" with or without emotional disturbance as well. Most cases
" of anxiety neurosis were wholly genuine to start with. Many
" remained so throughout, but some were consciously protracted
" and exaggerated later."

Asked whether he could distinguish genuine emotional neurosis
from simulation or perhaps from mere cowardice, the witness
said : " Frankly, I am not prepared to draw a distinction between
" cowardice and ' shell shock.' Cowardice I take to mean
" action under the influence of fear, and the ordinary type of
" 'shell shock ' to my mind was chronic and persisting fear. I
" think the situation really is that the emotional mechanism of
" fear habitually stimulated, or intensely stimulated even on one
" occasion, can pass into a condition of over-action and that is
" practically what ' shell shock ' is."

*Colonel J. F. C. Fuller, D.S.O., Deputy Director of Staff
Duties (Training), War Office, late General Staff Officer,
Tank Corps.*

Colonel Fuller said : " If a crowd of men are reduced to a low
" nervous condition ' shell shock,' so-called, becomes contagious.
" This was noticeable at the Battle of the Ancre, 1916, the only
" battle in which I had direct evidence that British troops deserted
" in considerable numbers to the enemy. I believe that this was
" due to the low nervous condition produced by the appalling
" surroundings of this battle. I have only witnessed one panic,
" namely, that which took place on the 30th November, 1917.

" I have little experience of this condition but consider that
" panic or crowd ' shell shock is normally a temporary con-
" dition. It constitutes a moral stampede and when once
" stopped a little rest will soon set the men up again."

Asked what he meant by " shell shock " the witness said,
" By ' shell shock ' I mean the sapping of morale by sudden or
" prolonged fear which subordinates a man's power of will to
" his instinct of self-preservation and ultimately reduces him to
" a state wherein he cannot control his emotions. I think,
" myself, that it is very difficult to define ' shell shock ' as it
" covers such an enormous ground. I have noticed that men
" begin by suffering from a type of nervousness which leads
" sometimes to complete mental breakdown. I think that the
" prevailing idea that the sudden explosion of a shell or some-
" thing like that will derange a man's mind and that this is
" ' shell-shock " is the wrong meaning of the term. I think
" what produces ' shell-shock ' much more than the sudden
" danger is prolonged danger in a static position, where the man
" cannot get away from it. It is the wear and tear and slow
" sapping of his nervous powers. From observations," said the
witness, " I have noticed that the normal, healthy man arriving
" from England showed definite signs of physical fear when first
" coming under fire. This fear very shortly wore off and was
" replaced by a type of callousness which sometimes increased
" until a man took very little trouble to protect himself. I
" noticed in several cases that when this condition was well
" advanced a man became liable to breakdown mentally or to
" show a nervousness which may be defined rather as a mental
" terror than a physical fear. What I noticed was that first of
" all the man was healthily afraid of what was happening, then
" he became callous, and after that he sometimes became
" obsessed with fear."

. Asked whether the callousness was an outward and visible sign
of wear and tear, the witness said he thought it was. He had
also noticed that isolated duties, especially those of a static
nature, affected the men's nerves. He thought that isolated
duties had resulted in breaking down the nervous power of many
men quite as effectively as shell fire. On duties which they were
continually carrying out, such as in observation posts, sap heads
running into " No Man's Land," and places like that, the men
used to get very jumpy. He also held that the incidence of
" shell shock " was greater among troops who had been in the
line some time, especially if these troops were subjected to
dangerous conditions. He was sure that a high morale undoubtedly tended to lessen the incidence of " shell shock,"
because morale is the acquired quality which in highly-trained
troops counterbalances the influence of the instinct of self-preservation. As the soldier's morale to a great extent depends on
the security and comfort of his surroundings, the conditions which
produce " shell shock " undoubtedly undermine this greatly.

Further than this, " jumpy " men make others " jumpy."
Example is the foundation of morale, and also the foundation of
its destruction. If a crowd of men are reduced to a low nervous
condition " shell shock " becomes contagious.

There is a great difference between one battalion and another
side by side in the line. A bad battalion may infect the good
one. In one case at Ypres the Guards refused to go into the line
with a certain battalion next to them. They said they would
take over the line themselves, but they would not go in with that
battalion.

Asked whether he considered that an excess of " shell shock "
in a regiment is a discredit to that regiment, the witness said :
" Yes, I think it is. There are exceptional circumstances, but
" in normal fighting I think it is a discredit and shows that the
" commanding officer and officers of the regiment have not estab-
" lished in the men a sufficiently high morale to push them
" through." He did not regard as discreditable " shell shock "
occurring in isolated cases, but, on the other hand, if it occurred
en masse there was something wrong, " something wrong with
" the training and organisation of the unit."

*Squadron Leader W. Tyrrell, D.S.O., M.C., Royal Air Force
Medical Service.*

Squadron Leader Tyrrell gave the following evidence. He
said : " ' Shell shock ' I define as exhaustion of the nervous
" energy which determines will-power and self-control, with the
' resultant loss of control. It resembles a paralysis of the
" inhibitory nervous system. I approach the problem by com-
" paring a man's store of nervous energy to a capital and current
" account at the bank.

" A man instinctively masks his emotions almost as a matter
" of routine. In trifling everyday affairs this is involuntary and
" automatic with a negligible expense of nervous energy. In
" minor crises the expenditure of nervous energy increases rela-
" tively with the man's estimate of the importance and necessity
" for concealing the emotion. This expenditure is usually out
" of his current account, consequently it is not missed and has
" no untoward effect. In great crises—fear, birth, death,
" marriage, murder, personal disgrace or dishonour—the emotion
" called forth is abnormal. The necessity for camouflage or
" repression is increased in ratio with a corresponding rise in
" expenditure of nervous energy, which quickly uses up the
" current account and draws upon the capital account for
" reinforcement.

" A continuous series of great crises without intervals for
" replacing spent energy ultimately exhausts the capital account,
" and you get a run on the bank, followed by loss of control,
" hysteria, irresponsible chattering, mutism, amnesia, inhibition
" of the senses, acute mania, insensibility, etc., with the
" diagnosis of nervous breakdown or ' shell shock.' The credit

" balance of nervous energy varies in individuals just as banking
" balances do. Some become bankrupt and succumb before they
" draw on their current account, or even scent the battle. Most
" real men take a lot of depressing, and even when really and
" justifiably exhausted their hearts are in the right place. They
" have spirit and soul, and so they draw on an overdraft, if neces-
" sary, and manage to carry on. A very few appear to have an
" inexhaustible store. They usually get killed, and always earn
" the description that they did not know what fear was, which
" is a misnomer. All men know fear. Some conceal it better
" than others. A few bury it out of sight, but it is there all the
" same.

" ' Shell-shock ' is born of fear. Its grandparents are self-
" preservation and the fear of being found afraid. Any emotion
" which has to be repressed or concealed demands an unrestricted
" but well-controlled output of nervous energy. Craven fear is
" the most extravagant prodigal of nervous energy known.
" Under its stimulus a man squanders nervous energy recklessly
" in order to suppress his hideous and pent-up emotion, and mask
" or camouflage that which if revealed will call down ignominy
" upon his head and disgrace him in the eyes of his fellows. He
" must save his self-respect and self-esteem at all costs.

" The most likely type of man for ' shell-shock ' is the brood-
" ing, introspective, self-analysing man, the type who was
" constantly estimating his chance of survival, whose imagina-
" tion added the terrors of the future to those of the present.
" Men of high intelligence, who recognise the necessity to cast
" their imagination and live for the hour at a time, taking no
" heed for what the future might bring forth, i.e.. who adopted
" the fatalist attitude, these men fortified themselves, and for
" the most part ' carried on.' Other men of equally high in-
" telligence had not used it to develop their character and
" will-power. Their imagination ran riot, wasted their nervous
" capital; they usually ended in breakdown. Controlled intelli-
" gence was a safeguard. Uncontrolled intelligence was a curse
" and a sure forerunner of ' shell-shock.' A characteristic
" common to all ' shell-shock ' individuals was fear. Several
" of the conditions named (in Question 15) were usually present
" at the final breakdown, but most of them had contributed at
" one time or other to the exhaustion of will-power and of
" vitality." He considered that " the most potent single cause
" of ' shell-shock ' and nervous breakdown was loss of sleep
" and inadequate rest. Associate with these the bursting of high
" explosives, and you have the combination most fruitful in
" ' shell-shock ' cases."

" Next comes severe mental stress grouped with fatigue, mud
" and blood, wet and cold, misery and monotony, unsavoury
" cooking and feeding, nauseating environment, etc."

" The incidence was certainly greater amongst troops who had
" been worn out by long spells in the trenches. ' Shell-shock '

" was an unfortunate and costly error in nomenclature. Before
" ' shell-shock ' days the unspoken but very evident scorn of
" the old soldiers acted as a wholesome deterrent to all but the
" genuine cases of nervous breakdown."

He did not deny the aptness of the term, or the existence of
the condition, but it certainly offered an honourable means of
escape to the faint-hearted.

" Later in the war, when the troops learnt the symptoms
" and signs of ' shell-shock,' the percentage of incidence amongst
" fresh troops undoubtedly increased."

" The period which produced the greater number of
" malingerers was the one or two sick parades immediately pre-
" ceding a return to the line from rest billets."

During the war he had no experience of " shell-shock " in
depots or barracks. " In rest billets it was usually associated
" with the history of insomnia, nightmares, hysteria, mutism,
" amnesia, melancholia, petty crime, and, in some cases, by
" self-inflicted wounds. In the field by melancholia, depression,
" hysterical fits, uncontrollable shivering and wringing of the
" hands, staring eyes, blindness, amnesia, irresponsible chatter-
" ing, acute mania, sudden insensibility, self-inflicted wounds,
" generally to the left hand or the feet; fear, and the very
" characteristic look of furtive fear—the hunted animal."

" An observant and knowledgeable medical officer who has
" put himself into the right and proper relationship with the
" troops (officers and other ranks) under his charge, can often
" detect very early the signs of approaching breakdown.
" Summed up in change of character :—
" The wild fighting type becomes quiet and moody.
" The sullen type becomes excitable and talkative.
" The careful man becomes suddenly reckless.
" The previously well-behaved man perpetrates petty
" crimes, etc.

" It requires knowledge of the normal characters of the men,
" with endless and patient observation of their characteristics on
" the part of the medical officer or the executive officer to detect
" these changes in character." Many executive officers and non-
commissioned officers whom he had known became expert in
detecting the early signs of breakdown.

He should say " shell shock " was more likely in a single
man, as his thoughts and interests are more self-centred and
selfish. The happily married man takes one thought for himself
and two for his wife and children. The unhappily married man
was generally a good soldier and usually got killed.

The recruit should be " saturated and interested in tradition:
" Pride of regiment.
" *Esprit de Corps*.
" The fighting spirit.
" Discipline.

" He should be given leaders (officers and non-commissioned
" officers) of proved character and ability who will inspire
" confidence in their leadership."

" Leadership is the most important factor in maintaining
" morale and reducing ' shell shock.' "

" The first three months of all training, in whatever arm it
" may be, should be regarded as probationary. At the expiration
" of this time, all recruits should be regarded by expert observers
" and judges, and detailed for branches of the service for which
" they are physically and temperamentally suited."

" The unfit should be rigidly excluded. They are better left
" at home, they fill the hospitals, clog movement, and later
" on swell the pension lists."

" To prevent ' shell shock ' in the field, promote good morale
" and good interior economy of units—food, sleep, rest, exercise,
" baths, clean underclothes, entertainment, music, reading, etc.,
" when in rest. Direct men's thoughts away from their own
" persons and their inevitable conditions of life. Inculcate the
" habit of cheerfulness and the gift of laughter, and a sense of
" humour. Attention to spiritual needs by the right type of
" Padre. The C.O. should avoid detailing one man for lonely
" and dangerous duty—two, not one, should be sent."

" It had been necessary to withdraw whole battalions, not
" entirely due to ' shell-shock,' but indirectly their general morale
" fell after a protracted series of ' shell-shock ' cases and heavy
" casualties."

" ' Shell-shock ' is lessened by frequent removal if in a bad
" sector, but increased by frequent removal if in a quiet sector."

A mine was blown under the German lines at Messines Ridge
on the 7th June, 1917. Debris and bodies were evulsed from
a depth of 60 feet—depth proved by strata of soil thrown up.
He visited it within two hours of the explosion and found dead
Germans, three in number, lying unsoiled—unmarked—one with
spectacles still on and unbroken—no visible sign or evidence of
violence. Eyes and pupils normal, the possibility of " gas " was
excluded.*

This, in the witness' opinion, is a classic instance of death from
commotional disturbance without visible injury. He had seen
other cases, but none so definite or so well proved as this.

He had diagnosed cases as insanity, which, in his opinion,
were due solely to the stress of war. He had not heard or traced
the ultimate fate of these cases.

He had seen cases of an emotive state in the form of irresistible
fear of danger, associated with crises of terror and anxiety at the
front, leading up to desertion from post of duty or reckless
behaviour; one of whom, a regular serving non-commissioned
officer, with an excellent pre-war character, was eventually shot
as a persistent deserter.

---

* This was possibly due to Carbon Monoxide poisoning.

He had seen men punished for minor offences who later developed authentic " shell-shock," indeed, a sudden recourse to minor crime by previously well-behaved men was one of the premonotory signals of impending breakdown.

As his experience increased he was able to obviate unjust punishment by communication with the executive officers.

The usual feminine outbursts of hysteria are equivalent to " shell-shock."

The witness went on to say that he recognised three kinds of " shell-shock "—commotional shock, breakdown from the wear and tear of war, and the acute breakdown which occurred especially during bombardments when the men, sometimes in large numbers, lost their heads and lost their control. Asked whether he thought that the acute breakdown which occasionally occurred in a man the first time he was under fire was really due to the exhaustion of his nervous energy, the witness replied, " Strictly " it could not be described as exhaustion, but as I said before, " some men were stricken with what is called ' shell-shock ' " before they had made any demand upon their current account " or their deposit account, that is to say, the mentally unsuitable " men or the men cunning enough and with foresight to get out " of trouble."

Asked whether he considered that the primary cause of nervous breakdown in the recent war was exhaustion, more than anything else, either physical or mental, or both, the witness said : " I would not say exhaustion was the only cause. The " cause of the breakdown was lack of control or the power of " control." He added, that loss of sleep was the most potent factor in the production of " shell-shock." He put them in this order, loss of sleep, inadequate rest, unsavoury feeding, exposure to the elements, and to danger.

" How a man will be regarded by his people at home and by " his fellow-men was one of the factors in preventing ' shell-" ' shock.' The good opinion of his wife and family and sweet-" heart and of the men round about him was a strong incentive " to control the expression of fear."

The witness added, " When I got to learn more about the " early signs of breakdown and acquired a certain amount of " skill in anticipating it, I was very often able, in communica-" tion with the Commanding Officer and Company Officers, to " withdraw a man and put him in the transport lines for a little " time or send him on a course of instruction ; give him, as it " were, leave, and get him out of it for three or four weeks, and " then he would come back good for another six months."

" With the men, the most fruitful period in the production of " ' shell-shock ' was :—
  " (1) The height of battle.
  " (2) The hour before going over the top.
  " (3) The evening before going back to trenches after a rest
        " period."

"With the officers it was a more gradual thing and would
"suggest that the officer who has more responsibility is not so
"self-centred. He will carry through what he has in hand. I
"am speaking of the majority of cases; and not having time to
"think about himself or time for booding, it is only when he
"comes back to a period of safety that he starts to think and
"breaks down."

"Training must begin on the day of enlistment if it is to be
"done properly. In the field you want good morale, good leader-
"ship, and good interior economy."

"Cases of breakdown of some sort or other in the early part
"of the war were rather looked upon as remarkable, and I find I
"can recollect the early cases much easier than the cases later
"on. We had in 1914 a battalion of 1,000 men and relatively
"few cases of breakdown. Perhaps I can remember them
"because it was a fact that it was considered rather a disgrace
"to go down with a nervous breakdown, and was looked upon,
"more or less with unexpressed scorn by the rest of his com-
"rades; later on, of course, there were greater numbers involved
"and one was dealing with greater bodies of troops. There was
"the recognised term ' shell-shock,' and it certainly opened up
"an honourable or quasi-honourable way of getting out of
"danger."

Speaking of an N.C.O. of his own battalion—a persistent
deserter, but a normal man and a good soldier—who was shot, the
witness said: "Candidly, I do not think if it had occurred in
"1917 and 1918 he would have been shot. The old Regular
"Army had a much fiercer way of looking upon anything
"approaching cowardice, because their standards were based
"upon wars previous to this war in which the calls made upon
"a man's courage were as nothing compared to this war. It
"was a much fiercer standard. This is not derogatory to the new
"Army, who were extraordinarily good, but they had a different
"system and standard."

"It is difficult to describe the clinical appearance of the men
"who broke down suddenly. The man looked obviously out of
"control; he gave way to involuntary movements, wringing
"his hands, his eyes became staring, and he got the look of a
"hunted animal—you cannot mistake it. When the crash does
"come he loses all shame and cringes."

The officers who had powers of observation used them, and
that was how they detected the officer or man who had come to
the end of his tether.

Under conditions such as existed in France it is inevitable for
the man to breakdown at some time or other, and it is proper
to take steps to prevent it. If these steps are taken the efficiency
of the unit is increased and prolonged.

"Might I emphasise the capacity," said the witness, "which
"the Medical Officer has for prevention. It depends upon the

" interpretation which the medical officer puts upon his duties.
" I have met medical officers in France (and I say this with all
" deference to my profession) whose duties were circumscribed
" and interpreted simply by the seeing of sick and the issuing of
" one or two tablets for half an hour every morning, and they
" undoubtedly failed, in my opinion, in the best interests of their
" profession and their country. The medical officer must learn
" to know his officers and men intimately to be able to adjudge
" the slightest variation in their characteristics. That is what
" they are aiming at in providing a special officer in the Air Force
" —to be able to estimate minute changes in the character and
" soul and take the sick man away early. It is the medical
" officer's personal approach to and interpretation of his duties
" that counts."

" Approached in the proper way and provided you gave a sound
" reason for your interfering I think the Commanding Officers
" saw it in the proper light. At least, the type of Commanding
" Officer whom I was privileged to work with saw it every time.
" They saw if you were out to maintain the fighting strength—
" the number of rifles at their disposal—it was very easy to
" convince them you were out for the good of the battalion and
" when they realised and recognised that they not only backed
" you up, but they would go further than you."

Questioned regarding sudden breakdown becoming contagious,
the witness said, " I can recall one instance in 1914. It was
" on the night of the 19th October. We were attacking what
" eventually became our line for four years. We were being
" counter-shelled rather heavily and had been repulsed. The
" battle waxed and waned for five days and about the fourth day
" a young officer suddenly collapsed without any reason what-
" soever. I was hurried up to him and found a history of
" becoming suddenly reckless and excitable and urging the men
" on to attempt impossible things. I went up and we got him on
" a stretcher and came away and three or four men came back
" with me crying."

" At that period of the war a nervous breakdown was regarded
" as a disgrace and looked down upon by the men and the men
" have their own subtle, humorous, but very pointed way of
" referring to such cases. It was regarded, whether you liked
" it or not, as a discreditable thing to breakdown nervously at
" that time. That is why I hesitated so much to regard these
" cases as a battle injury or wound, because I feel strongly that
" if it were so there would be a marked increase in the incidence
" and if they were regarded as discreditable there would be a
" marked diminution."

" Immediately I noticed a large number of such cases coming
" from one battalion, I would go for their interior economy and
" the general discipline and conduct of the battalion. I should
" look for the reason not in subordinate individuals but in the
" head of the battalion—the Commanding Officer. It is the

" want of discipline and morale of the battalion that produces
" the wholesale cases. In a battalion with the finest morale
" you must always have individual cases and the individual cases
" may arise from two causes : either from commotional shock
" or from emotional shock where there is a legitimate break-
" down in consequence of wear and tear."

" There is a difference between army discipline and discipline
" in civil life in this way, that proper discipline is built up on
" tradition, *esprit de corps* and pride of unit and battalion. If
" discipline is cultivated along those lines you get the right type
" of man and it differs in that respect from the discipline of the
" waiter or the ordinary man in civil life. The discipline in civil
" life is a much lower type."

Asked whether he considered that a military operation in the
field could be carried out and brought to a successful issue if
psycho-neurosis were recognised in the Army Act as an illness
like measles or mumps for which the man could be evacuated by
reporting sick in the ordinary way and treated in hospital, the
witness replied, " You must recognise it. If the man comes and
" says, ' I am feeling extremely nervous and I must go back to
" ' hospital,' you must leave the decision to the medical officer.
" It comes back to what I said as to the personality and dis-
" criminating power of the medical officer. May I outline my
" own procedure, when confronted with cases like that? I
" thoroughly examined the fellow and would not agree one way
" or the other. I probably knew him beforehand if he had been
" long enough in the unit. I thoroughly examined him from
" the clinical point of view, with special attention to his nervous
" system, and kept him in my own sick quarters. I then went
" to his company and platoon officers and one or two N.C.O.'s
" who knew him, and found out his character, how he had been
" doing his work, and if they had noticed any signs of a change
" in his character recently, or at an earlier period. If time and
" circumstances permit, the family and personal history are
" usually useful in these cases. I never decided that a man was
" malingering until I had thoroughly investigated his case, not
" only as a doctor but as a man, and from the point of view of
" the section commander and N.C.O.'s who knew him per-
" sonally."

" You cannot eliminate psycho-neurosis altogether, but cases
" which occurred immediately preceding going to the front line
" and just before going over the top were always regarded with
" suspicion."

" In my experience, every man executed by order of courts-
" martial was given every loophole of escape."

*Gordon Holmes, Esq., C.M.G., C.B.E., B.A., M.D., F.R.C.P.,
late Consultant Neurologist, British Armies in France;
Physician National Hospital for Paralysis and Epilepsy.*

Doctor Gordon Holmes in giving evidence said, " a consider-
" able number of men were admitted to the Base Hospitals in

" France with gross hysterical symptoms such as paralysis, or loss
" of speech during the first 18 months of war, but relatively
" few men with the symptoms which are now included in ' shell
" shock ' were seen.'' This he attributed to :

    (1) The higher morale and discipline of the troops.

    (2) The less severe form of fighting during the period that
        preceded the Battle of the Somme.

    (3) The fact that the idea of " shell-shock " was not dis-
        seminated among the troops and did not affect them
        by suggestion.

He could not say that " there were any characteristics common
" to men who became affected, but mental defectives and neuro-
" pathic individuals were probably more liable to suffer. Race,
" education and previous environment were probably more
" important factors. The incidence was high among fresh
" troops of short training and low morale, e.g., the reinforce-
" ments from England to the 2nd Army in April, 1918. The
" incidence was probably higher, other facts being equal, in the
" older men.

" The cases occurred in greater numbers during prolonged
" engagements, especially when not successful, e.g., Passchen-
" daele, much less frequently when success attended the
" fighting during the autumn of 1918. The statements made
" by men as to the cause of their breakdown were frequently
" unreliable. This was proved by the independent evidence
" afforded by Army Form W.3436. The most potent causes of
" ' shell shock ' in order of frequency were probably :—

    " (1) The stress of battle.

    " (2) Exposure to the bursting of high explosives.

    " (3) Prolonged mental stress.

    " (4) Prolonged service.

" Poison gas had comparatively little influence and alcohol
" less. Only a small proportion of all cases were due to commo-
" tional shock. The great majority were of emotional origin.''
In the witness's opinion " most of the commotional cases could
" be distinguished by properly trained medical officers.

" Responsibility, e.g., among higher officers, may have been
" the cause of nervous breakdown of the neurasthenic type, but
" it was relatively uncommon.''

Asked to what he attributed the very considerable rise in the
number of " shell shock " cases which came before him as time
went on, Doctor Holmes said : " In the first place, it was partly
" due to the fact that morale among the troops at the front was
" not so high as in the original expeditionary force ; secondly,
" fighting became more severe and battle more protracted, but,''
he thought, " the most important factor was that in the later
" stages of the war the men got hold of the word ' shell-shock.'
" Many of them regarded ' shell-shock ' as something to be ex-
" pected, and the ' will and wish ' factor had considerable
" influence. They recognised that if they had ' shell shock '

" they would escape further service in the line for the time
" being." He had no doubt in his own mind that " the great
" increase in these cases coincided with the knowledge that such
" a condition as ' shell shock ' existed." He believed that to
increase in every possible way the morale of the troops was the
secret of all preventive measures.

The witness had had opportunities of handling records describing what the men themselves thought as to the causes of
" shell shock " and the medical experience was that by the aid
of Army Form W. 3436 they found out exactly what occurred
to each man. That Form was received a few days after the man
had been admitted to the Centre. The men frequently said
their condition was due to being blown up by a shell or something of that kind but information from their units failed to
confirm their statement.

The medical authorities investigated the question of the proportion of " shell shock " cases due to commotional shock in
several Centres and came to the conclusion that between 4 per
cent. and 10 per cent. were actually commotional cases. In
battle areas the commotional cases exceeded 10 per cent., but in
quiet areas the proportion was very small.

Doctor Gordon Holmes further said, " The great difficulty
" was that a great many men came down from the front who
" were merely shaken up. These men slept for 24 hours and
" after a few nights' good rest were requesting to go back to
" the line, but we were bound to keep them longer than that.
" A man with loss of speech came in and we often found that
" next morning he had regained his speech. He had been sent
" to a ward where there were other men who had had the same
" experience and they said to him, ' You will be all right soon '
" and that helped him along. If that did not act, the Medical
" Officer treated him by the appropriate method. In many
" cases it was found sufficient to insist that there was nothing
" wrong and that there was no reason why the patient should
" not recover. It was found in most Centres that the quickest
" method was to tell the patient that we should give him
" electricity to help him along and almost invariably he got his
" speech back within half an hour. Then he was sent back to
" the ward and as soon as he got rid of his symptoms was given
" a good rest for a few days and then, if possible, was given
" systematic exercises. In the best organised Centres we had
" a drill instructor who took the men out in small squads or
" even individually and put them through a certain number of
" exercises."

" There was one interesting group of cases which troubled us
" for a long time until Captain Johnson, R.A.M.C., discovered
" a method of dealing with them—the man who was trembling
" all over. In the early part of the war most of them found
" their way over to England. In the Autumn of 1917, Captain
" Johnson discovered that we could get all these men well in a

" very short time. He had a large hospital tent divided into
" small compartments each big enough to hold a stretcher, with
" a passage-way in the middle. The man was told that he
" wanted absolute rest, and was placed here in isolation. Then
" the Medical Officer went and pointed out to him that he only
" trembled because he held his limbs rigidly and he taught him
" to relax. Gradually by suggestion the man relaxed the muscles
" and controlled the tremor. Then the man was kept on rather
" low diet and was not allowed papers or books for two or three
" days. We had a man who had been a trainer of one of the
" professional football teams. He had been a ' shell shock '
" case himself and we retained him. He had each of the men
" out daily and smeared him with some oil and massaged him
" rather vigorously. Under this method of treatment—a form
" of suggestion and education (teaching them to relax)—they got
" well. I can state that even during the severe Passchendaele
" fighting, almost every man who was sent down suffering from
" tremors recovered."

" Our Army had to learn by experience, exactly as the French
" and German Armies did. The French adopted practically
" the same system as ourselves, but were more highly organised
" than ours in December, 1914, and January, 1915."

In Dr. Holmes' opinion, no such condition as " shell shock "
existed. It was a very unfortunate term, and to him it meant
nothing.

The witness further said that in the 5th Army Centre, during
the Passchendaele fighting, 5,346 cases were sent through in four
months. The man who has had " shell shock " is more likely
to get it again than the man who has never had it. At the time
of his investigation nine-tenths of the cases were fresh cases and
one-tenth recurrences. The 5th Army sent back 3,963 cases, and
that army at that time consisted of 22 divisions, and a division
is well over 20,000 troops ; that means 4,000 cases out of half a
million men.

" One characteristic," said Doctor Holmes, " of a com-
" motional shock case was that a man did not want to be mixed
" up with cases of ' shell shock.' " They thought it involved
discredit. He agreed that the wounded man, especially the
severely wounded man, was the man with a mind at rest. He
had done his bit.

The doctor was asked whether he had any experience of cases
of " shell-shock " in men who had never been up in the line, and
he answered : " I have seen a large number of cases of ' shell
" shock ' in men who were never near the line." Asked what
sort of treatment he gave these men and whether it was a condition requiring treatment, he answered, " Yes. At one time a
" battalion of Russian Jews came out as a Labour Battalion.
" There was an air raid warning one night after they arrived
" and a considerable number of men of the battalion went sick
" and had to be treated."

Asked whether he could state the chief reasons for keeping
" shell shocked " men in the Army Areas instead of sending
them down to the Base, Doctor Holmes replied that " the reasons
" were both administrative and medical. Administrative because
" it was recognised, and recognised rightly in his opinion, that
" during the Battle of the Somme a large number of men
" deserted from the line on the claim that they had ' shell shock '
" and it was necessary to prevent that and to keep them within
" the Army area where they were still under the discipline of
" the Army and could be reached by their battalion and sent back
" easily. The second administrative reason was that only when
" the cases remained within the Army area was it possible to
" get suitable information on the Form 3436. The medical
" reason was that once the man got to the Base it was a struggle
" to get him back again. The man was in a better mood for
" returning while he was still in the Army area. The further
" men got from the line the more difficult it was to get them
." back. ' It was the atmosphere which was important.' "

*Lieut.-Colonel H. Clay, C.B.E., D.C.M., Chief Recruiting Staff
Officer, London District.*

In Colonel Clay's opinion " only men mentally, physically and
" organically sound are wanted in the Army. Men who are not
" A.1 should on no account be enlisted and should not be retained
" in a fighting unit, if they become lower category men. There
" is a class of man who on enlistment has no defects but after
" training breaks down. This man should be discharged forth-
" with because even if you patch him up he is sure to break
" down again in time of stress."

Colonel Clay said, " Let us start with the declaration of war
" in August, 1914. As soon as war was declared the machinery
" which was in existence for recruiting practically became non-
" existent because the machinery was carried on by officers,
" N.C.O.'s and men who were immediately mobilised and went
" into their regiments and left the recruiting organisation in a
" state of chaos.

. " Certain officers who were earmarked to take over recruiting
" offices were brought together, and got together and created
" recruiting machinery to deal with the vast number of men who
" responded to Lord Kitchener's call. After the opening of the
" recruiting campaign the whole of the country was simply seeth-
" ing with recruits. They were medically examined, I say it
" without fear of contradiction, in a most haphazard manner.
" 20 to 30 per cent. of the men were never medically examined
" at all. Their attestations were made out and they were fallen
" in and drafted to regiments of what was commonly known as
" Kitchener's Army. The system was this. 600, 700 or 1,000
" men went to the depot. The recruiting officer went outside
" and fell in the party and called the roll and the party was put

" under the command of an officer, an N.C.O. or a civil police-
" man, whoever was handy and marched off to go to, say, Shore-
" ham. Bill Jones in the back row would say ' I don't want to
" ' go to Shoreham.' Other men said the same, and before the
" party had marched off 20 to 30 had changed places with other
" men who had not been medically examined. The party
" marched to Shoreham with their documents and they were
" handed over.

" It was at this period that I was brought in by Major-General
" Adye to put things right. It was realised that in the Eastern
" Command alone 49,000 men were serving without attestation.
" The only way we could trace these men's attestations was
" through their enlistment so we got clerks in the different
" offices to work double time, engaged numbers of clerks to work
" during the night, because it had not been realised that men
" would join up who did not care whether they had been attested
" or not. Consequently when we checked with Pay Records we
" were in a position to find which men had not attested. Thou-
" sands of men were never medically examined, and, consequently
" we had to get an Army Order published that all men for whom
" attestations were not forthcoming were to be re-attested. That
" was the position which carried us on over Christmas until
" February, 1915. I spent weeks in going round the depots in
" the Eastern Command and I collected over 30,000 attestations
" which had not been sent in. That is exactly how in the early
" days men not physically fit for the Army, and who would not
" have gone into the Army had they received a proper medical
" examination went in without one."

The Colonel, asked further as to the medical examination of
recruits, said, " I know of one doctor who medically examined
" 400 men per day for ten days and he didn't work 24 hours in
" the day. That was the same right away through the country
" in 1914 and early in 1915 up to the time of the Derby Scheme.

" Things had got more sorted out by September, 1915, and we
" did not get the big rush until July. Then machinery was
" working better; but even then in one particular case a practi-
" tioner's bill averaged £20 a day, which meant he had exam-
" ined 116 men a day."

The Colonel was of opinion that we should have had little
" shell shock " if we had been able to fight the war to a finish
with the first 150,000 men. The men were trained to the last
pitch when they went out in 1914. It was different with the
poor unfortunate men taken straight out of an office. The man
was brought up and rushed in twelve weeks straight to the
trenches.

*W. Brown, Esq., M.A., M.D.; late Neurologist 4th and 5th
Armies, France; Wilde Reader in Psychology, University of
Oxford.*

Asked under what conditions he had seen " shell shock " and
mental breakdown arise, Doctor Brown said, " After severe

" mental stress, from bursting of high explosives, from prolonged
" responsibility, from long service alone."

" Shell shock " was greater amongst troops fresh in the line
and during or immediately after an engagement. " Shell shock "
due to emotional disturbance is the more common by far. He
would put the average age incidence of " shell shock " at 26
years. He had experience of emotional shock similar to " shell
shock " arising during peace, such as fear causing stammering
paralysis, etc., mental anguish and anxiety causing amnesia,
etc.

The witness said he felt " the term ' shell shock ' to be an un-
" fortunate one, although it was, perhaps, almost inevitable under
" the circumstances of war, because ' shell shock ' describes a
" disease in terms of its physical aetiology rather than mental—
" the external circumstances of shock or shell explosion—and
" they may give so many different results." He found the term
" shell shock " scientifically useless. He thought that less than
10 per cent. of the cases of so-called " shell shock " were due to
concussion. There were really very few cases of commotional
shock.

The witness drew attention to the fact that there was an
enormous difference in the cases of " shell shock " from the
different battalions. The doctors could not help being struck by
the fact that men from certain regiments came up again and
again. They also noticed that in certain units there were many
more court-martial cases. Where there was more " shell shock "
there was more " skrim-shanking." He had experience of
malingering. In his first thousand cases of " shell shock " there
were 28 cases of serious malingering. They all confessed to him.
They malingered with loss of memory which was not genuine;
some with paralysis. One case said his left leg was paralysed.
Most of the cases pretended loss of memory. In one case the
man pretended that he had lost all memory of his life since birth,
and it took the doctor a week to get him to confess.

Asked whether he was struck by the amount of " shell shock "
in one battalion compared with another, the doctor added that
on one occasion he had most of the officers and men of a certain
regiment in his hospital. The whole hospital seemed to be filling
with them. There was heavy shelling at the time, but that was
not sufficient to explain the cases that came down. It seemed
as if a panic arose and they all came down together.

Asked whether he had any experience of cases of men charged
with certain military offences, such as desertion, in which the
plea of " shell shock " was put forward, the doctor said he saw
many such cases. As Neurologist of the 4th Army, all cases
which put in a plea of " shell shock " as an excuse for desertion
were sent to him for medical examination and report, and he was
always asked to give evidence in courts-martial on these cases.
He confessed it was an extremely difficult and distasteful task,
and he very soon came to the conclusion that it was almost impossible for the Medical Officer to make a decisive statement that

the man had been responsible for his action when he ran away. " In fact," said the doctor, " after my first two or three courts- " martial I found I was practically in every case giving evidence " in favour of the man. The reason was that I felt that his state " of mind in the line, when he was under heavy shell fire, was " not the same as his state of mind when he was at the Base or " somewhere between the Base and the line."

Major-General Sir H. S. Jeudwine, K.C.B.

Asked when " shell shock " first came under his notice, the General said, " It is very hard to say, because ' shell shock ' as " I understand it is a very wide term applied to a great many " different things, and I have heard of people suffering from " shell shock who were perhaps merely badly frightened, and " other people purporting to be suffering from ' shell shock ' " who were really suffering from what was undoubtedly a de- " rangement either of nerves or of health, which was very serious. " There were some officers and some other ranks who were tem- " porarily unfitted to stand the strain of active service and all " these are included in the term ' shell shock.' "

Asked whether he considered the incidence of " shell shock " was greater in the middle period of the war than at the end, the General said he thought it was greater in the middle, and he attributed the small incidence at the end of the war to the fact that troops were advancing and our armies were more successful. He said it was the sitting still that knocked the men out. If you could run after the enemy and shoot him you would not get " shell shock." People got knocked out by " shell shock " by having to sit still and see people killed on either side of them, not knowing when it would be their turn.

Sir James Galloway, K.B.E., C.B., F.R.C.P., Senior Physician, Charing Cross Hospital; late Medical Inspector of Recruiting; and Chief Commissioner Medical Services, Ministry of National Service.

Sir James Galloway described the conditions under which recruiting was carried on during the war and said : " Under the " conditions I have tried to outline, it will be understood that " large masses of the male population entered the army with " very little medical discrimination. Under ordinary peace con- " ditions many of these would in process of time have proved to " be unfit from the nervous and mental point of view. They ' proved to be unfit under war conditions."

Brevet-Colonel J. G. Burnett, C.M.G., D.S.O., 1st Battalion Gordon Highlanders.

Colonel Burnett was of opinion that the term " shell shock " i.e., the result of being blown up or concussed by the close bursting of a shell—must not be confused with what may be con- sidered " nerve shock," i.e., loss of self-control which makes it impossible for the person so afflicted to continue to face fire. This latter must be looked upon as a disgrace in an army which hopes to retain its efficiency. He said " the number of cases of " actual ' shell shock ' was very few, but of breakdown and " nerves, enormous—hundreds of them."

Asked whether in " shell shock " he considered that the neurasthenic condition played a part, the Colonel said he thought neurasthenia might be a result of it. In one case, in the battalion he commanded was a regular soldier with 12 years' service. He had been blown up by a shell early in the war. When he returned to the battalion in 1916 he was perfectly normal to talk to, but in the trenches as soon as a shell came over he was simply filled with terror and except for the fact that he was well known throughout the battalion he might have been infectious.

The Colonel said his battalion was drawn entirely from agricultural labourers. He also commanded a brigade of West Riding Territorials. The standard of *esprit de corps* in Regular battalions was always better than in Second Line Territorial battalions and the experience was that after sustaining casualties in action it was always harder to get second line battalions trained up again. He was quite certain that in a pre-war Regular battalion so long as the officer himself did not go back with a nervous breakdown, very few of the men would. The officer would not find that the whole of the platoon had gone back with a nervous breakdown and he was advancing by himself. In a modern battle he added there is always a procession of men left behind who remain in dug-outs and say they have been blown up by shells. A large proportion of them are so left because they do not want to go on. There was the case of a man on the Somme in 1916 who did not go over the top with the rest of the battalion. His story was that he was blown down the dug-out by a shell. He was unable to prove the story and was tried for his life and sentenced to be shot. The sentence was held over, but the next time he went into action he got recommended for a Distinguished Conduct Medal. That man had made a final effort to control himself and had recovered.

Asked whether he was of opinion that it was a disgrace to the man to lose control of his actions or a disgrace to the Army, Colonel Burnett replied, " A disgrace to the man. Although a " man's nerves may break down we must look upon it as a dis- " grace, otherwise you would have everybody breaking down as " soon as they wanted to go home. People who have not served " with regiments are sometimes apt to sneer at Colonel So-and- " so, who commanded a battalion for two years and then failed, " without making allowance for the strain which a long course " of battle experiences entails."

Colonel Burnett added that he went out in October, 1914, with the 2nd Battalion of the Gordons, and did not remember seeing anything of the sort, *i.e.*, " shell shock," among the regular soldiers.

Lt.-Colonel G. Scott-Jackson, C.B.E., D.S.O., M.D., late Officer Commanding T.F. Battalion, Northumberland Fusiliers.

Asked what he understood by " shell shock " the witness said, " I take it from experience that there are two forms—the " concussion form where you may have some small lesion, " hæmorrhage of the spinal cord or brain centre, and the " emotional form, which is simply and solely want of power " in the highest nerve centres. These are the forms I recognise."

Asked which he saw most of, witness said, " of the emotional " form, which was due to some faulty action of the high nerve " centres." When he went out in 1915 in command of a battalion he had no " shell shock " for a year—he would not allow it. The man or officer was sent back to the line. It was only when it began to get into the papers and the men came back home and found the amount of sympathy at home for the man " shell shocked " that his battalion got it. When he left the battalion both men and officers were coming out, who never got further forward than the transport lines. He was expecting a good draft and when he went to find them he found that half of them had already gone home with " shell shock."

He went through the whole of 1915 and into 1916 before he saw " shell shock."

Asked of his experience as time went on, did he notice that the man exposed to long service in the trenches was more liable to the emotional type of disorder, he answered, " I noticed that when " we had a rough time in the trenches it was not the day we " came out that the man had ' shell shock ' as you call it, but it " was the day we were going back into the line that most of the " cases occurred. The man would be out of the line three or " four days without symptoms or without complaining of symp- " toms, but when the time came to go back into the line he " developed all the symptoms of ' shell shock.' "

The Colonel added that he thought trench warfare and the trench mortar produced most " shell shock." It was the effect of concentration. The man shelled by artillery could lie down, but if you were shelled by trench mortars and so forth you were watching them the whole time. " It is watch and watch and dip " to avoid it, and that goes on for any length of time." In his battalion they held some trenches in the Kimmel district which were badly trench-mortared and they had more cases of " shell " shock " there than anywhere else. The Colonel said, " You " can see the trench mortar coming and you have to watch him " and dodge him, and just as you dodge him there is another " coming. It is a very unnerving thing and I put it down to " the concentration necessary to dodge them. If bombarded by " heavy artillery you are practically stupid and your mind is " almost a blank. You lie down and pray for it to finish. But " you have to watch trench mortars, and if you are cunning " enough you dodge them ; it is the concentrated attention which " is the important factor." In his judgment the most appalling thing was the feeling of inaction, tied down in the trenches. If you could move on " shell shock " disappeared to a great extent. He had no hesitation in saying that he thought many cases of neurasthenia and " shell shock " were " skrim-shanking " of the worst type. The medical officer if the man pretended to have a physical disability could see that he had not got it, but when the man said he had not been able to sleep and was shaking and nervous, what could the medical officer do when he was not trained sufficiently to decide whether it was " skrim-shanking " or not.

He said he had one extraordinary case of a man who was possibly vicious, and he had had a good deal of trouble with him as regards drunkenness and other things. The man was trying to get home on the plea of " shell shock," and he was almost tempted to let him go, but the idea struck him (Lieut.-Colonel Jackson) to make the man a stretcher-bearer, and he had no more trouble and the man was one of the finest fellows he had. He was a blackguard in the ordinary sense of the term, but when he was a stretcher-bearer going out to get the wounded in he would work night and day, and there was no trouble with him after that.

The doctor added, " I should say that in 1915 we did not suffer " from ' shell shock ' practically at all. We began to suffer " from it in 1916, but we got out in 1916 for a good long time, " training for the Somme. We went in for the Somme in Sep- " tember, and after the heavy fighting had died down we had a " long period of fighting in badly-made trenches.

" We began to suffer with ' shell shock ' badly towards the " end of 1916, and it seemed to be progressing after that, and " then we began to get a badly-trained type of recruit. Some of " them were physically or mentally good, but were sent out with " nine or ten weeks' training. ' Shell shock ' got progressively " worse from the end of 1916."

Brevet Colonel G. C. Stubbs, D.S.O., 1st Suffolk Regt.

Colonel Stubbs said that it was a help to the young soldier to be told that 99 per cent. of the men were afraid of shells. The fear of being thought afraid is often a cause of trouble.

" I think there is an idea among young soldiers especially " that there should not be such a thing as fear. I do not know, " but I think I was in an awful funk the whole time, and I " think most people were, and if the young soldier were given " to understand that everybody is very much afraid and that it " is a natural condition to be in, but he should overcome it, and " if he were told about the effect of shells and that sort of thing, " and that it was up to him to control himself, it would have " some small effect. Many men are afraid of being thought " afraid, and it worries them. I think if it were pointed out " that it is not cowardly to be afraid, but it is cowardly to let fear

" get control of your actions, if that were rubbed into the young
" soldier as a part of his training, I think it would help to a
" certain extent."

He had seen men near whom a shell had burst
" (a) Dazed and stupid;
" (b) Suffer from trembling, rather like a jelly shaking."
The effect a high explosive used to have on him was as if all the
stamina had been taken out of him. This lasted for several
hours, and generally until he had had a long sleep.

He agreed that " shell shock " as a disorder was always most
rampant when things were at their worst, i.e., much worse when
they were sitting in the trenches and not getting forward at all.
By the end of the war, when they were up and away to victory,
it had practically disappeared.

Asked whether it was not the case that particular classes of
men in the war were not worth anything, and that as a result
of suggestion or otherwise they were practically suffering from
nervous disorder before they got near the fighting line for the
first time, Colonel Stubbs said, " I should say that was probably
" the case. At any rate it spread very quickly, and as soon as
" one started to come away the rest followed. They came away
" in two's or three's. My doctor collected about 20 or 30, and he
" wanted to send them back to the line, but I packed them off
" to the transport line and kept them in a very unpleasant spot,
" and eventually got rid of them to some division, who put them
" into a Labour Company."

Colonel Stubbs summed up as follows :—" There is the case
" of ' shell shock ' where a strong man is blown up and is shiver-
" ing and quivering like a jelly, and then the case of the fellow
" who, simply from being kept out there for a long time, is worn
" out. Then there are the other fellows who are not of the fight-
" ing type."

*Brevet Lieut.-Colonel Viscount Gort, V.C., D.S.O., M.V.O.,
M.C., Grenadier Guards.*

Lord Gort said :—" You must distinguish between ' shell
" shock ' and nervous breakdown. ' Shell shock ' is a word
" which has crept into the public vocabulary for use on all occa-
" sions, whereas most of the cases to which this term is applied
" are not ' shell shock ' at all, in my opinion, but nervous break-
" down caused through the soldier's nerves gradually wearing
" out. Among the regular battalions with a good class of men
" the circumstances were rather different to those in the New
" Army units, and there were few cases of real ' shell shock.' "

Lord Gort said he took over a battalion at the beginning of
1917. He remembered before that the case of an officer who was
buried at the first battle of Ypres and had " shell shock " and
came back to duty in 1915 in time for another battle. Unfortunately for him he came back at a time when the Germans were
attacking. Directly the enemy came over the top it was too

much for him, and his nerve went again. He was sent home and did not come out again until 1918, when he went to another division and, the witness believed, did well.

Lord Gort proceeded :—" The next case I recall was of a man " in my own battalion—a private soldier. He got a very slight " wound on the Somme, nothing more than a scratch. He was " put over the top again later on, but would not face it. He " avoided the battalion aid post and went to the advanced dress- " ing station. He was a cunning man, and insisted on having " his temperature taken. It was found to be between 99° to " 100°. When he came back we tried to get him court martialled " for desertion in the face of the enemy, and he was put up for " trial. He pleaded evidence of temperature and got off. We " put him over the top again on the 31st July and the same thing " happened, and again he avoided the battalion aid post and " went off to the advanced dressing station with the same old " story. I decided to have him up and talk to him. The man " was disliked by the whole battalion, as it was bad for *esprit* " *de corps,* and he was publicly talked about. I had him in the " Orderly Room and talked to him about the discredit and dis- " grace to his regiment, and then asked him finally, ' If nothing " ' comes of this last escapade will you go over the top next " ' time? I put you on your honour to do so ; you must control " ' your nerves.' He promised he would. The battalion " attacked again in October, and he was in a Reserve Company " and he went over with his comrades. The men were " enormously pleased about this, and when they came back said, " ' Private X (we will call him Private X) went over to-day.' I " was pleased myself, and had him up to the Orderly Room and " congratulated him on having played up to the regiment. We " went over the top again later—his company was in the front " line this time. He reverted to his old habits and went off to " the advanced dressing station. Shortly after that he was " killed. He was killed actually holding the line, but not in a " battle. He did not mind holding the line, but when there was " any question of going over the top he would cut it at once. " There was nothing odd about him except that his profession " was that of a tramp. The Orderly Room sergeant found this " out about him, and that he had never done any work in his " life. He was quite good physically and everything like that, " and to look at him you would not think he was a tramp. I " think he was a clever man.

" I remember a sergeant I had who had done very well. In " September, 1918, we had to take over from another division " in the middle of an attack. It was a night attack and it was " difficult to find where everything was. Two sergeants got into " a dug-out with some men and we could not find them for " twelve hours. These men had been jolly good fellows, both " of them, and it was simply a case of nervous breakdown. It

" was not ' shell shock ' as I understand it but they were worn
" out and finished."

Asked whether when Commanding Officers saw a man
obviously breaking down they sent him back to the Base, Lord
Gort said, " Yes, but it was a difficulty. If you once allowed
" people to go away you felt you were not playing the game to
" the Army." He added that he thought that it would be worth
while getting statistics of the incidence of " shell shock " in the
various divisions at different periods. He thought it would be
found that in first-class divisions there was practically no " shell
shock."*

Lord Gort added, " I think the whole question of training is
" one of morale and *esprit de corps* and that in face of strong
" morale and *esprit de corps* ' shell shock ' would be practically
" non-existent. Where there is a good battalion commander
" the men will always play up to him ; if he sets the example the
" rest will follow. In peace training the great thing is drill.
" No doubt you want something to help you over your fears
" and if you get control of the nerves, as you do in drill, it helps
" largely and it helps to drive the man forward in war. For an
" instance of that, the Canadians fell back on drill as an excellent
" way of improving the general morale of their divisions.
" Another form of morale raising is regimental history—to tell
" men of the deeds done by the regiment. The feeling of
" unionism—of moving together—is a great help and this is
" brought out by the soldiers' training—drill.

" Another most important point is that in France we put great
" store on drilling battalions every morning when they were out
" of the line. It made them move as a mass and undoubtedly
" created the feeling in them that they belonged to a body
" capable of moving as a whole and not as individuals."

Lord Gort added, " I think ' shell shock,' like measles, is so
" infectious that you cannot afford to run risks with it at all and
" in war the individual is of small account. If one or two go
" by the board it is extremely unfortunate and sad but it cannot
" be helped. A large proportion must be wounded or killed. It
" must be looked upon as a form of disgrace to the soldier. A
" certain class of men are all right out of the line, but the minute
" they know they are to go back they start getting ' shell shock '
" and so forth. If such a man had been in a bad condition it
" would have been seen by his Commanding Officer and he would
" have been examined by the Medical Officer and passed out of
" the line. Officers must be taught much more about man
" mastership in the same way as horse mastership. I
" think further care should be taken to teach commanders
" that at the Staff College, so that they do not overtax
" the men. It is all to a great extent a question of discipline

* *Note.*—The general evidence favours Lord Gort's opinion, but such statistics
are not available.

" and drill. The man with 14 weeks' training had not been
" taught to control himself. He was probably a Yahoo before
" he was taken into the army and he could not get his nerves
" under restraint. In the young soldiers' battalions the boys
" were gradually broken in."

Lord Gort thought that a large number of the men who two or
three years after the war were still suffering from " shell shock "
symptoms were probably bordering on lunacy before.

Major-General Sir Alfred W. L. Bayly, K.C.B., K.C.M.G.,
C.S.I., D.S.O. ; Late Inspector of Temporary Non-Effectives.

Sir Alfred Bayly was of opinion that it was probably impossible,
with any degree of certainty, to pick out before trial any particular type of man who cannot be made into a good soldier, except
degenerates from physical or mental causes or the results of a
vicious life. Many individuals, however, cannot be made into
good fighting soldiers.

All types of temperament and intelligence are likely to be
affected by " shell shock." Much depends on health and condition at the time of stress; previous mode of life, whether usually
outdoor active men, or whether they have led sheltered sedentary
inactive lives (bodily or mentally). If they have been burning
the candle at both ends they would certainly become liable to
" shell shock." There are no general characteristics.

During the late war numbers of officers were of the same class
as those in the ranks.

The cases of " shell shock " he had noticed were trembling;
sometimes there was apparent difficulty in speaking clearly, they
could not collect their thoughts, they had unsteadiness of gait,
often appeared as if the worse for alcohol; were always dwelling
on their condition; imagined they were worse than they really
were, and made no apparent effort to get fit; gave the impression that they were very frightened. · Frequent visits home would
tend to increase " shell shock "—such visits often spent under
conditions tending to lower mental control and there is also the
conscious or sub-conscious dread of return to active service.
Emotional " shell shock " is not completely curable during the
period of a war if the patient has any possible chance of being
returned to the fighting line.

The General said that his impression was, and he thought it
was unavoidable, that we pushed the recruits too much, recruits
of all ages. We were very short of men and everything was
forced. Many men were out of condition and not as fit as they
might have been. They were fit enough to go into the army;
they had no organic disease, but they were not in a good physical
condition, *i.e.*, the younger men. The elderly men over 40 were
in the same way. You suddenly took a man who had never done
anything in that way in his life since he left school, and put him
through physical drill.

The witness said that he had seen " shell shock " cases in groups and had also seen and spoken to the men individually. As a layman he must say he had formed the opinion that there were a good number of them not " shell shock " at all—a good deal of simulation. He would not say they were all malingering. He thought there was very little malingering in the army, but a great deal that was put down to " shell shock " was not " shell shock " at all. They had found out it was an easy way to get home.

He knew personally of a man who was taken prisoner and wounded. He was a prisoner in Germany for some time. He was a sergeant with three or four years' experience at the front. The witness was speaking to him the other day and said, " During your experience at the front and in Germany, how many cases of ' shell shock ' did you see? " He said, " Genuine? " The General said, " Yes," and he said, " One, Sir." The General thought that " shell shock " came less from the strain and stress of war, but that it was more the effect of always thinking how long is this thing going on; can I stick it much longer. The man broods over it.

We should not have had " shell shock " in the witness' opinion had it been a worse war as regards casualties but had not lasted so long.

Asked whether he had experience of the same sort of thing before this war, the General said, " I saw the men who " retreated from Maiwand. They had been a 50-mile march and " most of these men to look at were exactly the same as the men " who are now known as ' shell shock.' It was pretty much " emotional upset when they threw away rifles and everything " else as surplus weight. We also had it in South Africa in a " few cases and they were just the same sort of thing."

Asked whether " shell shock " becomes contagious in a unit the witness answered, " Panic becomes contagious. Whether " ' shell shock ' does or does not I do not know, or whether you " would describe ' shell shock ' as panic or panic as ' shell shock ' " I do not know."

As to visits home, he pointed out that the last thing he would recommend in civil life to a person who had a nervous breakdown would be to be nursed by his friends.

Professor Graham Brown, D.Sc., M.D.; late Neurologist, British Salonika Force; Professor of Physiology in the University of South Wales.

Doctor Graham Brown said that he had no meaning for the term " shell shock." He disliked the word intensely and he thought it was extraordinary that it was used. He used two terms himself—first, " concussion cases," which he believed to have been true cases of concussion, and secondly he used the term " nervous breakdown in the line," which covers any other disability (save organic lesions of the nervous system) which causes the soldier to be sent to the neurological department. He explained that in Salonika there was a special mental hospital and that he did not get cases of true insanity diagnosed as such He gave some illustrative cases of the sort of men who broke down. One case was a battery sergeant-major. He had a malarial attack and carried on during it and after it. His memory became bad ; in the line his efficiency suffered and when his battery came out of the line he was sent sick. He recovered and rejoined his unit. His unit again went into reserve, but previous to this in the time of stress his memory had been bad. He had malaria again but recovered. Next he was too ill to return to the line and was sent to a rest camp, and there he was given a Corps Order under which he was reduced to the rank of sergeant for inefficiency. Then he was sent to the neurological department. In this case the knee and ankle jerks were slightly unequal but there was no other trace of organic disease. Doctor Brown said he had lost the note with regard to the cerebro-spinal fluid, but was almost certain that it must have been a positive Wasserman reaction. He had seen other cases of the same sort. He also had a certain number of cases of alcoholism which he called neurasthenia. One was that of an officer in charge of a Trench Mortar Battery. He was put into a position where he expected to get it hot and he thought it was a death sentence. He began to drink. He should not have done so, but he did and he gradually broke down. It might be called a breakdown under neurasthenia or alcoholism or fear—all three things went together.

Another case was that of an officer who was in charge of a Field Ambulance. His was an interesting case. He had a severe shaking from a shell burst and in the succeeding year he had suffered from malarial relapses. He had the cocaine habit and gradually become more and more depressed. He had the cocaine habit before the period of stress started. With the habit and malaria he became very depressed and broke down. He was found wandering away from the unit one night and was unable to account for it. He was not court martialled.

If a man was isolated for a long time he often broke down. There was an officer who spent most of his time deciphering enemy wireless messages. He had a trying time of it in the marshes and he broke down simply because of the arduousness and loneliness of his work.

With regard to responsibility, there is a larger proportion of N.C.O.'s above the rank of Lance-Corporal in the concussed class than in the nervous breakdown class. The man who has a good billet does not want to break down if he can help it. In the case of the Lance-Corporal, whose billet is not so great a prize, the effect of responsibility is considerably less.

The doctor said he had gone into the question of nightmares and examined each case privately. 5 per cent. of the men under fire were having nightmares and 17 per cent. of the men who had never been in the line were having nightmares. 11 per cent. of the men under fire had broken sleep, and 31 per cent. of the men coming to the line had broken sleep. 11 per cent. of the men under fire talked, shouted and screamed in their sleep. He thought that the greater incidence of signs in the men under fire and of the dreaming and sleeping disturbances in the men just about to go under fire for the first time were very interesting and important.

Asked whether he had any suggestions to make with regard to the prevention of " shell shock," the witness said he did not think we should have had it if the name had not been invented. We should have been bound to have men breaking down in the line, but we should not have had the quantity. He thought the name had a great deal to do with the very big problem that we were faced with in " shell shock." The doctor felt strongly that the matter of infectiousness was an important one and he gave illustrative cases of men who actually did become affected and developed hysteria from other patients.

The first instance he gave was a treble one. A. had been many months in a base hospital. At first he went into hospital for malaria. After malaria he had dropsy and after dropsy he had hysterical paralysis. B. came into the same ward with malaria and was particularly interested in case A. because his own son had developed paralysis from a gunshot wound in the back in France. He took an interest in A. and helped him about the ward and so on. B. became cured of his malaria and was discharged. Then C. came into the same ward with malaria and he developed a hysterical paraplegia from A. B. was readmitted with a malarial relapse and came into the same ward and found A. still in his old state of paralysis. He began to dread that his malaria would go the same way and that he would develop paralysis, and eventually he did develop a hysterical paraplegia, so the three cases were in the ward at the same time. There was no doubt about the hysterical nature of the three cases. They were all sent to the neurological department and were immediately cured of their paralyses.

The second instance is that of a man admitted to a general hospital with malaria and placed in the next bed to a case of post-malarial paralysis. He feared that he would get it and sure enough he did get it. Such men have a fear that they will be affected. When they get out of bed their legs give way beneath them and the hysteria is fixed. They are naturally weak when they first get up, but they think it is the confirmation of their worst fears.

Another case was a bad one of syringo-myelia, and the physicians plotted out the areas of anæsthesia. On the other side of the ward there was a case of hysteria which was originally a case of hysterical loss of voice. This patient came to the physicians one day with a beautiful area of anæsthesia marked out by himself on his own arm. It was a case of infection. The man really believed he had a loss of feeling. All this proves the necessity of having cases early diagnosed and quickly treated, and emphasises the necessity of keeping this class of patient isolated as far as possible until he is cured.

Dr. Graham Brown agreed that the vast majority of cases of so-called " shell shock " used in its broadest sense were cases of psycho-neurosis, and not differing from the same conditions in civilians.

The late W. H. R. Rivers, Esq., M.D., F.R.C.P., LL.D.; late Consultant in Psychological Medicine to Royal Air Force; Prælector in Natural Science, St. John's College, Cambridge.

Dr. Rivers. asked what he thought of the term " shell shock," said he objected to it root and branch. The reason why he objected to the term was that so far as he could see the main factor had been stress, and the shock in most cases was merely the last straw. Any disturbance might have produced the same result. Stress, in his opinion, was really the important factor. Although one could not make a division accurately one ought to distinguish between two varieties of case.

One is the officer who breaks down soon after going to the front because he is unfitted for the position in which he finds himself, and the other is the officer who breaks down after long and continued strain. It is doubtful whether the cases of the first class ought to be called cases of neurosis. In his experience they were not very severe as a rule and got well easily, unless they were mismanaged when sent home. The other class of case, which is much more important, is the man who breaks down after long and continued strain. These were the men who, especially in the early stages of the war, after some shell explosion or something else had knocked them out badly, went on struggling to do their duty until they finally collapsed entirely. Cases of that kind presented specially severe symptoms. All these cases were much of the same order, only people who broke down before they went over to France did not want stress to cause them to break down; they were ready to break down immediately. The man who got to France had stress. There is no question of that; perhaps, for him, a very big stress indeed. The case of the man totally unfitted for warfare finding himself in the trenches meant a very big stress for him. Stress is relative. He had not immediate experience of men who broke down shortly after joining the army, but he was doubtful whether they ought to be called cases of war neurosis.

A man should not develop a real neurosis unless he had strain; it depends on the man. There are cases intermediate between the two classes. Men whom a small shock would knock out. If a patient was asked to compare the shock which knocked him out with his previous experience of shell explosion, the answer usually was that the shell explosion which knocked him out finally was trivial compared with his previous experiences. He had had much severer shocks after which he picked himself up and perhaps laughed at the experience. The final experience which knocked him out when compared with his previous experiences might be a comparative triviality.

That was the kind of experience which lead the witness to lay so much weight on the fact of stress, using stress as a wide term, including sleeplessness, anxiety, fatigue, responsibility.

Asked whether there was doubt in his mind as to the existence of a mental wound arising from emotional shock in contradistinction to any concussion, the witness said he should be inclined to put it in this way, that when the man began to have a number of disturbances of different kinds, such as loss of sleep, etc , he either consciously or more or less unconsciously looked for an explanation, and this tended to centre around some particular experience, in many cases a comparatively trivial experience. Asked whether it would be fair to say that there is such a thing as a mental wound arising under these conditions, the witness answered in the affirmative, adding that he had got into the habit of calling it trauma rather than wound ; but that if wound was recognised as the English term he would agree, certainly.

Asked as to morale, the witness said, " My experience is that " the whole object of military training is to produce *esprit de* " *corps* and other factors which give good morale, and that the " lack of them is a very strong factor in the production of " neurosis of certain kinds. It would tend to diminish these " varieties of neurosis, in which the soldier breaks down rapidly, " if the military training were successful as it was in the regular " army, where it was exceptional for a man to break down except " after severe stress. One influence of this was that when the " regular soldier broke down, particularly the private soldier and " the regular non-commissioned officer, he suffered severely from " shame ; the soldier serving only for the war had not that senti- " ment produced by the regular training. The reason why we " had such enormous numbers suffering with neurosis in this war " was the incomplete training."

The witness said that statistics were required as to the extent to which psycho-neurosis occurred in different parts of the army ; that he had found it very difficult to judge of frequency.[*] In the Air Force there were three different lines of work : the pilot, the observer, and the balloon section.

Dr. Rivers said : " The pilots frequently had severe concus- " sions and were much more knocked about than either of the " other two groups, but such psycho-neurosis as they had was " very slight indeed, almost trivial compared with the cases seen " in the army. All they wanted was a talk to get rid of the " repression and then to go off for a holiday.

" The observers had definitely more severe symptoms on the " whole, and those in the balloon section were the most severe " cases of psycho-neurosis that I think I have seen anywhere.

---

[*] *Note.*—Unfortunately these statistics are unobtainable.

" The explanation I give involves my special theoretical posi-
" tion that man's normal reaction to danger is what I call mani-
" pulative activity.   Every animal has a natural reaction to
" danger, perhaps more than one, and man's is manipulation of
" such a kind as to get him out of the dangerous situation.   Of
" course, the pilot is able to utilise that in a supreme degree.
" When in danger his whole mind is taken up with guiding the
" machine and so on.   The observer, on the other hand, although
" occupied in various ways, is not occupied to the same extent
" He has periods of considerable stress, especially when going
" up, when he has not anything to do.   He is not in charge ; he
" has his own special work to do, but he has not the same chance
" of manipulative activity as the pilot.

" The balloon man has a certain amount of observation to do,
" but most of the time he has no activity whatever and is sitting
" in the middle of a target.   I believe it was the absence of mani-
" pulative activity that led to his more frequent and severe break-
" down.

" That led me to the view that man's normal reaction to danger
" is manipulative activity.   If he cannot have that, or if it is
" restricted in any way, you have a prominent condition for the
" occurrence of neurosis in one form or another.

" That only confirmed my experience in the army—that the
" trying time was the period in the trenches when there was
" nothing to be done.

" Officers would tell me that they recognised this so well that
" they had sent men and junior officers on quite unnecessary jobs
" in order to keep them occupied.   I think the able officer in the
" army recognised that himself as an important factor.

" If that is correct there ought to have been considerable
" differences in the incidence of neurosis at different periods of
" the war, and it is the general impression that there was a
" distinct falling off in the amount of neurosis after March, 1918,
" when it became a war of movement.   I should like to know
" whether that is so."*

In the witness's experience, having to dodge shells was a help ;
what did produce fear was being between two barrages—a barrage
in front and one behind and nothing to be done.

He did not believe he had ever met a healthy officer who had
not confessed to him when he knew him that at certain times
during the war he was subject to acute funk, and the condition
producing it was being in a helpless attitude.   It was the same
in the Air Force, when the man lost himself and did not know
what to do.

The witness said he never used the word " neurasthenia."   It
had become an absolutely worthless word.   What was ordinarily
called " neurasthenia " he called " anxiety neurosis."   Hysteria
and anxiety neurosis might be combined and were in the majority

---

* *Note.*—The general evidence shows that the answer is in the affirmative.

of cases. The hysteria might get well and then the patient would develop an anxiety state. The witness said he had always laid stress on the fact that the repression was a normal process. Those who were repressing were using a normal mechanism for a cause for which it was not suitable. The things which the men were trying to put out of their minds were far too powerful. They were using an instrument of repression for a purpose for which it was unsuited and inadequate. "If," said the Doctor, "you think about the experience which men went through in "France, seeing their friends at their side with their heads blown "off and things of that sort, the process of repression is alto-"gether unsuited for an experience of that kind, and yet that "process was going on on an enormous scale and in the early "stages of the war was habitually recommended by everybody. "'Put it out of your mind, old fellow, and do not think about it; "imagine that you are in your garden at home.'"

F. A. Hampton, Esq., M.C., M.B.; Physician to the Hospital for Epileptics, Maida Vale; late Regimental Medical Officer and Medical Officer, Royal Air Force.

Doctor Hampton held that a commotional shock was the last straw, the precipitating factor in "shell shock." He said that in the early stages the men would tell you in confidence that they had become very nervous and that they were continually on the alert listening for shells coming, or perhaps if it was an officer, that he found his responsibilities trying and began to get uncertain. He was not certain whether he had the sentries posted or not and had to make doubly sure of everything. A man in that condition might get a momentary blow which would put him into a state of terror and he might not be able to recover from that, or he might develop conversion hysteria and be temporarily deaf or paralysed. Asked what importance he placed upon the history of loss of consciousness, he said he tried to determine whether it was amnesia or actual loss of consciousness. In many cases it proved to be amnesia. He discovered that chiefly by hypnotism. The man came up with a history of having been blown up and unconscious for a day or so. The doctors often found out that it was really amnesia, that the man was lying helpless and let people pick him up and carry him off; he was almost like an animal shamming death. The man was conscious all the time and described what had happened, how he was picked up and put on a stretcher. Unless investigation had been made by means of hypnotism you would have said the man had been unconscious.

Asked whether his general impression of "shell shock" was that it was an emotional disease, he answered in the affirmative and agreed that the explosion of shells had very little to do with it.

"The popular conception of 'shell shock' is that it arises "after and only after an explosion. That is known by the man

" and when a shell bursts near him, whether it causes a
" mechanical effect or not, he says to himself, ' Well, now I can
" have a reasonable excuse for giving way.' " Asked whether in
his opinion it was a good thing or bad thing that " shell shock "
should be looked at askance, that it should be considered as a
sign of weakness at a time when the men should do their best
to keep up, the witness said, " I think in training it would be a
" very good thing if it could be explained to the men that they
" will be afraid and that they are liable to develop neurosis by
" repressing that fear, but explain that everybody does feel
" afraid."

The witness was asked as to " shell shock " in the Flying
Corps, and said that it seemed to be different from the infantry
type. " The airmen seem to go more slowly. In the Infantry
" type a man breaks down through an explosion or otherwise and
" develops the thing suddenly, but in the Flying Corps they get
" more and more nervous until somebody sends them on leave or
" until they crash."

*J. I. C. Dunn, Esq., D.S.O., M.C., D.C.M., M.D., D.P.H.;
served in the ranks during South African War and as a
Regimental Medical Officer in the Great War.*

Doctor Dunn said " It would be going too far to say that a
" man who :—
"   " (a) was nervously unstable,
"   " (b) had been insane,
"   " (c) was mentally defective,
" cannot be trained into an efficient soldier, meaning thereby a
" man thought good enough to send into the line during a
" national war. In peace time high grade defectives were
" recruited and completed their colour service. Several such
" cases have come before the Pensions Appeal Tribunal—the war
" revealed them, in two instances after a long period of testing
" service (one had a markedly asymmetrical head and face; he
" had a mild malaria several months before his breakdown).
" The chances of a breakdown in training these men are great;
" of an eventual breakdown very great, according to my Pensions
" Appeal Tribunal observation. Such a man as (a) and still
" more (c), if he outlast training and be posted to a combatant
" unit in active service conditions, soon excites notice, is con-
" sidered unreliable or useless by a competent officer, and the
" Medical Officer is asked to get rid of him. It must depend on
" the officer and chance whether he is got rid of before he has
" been ' shocked ' or become confused. Labour units appeared to
" be very tolerant of defective and unstable men, almost to
" waiting until a breakdown occurred, even in the case of men
" whose appearance was suggestive of their condition. The
" standard of work in the labour corps was very low; the men
" were little tried and so would not attract notice. There is no
" economy in training such men; it is waste all round. On
" similar, but narrower, grounds, there should be exemption, at

" least from service in the War Zone, of men who merely had
" been insane. The mentally defective are the most liable to
" breakdown, and their liability is great.

" In the public interest, that of the individual apart, all these
" types should be exempted from all forms of service, except
" controlled labour that allowed them to live at home."
Further, Dr. Dunn said he would discharge permanently and
grade with these, every adolescent and young man after one
proved epileptic seizure.

" Commotional disturbance," said the witness, " can in my
" opinion account for an exceedingly small percentage of cases
" of shock and a consideration of the nature and onset of strain
" as I have seen it makes me doubt if commotion is such a factor
" in producing it—unless the residual signs of commotional shock
" simulate strain."

Windage, the air compression of a passing shell, the witness
discredited entirely as a cause of commotion. The draught of a
5·9 within a very few feet (about 4) is negligible.

" Shell burst; to be blown into a shell hole, into the air, etc.,
" is a conventional expression. It means much less than
" 'buried' or 'gassed.' Great is the number of men 'blown,'
" who have raised a smile or a jeer among those who saw them
" jump before the shell burst 10 or 50 yards off. Then the
" draught during a burst is so vertical, unless the burst be on
" a hard surface like a main road, that at three or four yards
" from a 5·9 it is scarcely felt.

" I have seen a man temporarily dazed when closer than that
" to a burst, but I have not had to evacuate one for shock.

" Once I saw one man and once two men together 15 to 20
" feet in the air. Once I saw a man blown as far along the
" ground (the shell burst beside him on a road). The last was
" killed. The other three were reported killed unwounded, but
" I had no chance of examining the bodies. I infer that com-
" motional shock is a very rare condition."

The witness said he could not contribute to the differential
diagnosis of emotional or commotional shock more than the suggestion that no man's statement that he had been " blown "
should be accepted by any clinician except after a most searching and informed cross-examination on every detail of the alleged
incident.

" The seriousness or levity with which different men in re-
" sponsible positions regard their responsibility is very striking."
This he regarded as a great factor in the incidence of strain.
" Many officers and senior non-commissioned officers take care
" of themselves to the neglect of duty and of the example due
" from their rank; they last long unscathed. It is on the good
" type of man that strain tells, the men who try to control
" events, not those who are content to sit down and await
" events."

The witness remarked that he had no very definite evidence to offer of the contagiousness of shock. He said :—

" I have seen three or four men at very brief intervals fall out " in a condition of acute shock. They were all fresh in the " field; no shell had burst within 20 yards of them. We had " had no rest all night, had been under a heavy dispersed fire all the morning, a constant stream of wounded had passed through " us, we were then moving parallel and close to a barrage ; our " own guns were on the other side, about 100 yards off ; there was " a lot of noise and noise alone jangles one's nerves.

" I have encountered a minor stampede started by an officer " of low *morale* calling ' gas ' when there was no gas. He had " already denounced the ' butchery ' to his platoon during the " action.

" I have seen the bad effect that the behaviour of a man " suffering from strain is calculated to have on others who looked " up to him."

Asked at what period he first heard something of " shell shock," the witness said, " The first case was that of an officer who had " already been out in the early part of 1915. Within a very " short time of going out he was sent home for inefficiency ; the " inefficiency was that he simply rolled into any odd corner as " soon as a shell came over. He came out again and joined the " battalion in the very peaceful trench warfare that was going " on after a battle had quite died down. He showed the same " signs again and was sent to me. I could find nothing about " the man. Of course at that time I did not know what the " physical signs of shock were, but I could find nothing about him " at all and he was eventually passed to the A.D.M.S. and was " sent home. He came out again a third time. He was with " us when we were in divisional reserve for a little but as soon " as we went up into the line (he happened to be temporarily in " command of his company) we were delayed in getting across " a river by the shelling of the bridges, and he suddenly dis- " appeared from his company. Nobody knew what had become " of him and the whole relief was held up for an hour. He was " afterwards discovered in hiding and was again sent to me. " I refused to take any action in the matter and said it must be " dealt with as a disciplinary matter as I could find no reason " for treating it as a medical case. He was sent to the G.O.C. " who gave him a job with a Labour unit.

" The other man was a very similar type of fellow. There " could not be a better man at ordinary times. but a machine " gun firing would send him 200 or 300 yards down the trench to " the rear. There were no physical signs and in conversation " he said he just found himself running. He was disposed of in " the same way. I could not say in looking at these two cases " in retrospect that either showed any of the signs that later on " I came to associate with the man who was suffering from strain " or shock in any of its degrees."

Lt.-Colonel J. S. Y. Rogers, C.B.E., D.S.O., T.D., M.D., C.M.
(R.A.M.C., T.F.), late Regimental Medical Officer 4th
Black Watch).

Lt.-Col. Rogers said " shell shock " was a misnomer; he went
on, " I consider that the majority of cases that one meets with on
" active service are not due to shells at all. The majority of cases
" are entirely anxiety neurosis and if you know your man you can
" see this gradually appearing. You see a variety of conditions,
" including fear and commotional ' shell shock,' but this latter
" is exceptional. You do not find a great many commotional
" 'shell shock' cases as far as I can see. I would put com-
" motional cases at 5 per cent. if as much as that."

He added, " If you leave out commotional cases every case is
" emotional and I agree with Sir Frederick Mott that fear plays
" a large element in all cases. I think every man, no matter how
" brave out at the front, has experienced fear. You cannot
" avoid it with the various things that are going on. A man
" in the front line is under constant stress of excitement. He
" does not know when he is going to be shelled or sniped or
" undergo the dangers of patrol duty. He may be mined under-
" neath; he does not know when the mine is going up. He has a
" fear of gas (that is a tremendous fear with the men), a whole
" battalion will go almost panicky with gas, and they are con-
" tinually living in such a stress that I do say that fear plays a
" large part in the emotions. They are not cowards. They are
" men who can keep that stress of fear under, but I think it
" enters largely into these cases."

Asked what temperament favours anxiety neurosis, Doctor
Rogers said, " It is difficult to say, but as a rule you will find
" that bright volatile people—people who are willing and anxious
" to do dangerous work, battalion runners, men who are anxious
" to go out on raids and patrol—are even more liable to this
" anxiety condition than others. On the other hand, you have
" this strange coincidence. I will give you an instance. There
" were three rather noted boxers. Two of them were in our
" battalion and one belonged to another battalion. They would
" stand up at boxing competitions and take a lot of hammering,
" and these three men suffered from ' shell shock,' from anxiety
" neurosis. They could face the boxing ring but they could not
" face the music otherwise. It is extremely difficult to lay down
" a type."

As to marching and exposure as a cause of emotional " shell
" shock " the Doctor said, " I think, in regard to that, that in
" many cases you are dealing with boys, some of whom are not
" properly grown, and it was always an anxiety to these boys to
" have a march of 10 to 15 miles carrying a matter of 80 to
" 100 lb., and a good bulk of that pressing on the chest. These
" boys used to dread the march and I know two or three that
" undoubtedly developed neurosis with that dread. They dreaded
" the weight and I only prevented these men developing neurosis

" by getting hold of them and carrying their packs. I prevented
" it by seeing the mental distress of these boys when they
" marched along the road. I made it a point always to march
" with the battalion. I never rode. I wandered up and down
" watching each man as he marched, singling out the men suffer-
" ing from distress. We had boys of 18 and 19, and at the
" beginning even boys of 17. They suffered severely from
" physical stress and it also gave them mental distress—the
" knowledge that they had to keep up with the battalion and
" could not do it.

" Gas was a potent cause of anxiety neurosis in the majority
" of cases. There were periods when we were gassed and some
" of the men were undoubtedly suffering from gas poisoning, but
" there were always a large number turned out that were not, in
" my opinion, gassed but were suffering from anxiety neurosis.
" During a very bad time we had in the Polderhoek sector about
" November, 1917, there were about 150 or 200 went down the
" line with so-called gas poisoning. There were only a matter
" of 30 or 40 who were really gassed, the rest were anxiety
" neurosis from fear of gas, and I have seen that happen so often.
" The very mention of gas would put the ' wind up ' the bat-
" talion at once, even if they had gas masks, which, they were
" told, were perfectly safe. I think gas was a very powerful
" factor in causing anxiety neurosis."

Asked whether so-called " shell-shock " was common after a
short period of rest, and before the men went back to the front
line, Dr. Rogers said : " A good deal depended upon the con-
" ditions of the front line. If the front line was in a bad state,
" with cold, wet or snow, or anything like that, or if the troops
" were having a rough time in any way, then he thought that the
" rest back did good and he thought the neurosis lessened. The
" men got very exhausted and upset if they had bad times in
" the front line, and especially if they had unpleasant conditions,
" such as those which existed in the Ypres salient. He said
" they were there for 14 consecutive months, and he always
" found if they got bad times a rest behind the lines did good.

Asked whether the bursting of a shell would not produce an
hysterical condition, the doctor replied, " Not unless the condi-
" tion was there before. I have seen so many men blown over
" and then get up and go on with their work none the worse.
" I remember one instance in front of Goudecourt where there
" was a big dug-out containing a great many non-commissioned
" officers. There were 10 in this dug-out ; a shell burst and nine
" of the ten were simply blown to pieces. Those that were not
" killed outright had their legs and arms blown off. There was
" one sergeant sitting close to the door, and the force of the
" explosion threw him out of the dug-out. He escaped concus-
" sion ; he escaped aerial compression. He was simply blown
" clean out of the dug-out. He was a bit out of sorts and

" nervous for a few hours. He came down to my dug-out and I
" gave him some food and a good night's sleep, and he went back
" to his work and never turned a hair over the incident. I think
" you must have the anxiety neurosis creeping up, unless you
" have distinct concussion or a commotional shock."

The handling of " shell shock " depends on a lot of things in
the field. " A good deal depends on the Medical Officer ; in fact,
" I think most depends on the Medical Officer attached to the
" battalion—his knowledge of men in general and his knowledge
" of the men of his unit in particular. He ought to know the
" men personally and take an interest in them. There is no
" reason why he should not have an elementary knowledge of
" psychology. I think that should be within the possibility of
" every qualified medical man. It is a great mistake to look on
" men as malingerers. I must confess that when I went to
" France for the first two or three months I was inclined to look
" on men far too much as malingerers, and I very quickly
" changed my opinion. I think there is far more in psychology.
" I do not think malingering is common ; I think there is
" psychology in the whole matter, and if the Medical Officer
" takes an interest in the man, if he sees that the men are com-
" fortable, well housed, kept clean with plenty of baths and all
" that sort of thing, if the men realise the Medical Officer is
" taking an interest in the general health and welfare of the
" battalion (asking them to do impossible things irritates them
" and tends towards a nervous element) ; if the men have any
" grievance see if you can get it redressed ; sometimes you your-
" self are personally guilty of giving a man a good talking to
" when it is unmerited ; if you do that you do not know where
" it is going to end as far as that man is concerned and perhaps
" his companions. You should have no hesitation in making a
" public apology to that man if you have done him a wrong.
" Take an interest in their sport ; see that they get plenty of
" sporting competitions. If you do all this the men will give you
" their confidence. Last of all, do not send your cases down the
" line ; that is a big mistake. You must send your commotional
" cases down the line. But when you get these emotional
" cases, unless they are very bad, if you have a hold of the men
" and they know you and you know them (and there is a good
" deal more in the man knowing you than in your knowing the
" man), and if the man knows you and you are able to explain
" to him that you have investigated his condition and that there
" is nothing really wrong with him, give him a rest at the aid
" post if necessary and a day or two's sleep, go up with him to
" the front line, and, when there, see him often, sit down beside
" him and talk to him about the war or look through his peri-
" scope and let the man see you are taking an interest in him,
" you will not have nearly so many cases of anxiety neurosis.
" The same holds good in regard to the combatant officers. Some
" of them have companies better than others, and you can

" always tell that the Company Officer who has the best com-
" pany will have the least number of cases of neurosis due largely
" to the personal example of the officer. One officer who was
" killed, Talbot Stevenson, as long as he was alive in charge of
" the company never had a case of neurosis.

" Then, in regard to the trenches, I think it is your business
" to see that the men are not exhausted in the trenches,
" especially if there is a rough time going on. In the Ypres
" salient, where we had a very bad time in the winter of 1917
" with the melted snow, the men were sometimes three days
" and three nights in nothing but shell-holes (there being no
" trenches) up to their thighs in water. They got trench feet,
" and it had a tremendous mental effect on them. You must
" have the men's condition in the trenches as good as possible.
" Then there is another point—change of front. To my mind
" that is most important. If troops are kept too long on one
" front they begin to know too much about it; they know
" ' Salvation Corner ' and ' Hell's Corner,' and so on; they know
" the road where a German machine gun is playing down at
" certain times in the day. The moment they begin to know too
" much about the place their anxiety begins to creep on. In
" returning to the trenches they know the places liable to be
" shelled, and they wonder will it be shelled as they are passing
" over it, or will they wait until they have got past. The men
" should be changed to another front. My own division was
" in the Ypres salient for fourteen months. Eventually I wrote
" up to the division requesting it to be sent to Army Head-
" quarters, saying I would not be responsible for the men any
" longer if kept in the Ypres salient. You could tell at once
" the condition of the troops. There was a feeling of tension,
" a feeling of jumpiness. Notwithstanding the work, the men
" had previously sung going up to the trenches and coming
" back, but they gave it up; they gave up all social business;
" they were getting into a state of nervous exhaustion. The
" troops were then moved to another part of the line, and the
" moment they were moved you would not have known them
" for the same battalion.

" Nervous exhaustion and nervous anxiety are very much the
" same thing. Physical exhaustion includes nervous exhaus-
" tion. Sport is useful; friendly competition, interchange of
" sport between the different battalions, brigades and divisions.
" Then you have men who are sometimes kept too long on
" dangerous work. I found that men who were often very will-
" ing to undertake dangerous work eventually broke down unless
" they got sufficient rest. You would have a good man who was
" always sent on raiding parties or sent out for night patrol
" work. Humanity has only a certain limit of endurance, and 1
" found if these men were kept too long on dangerous work they
" had a tendency to break down. Single-handed battalion
" runners were also apt to break down. It was not so bad in

" double-handed work, because there was company. In an
" engagement they always had battalion runners in duplicate,
" so that if one were knocked out, the other could carry on, but
" in the ordinary course of events a battalion runner did all his
" work single-handed. He would go along through a shelling,
" and it was very heavy mental stress. I have in my mind
" several battalion runners whose careers I followed, and a great
" number of them broke down with ' shell-shock.' "

" Those are just general points, but I think a lot might be
" done to help on these lines. It is all summed up in one word
" ' morale.' If the morale is good in a battalion, you will have
" less so-called ' shell-shock ' or war neurosis. The better the
" morale, the less the neurosis.

" I regard ' shell-shock ' or war neurosis as a very contagious
" source of trouble when it gets into a battalion. I saw it very
" markedly in the retirement of March, 1918. I came through
" the whole of that retirement, and my battalion, I am pleased
" to say, was mentioned by Mr. Lloyd George as the Scottish
" battalion that held the line so well. We came through with
" only one Second Lieutenant and 35 strong at Villers Breton-
" neux. I saw a lot of other troops in an absolutely terrified
" condition (there is no other word for it) during that retirement.
" Then again at Givenchy, I saw it to a certain extent in my
" own battalion. There was a mine blown up at Givenchy, just
" near to the biggest mine in France, the ' Red Dragon.' This
" mine got the 2nd Black Watch, who were on our right, rather
" badly, killed a good number of them and killed two or three
" of our men with the falling debris, sandbags, and so on. The
" 2nd Black Watch had a considerable number of commotional
" ' shell-shock.' From that time some of our men began to go
" down ; there were about 40 of them with 3 non-commissioned
" officers. I knew the men quite well, and I sized them up.
" There was no such thing as ' shell-shock ' wrong with these
" men at all. They had ' the wind up,' and they were
" frightened, and I knew perfectly well it was deadly to allow
" this contagion to spread ; I saw it had to be stopped, I therefore
" told the men that they had left the front line without per-
" mission. I said they were going straight back and would be
" punished for it afterwards. I promptly marched these men
" myself up to the front line, and handed them over personally
" to the Company Officer. In none of those men did this condi-
" tion go any further. They saw that it was more fear than
" anything else, and if I could go up and share their dangers
" they were quite willing to settle down. I took their names
" and followed their careers, and they did quite well, but it does
" show how it may become contagious.

" I know there is a severe emotional neurosis ; I know there
" is a difference of degree. I will give you an example. In front
" of Dead Cow Farm there were two officers, who were going

" up with a battalion orderly. They were just by the communi-
" cation trenches, when they were shelled badly. The two
" officers stood it quite well, but the man simply collapsed and
" crumpled up. He was brought down to my aid post and I saw
" it was a case I must evacuate. He was there with terrified
" expression, cold face, sweat pouring off his body, unable to
" speak though he tried to do so, tremors of body. As far as I
" can tell, I do not think blood pressure is important, we had
" no means of finding the blood pressure except with our finger.
" One could not say definitely whether he had high blood
" pressure or not, but a case like that ought to go down the line."

Asked whether there was any possibility of distinguishing
between intense fear and the condition that we usually designate
" shell shock," that is to say, conditions associated with neurasthenia and hysteria, Doctor Rogers said, " I do not think you
" have any distinguishing point. You may get the history,
" which helps you. You have a lot of men who tell you that
" they were buried by a shell, who are not telling the truth at
" all. They only think they were. These cases are psychas-
" thenic and neurasthenic. The thing becomes real to them—
" it is what they are thinking of day in and day out. They
" think they were buried by a shell and they gradually begin to
" believe that it was absolutely true. I would not take that
" from any man unless he had a witness, because there are not
" many men who have been buried by shells. There were some
" certainly but if they showed any effects they showed com-
" motional ' shell shock ' and were bad enough to go to hospital."

Asked whether it was his opinion that the great likelihood of
breakdown in officers and men was sufficiently recognised by
executive officers as a whole, first in the early stages of the war
and secondly in the later stages, Doctor Rogers replied, " I
" think in the early stages of the war the officers were inclined
" not to judge things in their proper light. It was only ex-
" perience that taught us such a lot in this war. The combatant
" officer is not a very good judge from a medical point of view.
" For instance, these highly neurotic men were often good
" soldiers. They were active, bright and willing to do their
" work and yet they fell at the critical moment. Perhaps in the
" dark they imagine some post is moving and fire off their rifles
" and alarm the whole neighbourhood, because of nerves."

" Then the combatant officer is not able to judge of the mental
" condition of a mental deficient. The only thing he sees is that
" the man is always turning left when he is told to turn right and
" is a nuisance to his company."

He did not think that even in the later stages of the war the
combatant officers recognised the importance of the liability to
breakdown under the stress and strain of war.

Asked for his experience in regard to the use of the rum
ration, Doctor Rogers said : " I must certainly say that had it

" not been for the rum ration I do not think we should have won
" the war. Before the men went over the top they had a good
" meal and a double ration of rum and coffee."

Henry Head, Esq., M.D., F.R.C.P., F.R.S. : *Consultant
Physician, London Hospital, late Neurologist Royal Air
Force Hospital, Hampstead.*

Doctor Head said : " The term ' shell-shock ' has been made
" to include an enormous mass of conditions. It includes a great
" deal of the after effects of concussion and the whole of the
" neuro-psychoses. I take it that there was no definite difference
" between the people who suffered from such accidents as
" occurred in the Air Force and those who were supposed to be
" suffering from ' shell-shock ' in consequence of a shell explo-
" sion. Although a crash in an aeroplane has nothing to do with
" the bursting of a shell, yet the morbid stages we saw under
" those conditions were identical. So it includes, on the one
" hand, the after effects of concussion and commotion and, on
" the other hand, the functional neuro-psychoses.

" I have been accustomed to dividing neuro-psychoses into first
" of all hysteria, which is the effect of suggestion or substitution :
" secondly the anxiety neuroses, which have usually been called
" neurasthenia, when the fear is generally transformed into such
" conditions as lack of sleep, want of concentration, tremor, and
" so on. Lastly, the obsessional psychoses, which have usually
" been spoken of as psychasthenia, where the man has fear of
" closed or of open spaces, or some similar phobia—he cannot go
" into dug-outs or he dislikes going into the open. All these
" conditions have been included popularly under the term 'shell-
" ' shock,' whether they arose from the effects of a shell either
" physical or mental, or whether they arose from any other
" cause."

Then comes the influence of fear. " Fear may be transformed
" into any of those various conditions. The common soldier and
" the non-commissioned officer suffered mostly, I think, from
" hysteria ; officers suffered from anxiety neurosis. When a man
" was being heavily shelled in the trenches he knew he could not
" run away. He had no intention of running away, but he then
" fell a victim to a substituted condition in which he was para-
" lysed from the waist downwards or had some other disability
" which made it impossible for him to remain in the trenches.
" That is where fear is transformed in the direction of hysteria.
" Fear producing anxiety neurosis led to want of sleep. The
" man repressed his fear all the time and in the case of an officer
" determined not to show it. He sat on the safety valve. He
" had no means of expressing his fear and therefore the fear
" expressed itself in the form of tremor, crying, depression, or
" want of sleep, war dreams and the like.

" Then again, supposing that he tends towards the third form
" —an obsessional psychosis. Very often some obsession will

" come up. It may be of recent origin or may go back even to
" childhood. I saw a man, a regular officer, who went out to
" Gallipoli and went mad upon the beach. He saw the whole
" beach covered with jewelled spiders of enormous size. They
" did not know what to do with the man so put him on one of the
" boats, and as the barges came up with the wounded he saw his
" wife and child on a barge cut in pieces. These two obsessions,
" which he took a long time to get rid of, were accounted for as
" follows :—When his services were enlisted in England he was
" sent to a part of the country where he could not get proper
" lodgings. His wife and child were ill. He had a miserable
" time training soldiers he neither liked nor understood and all
" the time his wife and child were ill. He was sent abroad while
" they were still ill and it was at the bottom of the obsession that
" he saw them mutilated in the barges as they came up. It was
" not for some time that I got to the bottom of the other obsession,
" but I found out that at the age of three he had had a psychosis,
" some nervous condition in which he saw a jewelled spider which
" his mother wore in her dress."

" Thus in the third group—the obsessional group—you get
" ideas coming up in consequence of the removal of control pro-
" duced by fear. You get fears reappearing which may go back
" to childhood."

Asked whether, in order to cure persons suffering from one of
these conditions, it was necessary to bring up past experiences,
Doctor Head replied : " Yes, in so far that you must explain them
" to the patient. He must know what the terror is. The danger
" lies in the fact that they are unknown and unexplained. I
" remember well a young flying officer, an able pilot, who had a
" terrifying dream with hallucination. It was a condition which
" started in a dream, waking him up, and then continued after
" he had waked. He had a curious idea of white birds of peculiar,
" ill-defined form that were first in the extreme distance and then
" gradually came closer and closer to him. This woke him up
" screaming and spoilt his sleep. He had no idea what they
" meant, but when he was gradually made to think it out there
" was no doubt that they were the puffs of anti-aircraft shells.
" He had been shot down, and the birds represented the gradual
" approach of the white puffs. From that time onwards he was
" no longer afraid of the birds, although he had the usual fear of
" being shot down."

The doctor added that he thought tremor was one of the
earliest physical signs indicating that control had broken down.
This applies not only to war cases, but also to civilian cases.

Another disturbance was loss of memory, which is common to
both commotional and emotional shock in consequence of mental
stress. The amnesia due to concussion extends over a comparatively short period, whereas the amnesia of hysterical and mental

origin extends very often over a long period. A man cannot remember going to France or being trained as a soldier. Such an amnesia can be brought on by the bursting of a shell in the neighbourhood of a person or by wear and tear. How it comes on it is difficult to say. We can detect it coming on in the case of a man in the Air Force who has had a crash. A man has a crash and does not seem to be badly hurt. He gets up and walks about; goes to his hut and lies down for a bit. Presently he is looked at and they do not think he is very well and he is therefore sent to hospital. One such patient came to hospital, and when he was examined he was found to have a complete amnesia for the whole of his period in the Air Force; so much so that when he was seen for the first time it was not appreciated how deep his amnesia was. He was sent back to his squadron after a few days rest, but when he got there he said he had never seen an aeroplane, he had no idea what it was like. They thought he was malingering, and sent him to the witness for examination, but he could not get out of him any knowledge of the mechanism of an aeroplane or that he had ever seen one. He had not been concussed

Asked for the reason why a private soldier develops the hysterical variety and the officer the anxiety neurosis, Doctor Head said, " Because the private soldier has simply to obey. " He has no responsibility of his own. The officer, on the " other hand, is repressing all the time because, first of all, he " must not show fear in any circumstances. In some circum- " stances all men are afraid, therefore he has to repress all that. " Then again. he has, at any rate in the English Army, to think " of his men as a father thinks of his children. Therefore, here " again he has an enormous responsibility thrown upon him. It " is to a great extent anxiety on behalf of others." It was that sense of responsibility, the witness thought, that made so many young officers break down.

R. G. Rows, Esq., C.B.E., M.D., D.Sc., Director of Section of Mental Illnesses, Special Neurological Hospital, Tooting.

Asked whether breakdown was necessarily the effect of shell explosion, Doctor Rows replied in the negative and added, " the " breakdown follows from some incidents which disturb the " patients so that they could not carry on in the line and had to " come down , not merely the bursting of a shell, but a scene of " horror or a period of exhaustion. Long service, which must " lead to exhaustion, would be quite sufficient to so unnerve a " man that he would have to retire from the line. ' Shell-shock,' " as the result of a shell explosion applies only to the minority ' of the cases which have come under my care. It was the final '' result of shells exploding around them, and severe bombard- '' ments, but I should not say that the majority had actually been " blown up. They were in an emotional state which had been

" produced by a series of causes, some of them not connected
" with the war at all; maybe a letter from home with bad news,
" the mother dead or something of that sort, which has so upset
" the control of the man that he can stand the line no longer.
" That is after a long period of service which had lead to ex-
" haustion. Any strong emotional shock, quite unconnected
" with shell explosion or bombardment is sufficient to produce
" the condition. Even where there has been an actual explosion
" the explosion is simply the last straw. You will find a lot of
" men who will tell you that they realised in themselves that they
" were not the men they were, that they could not stand the
" bombardments, that they were gradually becoming more nervy;
" 'then some shock occurs, and they could no longer carry on.

" I will give an instance," said Dr. Rows. " A man had
" done something in France which he thought justified him in
" calling himself a coward. That made him so miserable that
" for some time before being blown up he exposed himself un-
" necessarily in order that he might get killed. Then when the
" shell exploded by him he went to pieces at once. For the first
" few days he was in a state of confusion, and when he got over
" that state he began to be depressed. Remorse seized him and
" he was incapable of doing anything. He did not remember the
" time immediately following the blowing up. The man was in
" hospital and he did not get much beyond that for a time; but
" gradually his mental capacities came back. Perhaps he might
" have been able to describe the journey home, or the amnesia
" might have lasted until he reached England."

The witness believed that in the majority of cases you can get
the memory back without hypnotism, but there are some cases
where he thought hypnotism was advisable, as you sometimes
come up against a blank wall where the man could not help
himself and then a slight hypnosis would give good results.

In the witness's view it should be explained to the men how
they come to be in a condition of war neurosis. In civil life
doctors explain to a man that if he falls off a wagon and his head
is hurt he becomes unconscious. It should be explained that
the explosion of a shell produces the same effect. The dread of
war neurosis is great. The witness explained that if the ordinary
civilian goes through a similar experience it produces the same
results. It should be made clear that the man's condition is not
something specially connected with war.

*Professor T. R. Elliott, C.B.E., D.S.O., M.A., M.D., F.R.S.,
late Temporary Colonel, A.M.S., Consultant Physician to
British Armies in France, Professor of Medicine, University
College, London.*

Professor Elliott defined " shell-shock " as a state of persistent
or recurring fear, which overrides the self-control of the
individual.

He said "shell-shock was, in my experience, uncommon
"amongst casualties from poison gas, though more frequent
"than with men who had received actual bodily wounds.

"Men who were badly gassed were sometimes very appre-
"hensive of death, but such loss of self control as they might
"exhibit was of brief duration and ceased when their physical
"sufferings ceased. Milder cases looked forward with tran-
"quillity to a fairly long period of detention under medical care.
"On recovery from the obvious features of gas poisoning, many
"of the men developed neurasthenic features of general debility
"that were closely akin to those seen in milder forms of disa-
"bility from ordinary ' shell-shock.'

"With mustard gas there were also examples of undue pro-
"longation of symptons, which persisted after the period needed
"for actual cure in organs that had been originally injured by
"the gas, such as the larynx, the stomach or the eye.
"Similarly with ' blue cross ' casualties from the arsenic com-
"pounds there were cases in which the nervous palsies and
"numbness produced originally by the poisonous substance
"tended to be perpetuated in a ' neurasthenic ' after effect;
"though such cases were not resistant for very long to deter-
"mined treatment.

"Some of the men who had been unconscious and half
"asphyxiated for a long time after exposure to phosgene, did
"subsequently develop very pronounced neurasthenic features,
"which, as far as I know, are indistinguishable from those of
"chronic shell-shock. I am inclined to think that ' neuras-
"thenia ' after gassing was a phenomenon that was less de-
"pendent on the temperament and character of the individual
"affected. But this neurasthenia runs very nearly into that
"group of exhaustion neurasthenia which affected many men as
"the result of long and unceasing effort in the war."

*Colonel A B. Soltau, C.M.G., C.B.E., F.R.C.S., M.R.C.P.,
A.M.S., T.F., Consultant Physician in France for Gas
Cases and also to Ministry of Pensions.*

Colonel Soltau said that for the purposes of the inquiry he took
"shell-shock" to include all functional conditions resulting
from active service as well as the true commotional conditions
resulting from actual explosions. His opinion was that the
imaginative city dwellers were more liable than the agricultural
type. Staff officers holding responsible positions were liable to
nervous manifestations and more particularly after prolonged
activity in consequence of heavy fighting. On the Western
Front trench fever was undoubtedly a precipitating factor in the
coming of neurosis. Any toxin appeared to act as a precipitating
cause Exposure to the effect of modern explosives, whether as
an isolated incident in close proximity, or from the continuous
strain of living in an area intermittently shelled, was a frequent
cause. Bombs or aircraft had, in his opinion, even greater effect

owing to the time of expectancy before their arrival and the entire absence of any possibility of gauging the site of their fall. Aerial torpedoes were far less important as a cause as they were usually visible and the sporting element of dodging was introduced. The witness said that none of them could remember seeing " shell-shock " until May, 1915. Neuve Chapelle did not produce anything that they could recollect as " shell-shock." There were one or two cases in the fighting line in May, 1915, and September, 1915, but nothing which really attracted attention. He had to jot down a few cases with nervous symptoms. He was now talking of emotional shock. It was not until the Somme that it became an appreciable problem in the Field Ambulance which he was commanding. " We were " flooded " he said, " with cases in the latter stages of the " Somme "

The man who finally breaks down after a prolonged exposure, is the man who is in a state of physical exhaustion and the tremulous, neurasthenic type of man. The man who breaks under barrage is the man who is in an acute state of panic, of emotional disturbance. It is a great thing for a medical officer to watch the men from day to day and say to one or another, " You are getting done up. You had better go away." He had seen that done. The medical officer used the wagon lines, and the number of break downs in his battalion was appreciably less than in any other battalion in the division. He was supported by the Battalion Commander.

The witness laid emphasis on the importance of poison gas as a factor in the production of nervous disorders.

In the early stages of the war it was an unknown weapon and he thought the unknown has always a powerful psychical influence. In the latter stages it was a weapon which was largely taught to the men—the effects of it—and he thought that the instruction in itself was to a certain extent valuable. It was also in many cases overdone so that it set up undue fear of gas. In 1918, during the retreat in the North of France, big drafts were sent up and these men, most of them youngsters, had been drilled pretty completely in gas warfare. The result was that they were terrified of gas. Their instruction had not been carried out at all in a sane manner.

Another reason why gas is liable to produce emotional disturbances is that in all serious forms of gas the respiratory organs are attacked, and there is nothing probably more liable to cause panic than the idea of being choked. It is rather akin to being buried alive—the dread of being slowly strangled. He was inclined to think that that in itself is one of the reasons why gas has such a moral effect.

Again, it is impossible to be certain that gas is present. When it is present in obvious concentrations anyone can spot it, but when in low concentrations many men are unable to smell it, and in many cases it is comparatively odourless. Consequently, if exposed to the possibility of a gas bombardment, the constant anxiety of looking out for it in itself wears out a man's resistance; he is always on tenter hooks and dare not go to sleep in the dugout in case of an alarm.

Further, the wearing of protective apparatus reduces both mental and physical resistance to a very low ebb.

Gas is a very potent cause of functional disturbances—more particularly the arsine group of arsenic compounds. Arsines in minute doses have a profound mental and moral effect in addition to their slight physical effects.

Many of the men who had had an appreciable dose developed mental symptoms and the most extraordinary paralytic conditions. The witness had seen a man develop hemiplegia within half an hour of exposure which had passed off entirely in three hours. Whether that was functional or arsine poisoning of his cortex he did not know.

The witness said that in cases of mustard gas poisoning the tendency to conversion hysterias was pronounced. A large number of men would have functional photophobia. Another large group had aphonia and hysterical cough. A third group had persistent vomiting which was a functional condition aggravated beyond the original vomiting which was common to the first twenty-four hours after gassing. He thought that the group suffering from tachycardia—irritable heart—might safely be added to a fourth group.

The witness held very strongly that minute doses of gas may be the final blow to a nervous system already tottering.

Discussing the differential diagnosis between carbon monoxide poisoning and shell-shock, the witness said he had seen many cases of poisoning by this gas amongst men rescued from burning dugouts and some from tanks and from enclosed machine gun emplacements. He had seen men die from acute carbon monoxide poisoning and post-mortem examination showed hæmorrhages right through the brain. He agreed that some of the cases called shell-shock might really have been due to the patient being unconscious and being poisoned by carbon monoxide when lying partially buried in turned up soil right over a crater.

He thought that many more suffered from this form of poisoning than was suspected.

E. Farquhar Buzzard, Esq., M.A., M.D., F.R.C.P., Physician, St. Thomas' Hospital.

Doctor Buzzard said, " ' Shell-shock ' is a misnomer which " has been widely applied to the manifestation of failure on the " part of soldiers to adapt themselves or to maintain their " adaptation to the stress of warfare.

" These manifestations do not differ in kind from those which " characterise the failure of persons of either sex to adapt them-" selves to various forms of stress in civilian life.

" Failure of adaptation occurs when, for a variety of reasons. " primitive instincts and emotions cease to be corrected or con-" trolled by higher mental activities which, both from the

" individual and the racial point of view, are of later develop-
" ment.

" In any individual, therefore, the liability to ' shell-shock '
" must depend on the relative potency of his primitive instincts
" and that of his higher mental activities.

" The strength and quality of primitive instincts, although
" varying enormously in different persons, appear to be fairly
" constant factors in each individual. On the other hand, the
" strength of the higher mental activities is greatly influenced
" by a number of factors of which fatigue is perhaps the most
" important.

" Fatigue may be the result of mental or physical stress, of
" prolonged exposure to responsibilities, of constant anxiety,
" and particularly of insufficient sleep.

" In addition to fatigue other factors may play an important
" part in impairing the higher metal activities. As examples
" of the most common in warfare may be mentioned :—
" 1. Intoxication by organic poisons, such as influenza,
" trench fever, malaria, etc.
" 2. Intoxication by inorganic poisons, such as alcohol and
" poison gas.
" 3. Insufficient or inadequate food.
" 4. Commotional disturbances of the brain due to injury,
" concussion, etc.

" In warfare the soldier is usually exposed to more than one
" of these factors, and breakdown on the part of the higher
" mental activities can rarely be attributed to one factor alone.

" It is impossible to define or specify the cause of ' shell-shock '
" in regard to a large body of men. . Each individual has his
" own emotional reactions, which differ from those of his
" neighbour, and this inherent difference of individuals forms the
" chief obstacle to standardising rules for preventing the
" occurrence of ' shell-shock ' in a unit, still more in an army.

Asked whether the appearance of the symptoms of so-called
" shell-shock " gave him cause for astonishment, Doctor
Buzzard said, " I have seen practically all the manifestations
" of ' shell-shock ' in civil life. It was not new to me; the
" only thing was the quantity of it. It has been at the bottom
" of a great deal of the trouble that we have shut our eyes
" to the fact that there are such things as nerve conditions."

On discussing the difficult question of cowards, and what is
cowardice in relation to the lack of control over their nervous
systems shown by many men who broke down, Doctor Buzzard
said : " If a boy refused to go to an examination because he was
" afraid of coming down, I should call him a coward, but if he
" faced it and did his best and failed, I should not call him a dis-
" grace. Whether ' shell-shock ' is regarded as a disgrace will
" depend upon the atmosphere created in a regiment. I should
" like the man to know that if he refuses to face a situation he
" will be regarded as a coward, but if he faces it, and in the

" opinion of his officers, and medical officer particularly, did his
" best, he would not be regarded as a disgrace."

He could not agree that all forms of nervous breakdown during
the war were a disgrace to a man.   In the first place, that did
not agree with the facts at all, and secondly, in making an exception of the man who goes off his head, it becomes absurd.   " One
" man will break down nervously and another will go off his head.
" That the one who goes off his head should not be a disgrace
" and the other should, is beyond my comprehension."

*C. M. Wilson, Esq., M.D., M.R.C.P., late Regimental Medical
Officer in France, Physician, St. Mary's Hospital.*

Doctor Wilson said he thought each battalion did ultimately
arrive at some conclusion by which " shell-shock " throughout
the battalion was looked upon as a disgrace.   The man knew he
would be looked upon with little sympathy.   No doubt there
were cases of hardship, but it was the only way of keeping up
morale, as " shell-shock " is very infectious, like measles.   He
agreed that there was not much " shell-shock " before the
Somme.

*Captain F. E. Hotblack, D.S.O., M.C., Tank Corps, Staff
College, Camberley.*

Captain Hotblack said that he believed very strongly that the
man who has never thought about fear, or been told anything
about fear is much more likely to lose control and to panic than
the man whose mind has been trained to expect to be afraid.
He thought that to a certain extent training taught the man to
avoid the idea of fear, and he thought you were much safer by
training the man to expect to be afraid, and impress upon him
that when the emergency comes it is up to him to struggle for
his self-control.   That is what he called preparing the mind.
The man who goes out and thinks it will be rather a good joke,
is overwhelmed by the horror of it and gives way.

*Bernard Hart, Esq., M.D., Physician, Mental Diseases,
University College Hospital.*

Dr. Bernard Hart said : " I believe that in the causation of the
" various conditions termed ' shell-shock ' a multiplicity of
" factors may play a part, and that some of these factors are
" no doubt physical in character.   The latter, however, probably
" either merely prepare the soil or act as exciting causes, just
" as they may in every type of disorder.   The essential causes,
" that is to say, the causes without whose presence the disorder
" will not appear, are causes of a mental order.   These, again,
" may be of many different kinds, and their varying combinations
" no doubt account for the various types of war neurosis which
" are encountered.   Among these mental factors is, however, one
" which is so constantly met with that it may be regarded as the

" nearest approximation to a specific cause of which we have
" knowledge. This consists in a certain type of mental conflict,
" and in processes resulting from the conflict. In order to make
" its nature clear, however, it will be necessary to digress for a
" moment and to explain certain general principles."

" When we endeavour to analyse mental causes into their
" ultimate constituents we are led back in every instance to the
" great instinctive forces of the mind. These are the driving
" forces of the mind, and the answer to the question, ' Why do
" these phenomena occur? ' consists in describing what instinc-
" tive forces are concerned and how they act in the particular
" circumstances presented by the situation in question. For
" example, the explanation of the fact that a man will not only
" have an affection for his son, but will slave to provide him with
" an education, anxiously plan out his future career, and so forth,
" is to be found in the workings of the parental instinct. That
" is to say, this instinct is the constantly present driving force
" responsible for a large section of the individual's thoughts and
" actions. Sometimes the great instinctive forces act singly,
" sometimes harmoniously together, while sometimes they are
" in conflict with one another, so that discord arises until some
" solution of the conflict has been found."

" Now the great instinctive force with whose actions we are
" particularly concerned in the causation of the war neurosis is
" the instinct of self-preservation. This is responsible for a
" large part of our behaviour, and in ordinary life it is allowed
" comparatively untrammelled play. Thus if I am standing in
" the road and a motor omnibus appears I immediately step out of
" the way, and am not expected to remain until the omnibus
" annihilates me. Very occasionally in civilian life the self-
" preservation instinct is not allowed free play. If, for example,
" there is a child standing in the road in front of the omnibus, my
" self-preservation instinct would tend to keep me on the pave-
" ment, and it thereby comes into conflict with other forces
" which may be summed up as ' duty,' which tend to drive me
" to run out and pick up the child."

" In the case of the soldier on active service, however, this
" conflict is continually arising. He is required to remain at
" the post of danger in spite of the impulsion to remove himself
" which is constantly proceeding from the self-preservation
" instinct. The processes which are occurring here may be said
" to consist in a conflict between the self-preservation instinct
" on the one hand and on other a group of forces compounded
" of self-respect, duty, discipline, patriotism, and so forth. For
" simplicity of description we will designate all this latter group
" simply as ' duty.' The object of training the soldier is so to
" enhance and magnify the power of this group as to make the
" issue of the conflict a foregone conclusion. That is to say, in
" the trained soldier the two opponents should be so unequally
" matched that ' duty ' is overwhelmingly victorious."

" Under certain conditions, however, perhaps by a magnifica-
" tion of the self-preservation stimuli, perhaps by an attenuation
" of the ' duty ' forces, the two opponents become more equal.
" The conflict then becomes acute, and a state of tension is
" produced which cannot persist, and which inevitably demands
" speedy relief. This relief, or solution of the conflict, may
" occur either by extraneous circumstances or by processes
" occurring within the individual concerned. Thus in the first
" place relief is obtained if the soldier is wounded or taken
" prisoner. If either of these events happens the conflict ceases
" because both the opponents are satisfied, the self-preservation
" instinct by the withdrawal from danger, the ' duty ' forces
" because the soldier is no longer called upon either by himself
" or others to remain "

" There is another solution, however, which occurs from
" within, and this consists in development of a psychoneurosis.
" In this event the conflict is solved as satisfactorily as in the
" case of a wound, because the disablement withdraws the
" soldiers from danger while the ' duty ' forces are satisfied,
" because the withdrawal is necessitated by illness. That is to
" say, self-preservation is satisfied without any loss of self-
" respect. It will be seen therefore that the *psychoneurosis*
" *serves a purpose*, namely, the removal of an intolerable
" conflict."

" Now in any organic disorder the fact that it may happen to
" be useful in some respect is merely an adventitious circum-
" stance. In the case of a psychogenic disorder, however, that
" is to say, a disorder in which mental causes play a predominant
" part, this fact becomes of fundamental importance. The
" circumstances that the psychoneurosis *will* provide a solution
" of the conflict becomes one of the causes leading to its appear-
" ance. In other words, there is a motive for the illness, and
" this motive is one of the driving forces which produces the
" illness. In this connection it is interesting to note the
" frequently stated fact that ' shell shock ' is rare in the wounded
" and in prisoners. It is rare because the motive for its appear-
" ance has become inoperative. It must be very clearly under-
" stood that this motive is an *unconscious* motive. The patient
" himself is in no sense aware of its existence or of the part it
" plays. Indeed, if he were so aware of it, a psychoneurosis
" could not arise, because the ' duty ' forces would not then be
" satisfied, and hence no solution of the conflict would be
" obtained."

" The existence of unconscious motives of this type is familiar
" to us in civilian nervous disorders. I may mention such well-
" known examples as the hysterical girl who rules the whole
" household by means of her illness, and the sufferer from a
" traumatic neurosis following a railway accident, in whom
" recovery is greatly impeded during the subsequent litigation,
" but occurs rapidly as soon as the verdict has been given and
" satisfactory compensation paid."

" The unconscious motive in the case of the war psychoneurosis
" would seem to be a factor of the first importance, because the
" conclusions to be deduced from its presence indicate possible
" lines of prevention. Before passing on to these conclusions,
" however, it will be profitable to trace briefly the effects of the
" unconscious motive throughout the course of the illness. These
" may be summarised as follows :—

" (1) It is one of the causes responsible for the outbreak of the
" illness.

" (2) It is one of the causes responsible for the persistence of
" the illness so long as there is any question of returning to active
" service.

" (3) If the patient is returned to a home hospital he becomes
" surrounded by an atmosphere of sympathy, consideration, and
" comfort which tends to enhance and fix the working of the un-
" conscious motive. The efficiency of the compromise which the
" psychoneurosis has achieved between the forces of self preser-
" vation and ' duty ' is greatly increased, because public opinion,
" particularly the public opinion provided by the friends and ac-
" quaintances which the soldier acquires in the neighbourhood
" of the hospital, regards the illness as absolutely equivalent in
" disabling power to a severe wound, and does not regard its
" presence as in any way damaging to the self-respect of the
" soldier.

" (4) If ' shell-shock ' is one of the avenues which not only
" lead to temporary withdrawal from active service, but to dis-
" charge from the army, the strength and effects of the uncon-
" scious motive are naturally greatly increased. If the soldier
" is sent to a hospital in which, as was the case in the special
" neurasthenic hospitals in this country for a considerable period
" during the war, all the patients are ultimately invalided from
" the army and none are sent back to duty, a further stimulus to
" the working of the unconscious motive is clearly given. When
" a tradition of this kind is once firmly established, it becomes a
" matter of extreme difficulty to combat it, and, so far as I am
" aware, the attempts subsequently made to send soldiers back to
" duty from hospitals in which for a considerable time previous
" all the patients had been discharged from the army, almost
" always miscarried, the soldier relapsing immediately he reached
" his unit.

" (5) If the soldier is discharged from the army and becomes a
" pensioner, the unconscious motive tends to transfer itself from
" its original aim to the pension, so long as there is any question
" of the pension being capable of reduction or withdrawal. That
" is to say, treatment is rendered difficult because recovery means
" the loss of the pension, and improvement means its reduction.
" The unconscious motive acts, therefore, as a resisting force to
" recovery, and the situation is precisely similar to that with

" which we have long been familiar in accident compensation
" cases. The great difficulty of treating neurasthenic pensioners
" is well-known, and in my opinion this difficulty is mainly due
" to the system of pensions which has been established.

" It is apparent, therefore, that if these considerations are
" correct, the unconscious motive lying behind the psycho-
" neurosis of war should be combated in every way in which it
" is possible to do so. In practice this will largely consist in
" limiting so far as it is feasible the ends or aims to which the
" unconscious motive may attach itself. For this purpose the
" following preventive lines may be suggested :—

    " (1) ' Shell-shock ' should under no circumstances be an
        " avenue leading to discharge from the army during
        " the continuance of the war.

    " (2) So far as it is possible ' shell-shock ' patients should
        " not be sent back to hospital in this country.

    " (3) When the question of discharge ultimately arises
        " fluctuating pensions dependent upon the severity
        " of the symptoms should not be given. The soldier's
        " disability should be assessed forthwith and finally,
        " and he should be allotted either a definite gratuity,
        " or a definite pension not liable to any subsequent
        " alteration."

*Spencer Hurlbutt, Esq., M.R.C.S., L.R.C.P., late Recruiting
Medical Officer and Deputy Commissioner, Medical Service
(Ministry of National Service).*

Doctor Spencer Hurlbutt dwelt upon the importance of not
regrading the men who were passed into the army without the
assent of some competent tribunal. It was a danger to put men
who were passed into the second grade up into the first grade
when men were required. In this way unsuitable men were put
to duties for which they were wholly unfitted, hence breakdown
and " shell-shock."

*W. Johnson, Esq., M.C., M.D., M.R.C.P., Physician, Royal
Southern Hospital, Liverpool, late Neurologist with the
British Armies in France.*

Doctor Johnson said he was Neurologist to the 5th and 2nd
Armies and in charge of the Army neurological centre, June,
1917, to November, 1918. His centre was situated in the forward
area near Poperinghe and was 10 to 12 miles behind the line.
Some 5,000 cases were admitted into his centre during the heavy
battle of Passchendaele, August, September, and October, 1917,
which was approximately 1 per cent. of the troops engaged.

He said that a certain small percentage of individuals could never become reliable and efficient members of a modern fighting service. They consist largely of the emotional and temperamentally unstable persons who under ordinary circumstances show definite deficiency in self-control. They are in fact pronounced neuropathic individuals. Such men after a period of training have undoubtedly given valuable service in the line for short periods during which they have proved fairly efficient. Events in the line affect them very deeply, however, and it is usually only a question of time before a breakdown occurs. A slightly dull-witted soldier not infrequently was an efficient fighter. Lack of imagination at times was not a draw-back.

" Shell-shock " is a misnomer, and its introduction as an official term was deplorable. Soldiers developed the belief that a bursting shell produced mysterious changes in the nervous system which destroyed their self-control. In France the term was definitely abandoned after much discussion in September, 1918. There was never any necessity to go beyond the ordinary existing medical terminology ; concussion (cerebral or spinal) ; neurosis (hysteria, neurasthenia) ; psychoses (exhaustion psychosis, confusion insanity) ; and simply physical and mental exhaustion. So-called " shell-shock " consisted of a motley of conditions. Its use was a loose proceeding which both obviated the necessity for an accurate diagnosis and at the same time tended to obscure treatment and prognosis. Stated in broad terms he would say that 80 per cent. of the total cases admitted were due to emotional disturbance, and 5 per cent. to commotional disturbance. The remaining 15 per cent. he regarded as being due to the presence of both factors.

The information obtained from Army Form W.3436 indicated that from 40 to 50 per cent. of patients admitted had been in the immediate vicinity of a bursting shell. This evidence was not always to be relied on, and in any case it is possible to be very close to a shell burst without sustaining any physical damage. He saw numerous cases of acute confusional insanity and was able to observe them usually from four to six weeks ; also reckless behaviour and desertion due to irresistible fear. Such cases frequently gave a history of sleeplessness for varying periods preceding the incident. At the time of this occurrence the anxiety state had reached its height, and the impulse to act was practically uncontrollable.

In his view the war produced nothing new in psychoneurosis.

The man, on the other hand, developed the belief that " shell-" shock " was a definite disease and that the term meant some mysterious change in the nervous system. The usual thing when one admitted a case and asked the man, " Well, what do you " complain of?" was to have the almost invariable answer : " Shell-shock, sir," as if it was a concrete disease.

The doctor said : " I have had men coming up with photo-
" graphs of themselves from the illustrated papers—Private A.
" B., suffering from ' shell-shock.' They carried them about
" with them. Young soldiers prepare to become a case of ' shell-
" ' shock ' almost before the first shell drops near them. The
" very fact of the noise of explosion causes a certain amount of
" emotional upset and that is sufficient to send them over the
" border line."

Asked whether he had seen " shell-shock " occurring in numbers of men at the same time, the doctor said : " I saw that
" happen before I had anything to do with the centre. I was
" with a field ambulance, in the first Somme battle, 1916. The
" division was kept in until practically everybody was done up
" and there one saw the men streaming down. There was
" nothing wrong with them, except that they were absolutely
" fagged out, and could not go over the top again. They had
" been over about 11 times in a fortnight and simply could not
" do it again. The only thing was for them to come down sick.
" It was at that time, before the centres were formed, that
" thousands of men got to England. Had they not been sent to
" England their treatment would have been less difficult."

*L. C. Bruce, Esq., M.C., M.D., F.R.C.P., Medical Super-
intendent, Perth District Asylum, late Lieut-Colonel,
R.A.M.C.*

Dr. Bruce said the word " shell shock " is used so loosely that
it was doubtful whether it could be defined. To him it conveyed
no meaning.

He had seen mental breakdown in all sorts of men amongst
his hospital patients ; he was struck with the number who had
marked nervous heredity—over 77 per cent. He had seen
mental breakdown occur in camp, during training, in the
Gallipoli attack, as a result of strain and lack of sleep in the
trenches, and in the mental hospitals as the result of malaria.
Prolonged strain and insufficient sleep were, in his opinion, the
most potent cause of mental breakdown.

He had had cases of true epilepsy under his care in hospital,
men who claimed that the fits came on after concussion from
shell explosion. It was difficult to arrive at the truth in these
cases as both the patient and the friends were fully alive to the
fact that there was money to be made by supporting the claim
that the epilepsy was the result of the concussion. He had twice
seen mental stress arising suddenly as the result of emotional
shock in peace time which resembled the states he met when on
service. In one case a workman heard of the death of his brother
by accident and immediately passed into a state of stupor. In
the other a lady who heard by telegram of the loss of her means
at 12 midday was acutely melancholic by 8 p.m.

Miss Cockrell, R.R.C., late Matron, Maudsley Neurological Hospital.

Miss Cockrell said she knew that in the first instance patients were admitted as neurasthenic and then afterwards as " shell " shock." " The word ' shell-shock ' was taboo, and eventually " they did not come down except as N.Y.D.N., or something " like that. On arrival these patients showed all different kinds " of symptoms—some were comparatively mild and had mild " neurasthenic symptoms, or they were visibly shaken in nerve, " jumpy and emotional, or they were unable to walk because of " extreme tremor of the limbs, or they were hemiplegic " or paraplegic. A few were blind, but there were many " deaf, mute, or stuttering, and many suffered from terrifying " dreams. Their memory and concentration was very much " impaired, and their confidence and decision for the moment " was lost entirely. Their memory also was subject to marked " disturbances. As a rule they could give a clear history up to " the moment that they were ' shocked,' and they could even " describe the particular form of explosion which caused the " shock, but from then onwards they would not be able to re- " member. The men deserved much sympathy."

Asked whether the tremors from which the men suffered occurred on the slightest excitement, Miss Cockrell replied in the affirmative. She said it was extraordinary. " I have seen them " all sitting at dinner quite quietly, and perhaps there would be " a clap of thunder, and immediately they would all go under " the table or tumble down." They were not so badly affected by the warning of an air raid, because they were prepared for it, but not for the clap of thunder. Something which occurred suddenly would upset them, even the banging of a door.

Air Vice-Marshal Sir John Salmond, K.C.G., C.B., D.S.O.

Sir John Salmond said that he defined " shell-shock " as " a " nervous state which seriously interfered with the patient's " capacity for all forms of work, and in many cases rendered him " unfit to carry on the ordinary forms of everyday life without " constant attendance." He was also of opinion that there were " certain individuals who, in spite of their best endeavours, " could never be made efficient members of a modern fighting " force. The majority of individuals, if subjected to forms of " treatment according to their different temperaments, could be " brought to varying states of efficiency. The type on whom " all effort spent is wasted effort is that of the ' non-trier.' "

The witness said that in his experience highly-strung and nervous individuals are the type most likely to be affected by " shell " shock."

Speaking of the Air Force, he said that cases were known where pilots, having undergone some arduous experience, coupled with miraculous escape from death, such as falling out of control from a great height, have been reduced to a state of mental collapse.

He said that there was on record the case of Lieutenant A., which was related to the witness from first-hand sources. Lieutenant A. had just arrived at the front, and showed every prospect of being a successful war pilot. One day, when flying above the trenches, his machine was brought down in flames from 1,500 feet. He brought his machine safely to the ground burning, but his aerial gunner in the back seat died of burns; immediately the aeroplane touched the ground Lieutenant A. jumped clear. The petrol tank then exploded. Lieutenant A., though escaping bodily injury, was in hospital for some months suffering from shock, described by doctors as " shell shock," and since that time had never been in the air again.

He added that it has been noticed that some pilots, if not watched by medical authorities for signs of fatigue, have sustained themselves by indulging in alcohol.

The witness was of opinion that all war pilots would inevitably break down in time if not relieved. The period of time before breakdown varies according to the temperament of the individual pilot and the nature of his flying duties.

He noticed that when officers in positions of responsibility break down the breakdown usually took the form of complete mental and physical exhaustion brought on by constant overwork.

" Shell shock," he noticed, is in most cases greater among pilots who have been in the line for some length of time, as their powers of endurance and determination are to a large extent used up. If a battle, or a particularly strenuous time has been passed through and overcome, pilots who had used up and called out all their forces were wont to give up as the need for further effort was over Extreme youth or extreme age for war flying was found likely to precipitate " shell-shock " and war neuroses. Example, determination, and bravery will greatly strengthen any mentality which is inclined to waver or give in to adverse circumstances. If the leaders of units, such as Flight Commanders of a squadron, are allowed to get into a fatigued state with regard to their work, their lethargy will be caught by their juniors, who look to them for example, energy and initiative.

Sir John was of opinion that in certain instances a pilot who has once suffered from " shell shock " is perfectly capable of further active service, and is often capable after the needed rest of services better than those previous to his " shell-shock." He quoted an instance of which he had knowledge. " Captain X. " was serving for some months in a reconnaissance squadron " which underwent as bad a time as any other squadron of the " Royal Flying Corps in the year 1917. Captain X., who had " worked well, but was completely used up, should have been " sent to some home establishment a considerable time previous " to the actual time when he was sent. On his arrival in " England he was a nervous wreck, and stated that he never

" wished to fight or fly again. He was given two and a half
" months' leave, and at the expiration of this period was sent to
" a flying training squadron where his Commanding Officer
" saw that he was unfit for any continuous flying work. This
" Commanding Officer left Captain X to his own devices, never
" worrying him, but leaving him to fly or not as he himself
" wanted. Four months later Captain X. was doing good work
" as an Instructor ; ten months from his return from the Front
" he went back to France and joined a squadron which was
" possessed of good morale, but he was captured five months
" later. Up to the time of his capture there was no sign of his
" nervous trouble recurring, in fact he performed wonderful feats,
" gained the Military Cross and Bar, and two days before
capture shot down six German aeroplanes in one day."

*Lieut.-Colonel E. C S. Jervis, D.S.O., late 5th Lancers and
Machine Gun Corps.*

Colonel Jervis said that " shell-shock " is when one has been
knocked out by the force of the explosion of a shell, *i.e.*, by
the concussion, and not by the fragments. Loss of nerve is not
" shell shock " and should never be called by that name, but,
for the purpose of answering questions put by the Committee,
he would regard " shell-shock " as loss of nerve. In such a
state a man's mind is not under control. He would not run
away, but was so distressed and overpowered that as an officer
he would become perfectly useless, and it was painful to watch
him.

The witness said he had not seen much " shell shock " at the
front, but when he had been down in hospital he had seen much
more so-called " shell-shock." He would have said most of it
was nothing at all. Then when he was in the line he had seen
men go quite off their heads for the time being, and that sort
of thing, but they very often came back quite all right after a
little rest.

Asked whether he would look with severity upon a regiment
producing an abnormal quantity of emotional " shell-shock,"
the Colonel replied, " I should at once put it down to bad regi-
" mental officers, or to bad handling of the regiment by the
" Staff." He was sure that rest was absolutely essential. He
had always relieved his men the same night when they had been
over the top, but they were machine gunners. It might not be
possible to do that with infantry. Esprit de Corps was also
absolutely necessary. There is a breaking strain, but the breaking strain could be avoided if the troops are properly handled.

He advocated the greatest care of the troops by the Commanding Officer and by the Staff. The fighting troops should be the
best paid and the best rewarded; good food and amusements
also. Troops fresh in the line should not be given a hard job,
and the prestige of a regular officer among irregulars is
enormous.

Asked whether he held that emotional " shell-shock " was a disgrace to a regiment, he said that he was inclined to think it was.

Squadron Leader E. W. Craig, M.B., Medical Service, Royal Air Force.

Lieutenant Craig put in a statement of some of the causes which, in his judgment, led to nervous breakdown in the flying personnel.

(1) Flying at high altitudes for prolonged periods, cold, oxygen want, failure of respiratory mechanism, cardio-vascular and nervous systems leading to breakdown.

(2) Flying at low altitudes, contact patrols with infantry tanks, etc., " ground-straffing "—strain of flying and fighting in an area where the machine is the target of machine guns, rifles, trench mortars, etc.

(3) Long periods of flying day after day without leave, or little leave or transfer to Home Establishment, but less breakdown in winter months, probably in part due to less flying.

(4) Returning to flying duty within a short period after illness, *e.g.*, influenza—malaria—dysentry, etc. A man feels a " dud " for some time after, and is not happy in the air.

(5) Returning to duty within a short period after minor crashes, starting flying too soon, concussion, shock, etc.

(6) Excessive use of alcohol—resistance powers to stress lowered ; takes more to keep him going, etc.

(7) Excessive use of tobacco, especially cigarettes, gives rise to irritable heart, and has a bad effect on respiratory system. Most pilots were moderate smokers and preferred the pipe.

(8) Insufficient training. In great part due to necessities of war, short period of instruction, *e.g.*, a man may never have flown the type of machine he was called upon to fly on going overseas

(9) Conditions which interfere with or impede free passage of air to the lungs, *e.g.*, hypertrophied tonsils, adenoids, tonsillitis, nasal catarrh, pharyngitis, etc.

(10) Night flying. Abnormal mode of life, meals at irregular hours, lack of sleep, sleeping in day and working at night. Strain of night flying, cold, etc.

(11) Severe mental stress, fear, worry, anxiety and " wind up."

(12) Unsuitable employment. Employed on high flying when more suitable for low and *vice versâ*. Scouts, bombers (day and night) Reconnaissance, etc.

(13) Youth and immaturity. Age—type of previous employment.

(14) Causes which lower *morale*. Many casualties in unit—lack of confidence in certain types of machines—discomfort and privations in mode of living—machines in the open, quarters in 1918—in case of observer lack of confidence in pilot—obsolete type of machines.

(15) Responsibility. Flight Commander's responsibility for his flight, observer taking new pilot on first flight over enemy country—decision as to whether to attack enemy formations or not—worry over lost pilots, etc.

(16) Neurasthenia. Brooding over trivial matters in connection with his work. Believes he can not do certain things right. Obsessions, etc. Feels that he cannot cross "the Lines."

(17) Severe physical strain—especially repeated in a short space of time. Machine much "shot about" much shelled, etc., in successive flights, continuous flying on "Contact Patrol" under the path of shells from our own guns, etc.

(18) Insomnia. Early morning patrols in summer months, lack of sleep—Dawn patrols, etc.

Major W. Brook Purdon, D.S.O., M.C., M.B., R.A.M.C.

Major Purdon asked what he understood by the term "shell shock" said, that he recognised it in three forms,

(a) "Shell shock" proper.
(b) Shell exhaustion.
(c) Funk.

"Shell shock" proper is the abnormal condition which follows the explosive and concussive effects of shells bursting near by, manifesting itself by symptoms of cerebral concussion and without causing visible wounds.

(b) Shell exhaustion—the emotional neurosis, such as stupor, amnesia, nightmares, hysteria and simple neurasthenia, occurring as the result of active service under conditions of prolonged danger, discomfort and noise.

(c) Funk—the result of the dread of the conditions in (b) and the determination to avoid them.

Major Pritchard Taylor, D.S.O., M.C., M.B., R.A.M.C.

Major Pritchard Taylor defined "shell-shock" as a loss of control generally of the higher centres, but also of others, e.g., motor.

He said: "You cannot express any firm opinion as to the " type, temperament and intelligence of men most likely to be " effected by ' shell shock.' There was no general characteristic " in the individuals so affected."

" You can never tell how a man is going to do in action until " you have seen him there. Some gay and sporting types which " one imagines should do well are useless ; other foppish, idiotic " types do splendidly. Breeding and family tradition count " much among officers. The typical Irishman does well, pro- " bably brilliantly up to a point, but will not stick it like the " typical Scot."

" The stress of an action, or strain of an impending action, is " likely to produce mental breakdown in one whose mental health " is low. New divisions often got ' shell shock ' because they " imagined it was the proper thing in European warfare, and

" because they had not had sufficient propaganda to negative the
" impression."

" Prolonged intensive responsibility without rest led to a
" ' rattled ' condition in senior officers and non-commissioned
" officers. Possible dangers were magnified, and the power of
" rapid, cool decision impaired. The man affected would sleep
" badly, if at all, refusing to recognise the necessity for it. A
" tendency to be irritable over small things and to take the whole
" matter too seriously was a common symptom of ' shell shock.'
" *Morale* is the secret of the whole business, the training of the
" man and the unit, and the knowledge that it is a disgrace to
" give way."

*Major-General Sir B. E. W. Childs, K.C.M.G., K.B.E., C.B.;
late Deputy Adjutant-General and Director of Personal
Services, War Office.*

Major-General Childs said that he was A.A.G. of the Expeditionary Force from the commencement of the War until February, 1916, when he became D.A.G., and remained at the War Office until 23rd March, 1921.

He described the steps that were taken at the Front and at Headquarters for dealing with court-martial cases, and the methods adopted for ensuring that any plea or suggestion as regards war neurosis put forward by or on behalf of an accused was thoroughly examined under expert advice before a capital sentence by courts martial was confirmed.

He assured the Committee that the greatest care was taken by the Commander-in-Chief not to confirm any such sentence until the prisoner's case had been fully examined by experts in nervous disorders. The procedure controlling this court-martial procedure was put in force in the autumn of 1914.

The witness said he did not believe there was much cowardice, but there were certain types of men who could not control their nerves, and under certain conditions they became deserters. " Where discipline is bad you get desertion ; where there is no " esprit de corps you get cowardice ; where you get esprit de " corps plus discipline you will not get that kind of thing at all. " It was all a question of *morale*.

" In some cases a battalion became dog-tired, absolutely done " to the world : the wise Divisional Commander would recom- " mend their removal to a rest area."

An Anonymous Witness.

This witness, a man distinguished in the war, having stated that he had himself temporarily suffered from " shell shock " caused by wear and tear, was asked whether he would feel any difficulty in giving the Committee an account of his painful experience.

The gallant officer said, " I knew the thing was coming on
" for months before it actually arrived.   I was always consumed
" with fear, and it was difficult to conceal that fear.   That is
" the mainspring of my evidence.   It is the repression of fear;
" the repression of the emotion of being afraid, that makes the
" greatest tax upon the man's mind and strength."

" During the three months of the 2nd Battle of Ypres the
" battalion to which I had the privilege to belong occupied
" practically every sector in the Ypres salient.   The personnel,
" officers and other ranks changed, I should say almost com-
" pletely, four times.   After the third time I knew I was ' for it.'
" You can understand what I mean.   I knew I was approaching
" the end of my tether, I had had no leave from August, 1914,
" except a rather tragic 72 hours in December, 1914.   I do not
" think the people in the battalion would tell you they noticed
" signs of it coming on, but somebody must have noticed some-
" thing, because at a time when we were rather pressed and all
" leave was stopped and just prior to the battalion going into a
" specially difficult attack I was sent on ten days' special leave
" to fit me for this attack—' to fatten for it,' was our word.   I
" knew that, and I spent five or six days at home, and on my
" way back spent three days in London, and during these three
" days I tasted life in practically every way that I could taste it.
" I had my own thoughts about it, and I did not think I should
" have another chance."

" I arrived back in France, and found my battalion on the
" extreme north of the British line lying in wait to proceed up
" to attack.   I slept for 48 hours, and then went up with the
" battalion, and we lay in support.   We attacked and were suc-
" cessful and took the German trenches and, if you understand
" trenches,   the   German   front   line,   immediate   supports,
" secondary supports and reserve became our front line and their
" front our battalion headquarters.   The Bosche line was really
" running   right   through,   so   that   this   part   of   the   line   was
" enfiladed.   After we captured it and it came in our line they
" were able to enfilade our whole position."

" Our troops got up there with relatively few casualties, and
" as always was the case during the war the greater casualties
" came when there was counter-attacking and shelling following
" a successful attack.   On a certain night two regiments were
" withdrawn and another pushed up to hold the new position.
" This was the third time that regiment had been built up to
" war establishment, and they had a full complement of com-
" manding officer, second in command, adjutant, company
" officers, machine gun officer and specialist officers who were
" just beginning to develop at that time.   They went in with a
" full complement of officers and men.   They were very cheerful
" and everybody was quite happy about it."

" At dawn the counter-attack started after considerable shell-
" ing all night, and, to make a long story short, during the suc-
" ceeding 48 hours the battalion lost about 70 per cent. of their
" personnel. And now I am coming back to my own personal
" story, which is rather difficult. I had had this leave, and
" apart from the five quiet days at home, I had enjoyed life. I
" came back dreading every moment. On the evening of the
" counter-attack I was sitting in an old German trench. It
" was the old German front line trench and was very well con-
" structed; much better than any of ours, with huge trees laid
" across the roofs of the dugouts on the far side of the canal
" bank. The reason for that I will come to later. We were
" sheltering in their dugouts of which they had absolute range,
" and the result was that we were subjected to the most terrific
" counter-fire, the most terrific fire I had been through during
" the war. I never had an experience to exceed it; perhaps my
" condition exaggerated it, but I do not think so. Things were
" not going well; the trenches had been wiped out, and while
" we were having a conference one 5·9 shell came in amongst
" us, killed three on the spot, severely wounding three, and as
" for myself—I believe my moustache and eyebrows were singed
" and my hair, otherwise it left me unhurt, visibly unhurt. We
" got rid of the wounded and the dead were pushed on one side,
" and we tried to carry on with the supply of bombs, ammuni-
" tion, water and rations. All this time the casualties in the
" front line were heavy. I do not want to exaggerate anything,
" but I told you the number of our casualties, and it became a
" question of holding on at all. In response to entreaties for
" help they could not get people up for some time, and our
" fellows had to carry on. Well, they did carry on, and it was
" not for some time afterwards that we did get help, and my
" help personally came in the shape of two officers of another
" regiment. I knew then that my time had come absolutely.
" I knew as soon as they arrived that my time had come. I
" took them over the ground and showed them round and what
" had happened. We got two companies and also a lot of
" details from the transport lines of a brigade to fill in our gaps,
" and as soon as the two officers had more or less taken over
" responsibility I in my turn shrunk into one of these deep dug-
" outs. Now I had time to think, I do not mind telling you, I
" was in absolute terror. The following observation is interest-
" ing. At this time I looked at my watch and noted the time.
" It was about 3.30 a.m. Then after what seemed to me to be the
" whole day, and with the hope that it would be time for the
" twilight lull, I looked at my watch again, and found to my horror
" that only a few seconds had elapsed. This added to my alarm.
" I repeated the experience; each time I told myself : ' Surely it
" is evening now,' but the intervals between looking only
" shortened. The watch showed only one second. Yet I had
" lived in my mind a whole day. This fact made a profound

" impression upon me. I told myself that my brain was
" going. Then the dugout was struck with an exceptionally'
" big shell which blew the whole thing down, on top
" of me, and that is all I remember until I awoke, I think,
" about three or four hours later, in another place to which I
" had been taken. What saved me was the huge trees, which
" jammed and left me a breathing space, and one or two stout
" fellows who came back dug me out about an hour afterwards.
" I came to and recovered consciousness. I had three-quarters
" of a glass of neat whisky, and I saw a medical officer whom I
" knew to be a field ambulance officer, and I asked him what the
" hell he meant by being there, and he said he had come up to
" relieve me, and he showed me a wire reporting me dead. I
" used some other bad language and told him to go away. I
" stayed with the battalion for another 24 hours until we were
" finally relieved. We were relieved, and I remember some of
" the relieving regiment coming in in tears. It was no shame
" or disgrace to them. They knew the trenches were nothing
" but mud and blood. There was nothing to take over; the
" supply of bombs had been blown up, and they simply walked
" into the open and laid down in whatever sheltered places of
" cover they could get. I got a good many caustic comments
" passed upon me (not knowing I was a medical officer) as to the
" state of things, and I replied rather bitterly to one or two, but
" I was all right and had good control of myself. I was per-
" fectly all right until what remained of the men, approximately
" 300, three young boys (officers) and myself were mustered
" behind the lines and proceeded to march out. Just about
" dawn we got back as far as where the quartermaster had come
" to meet us. He brought up all the officers' horses and there
" were no officers to ride them, and when I saw the horses and
" realised what had happened I broke down and I cried. That
" finished me. The D.D.M.S. sent for me and put me in his
" own bed, and after I had had a good sleep I was quite all
" right. I went back to the battalion and stayed with them
" and went on to the Somme. We took over a piece of French
" line and stayed for a long time, but eventually I was sent to
" General Headquarters.

" That gives very little medical detail, I am afraid; but it is
" appropriate to one of the questions you ask : ' Have you heard
" ' of anybody who suffered from shell shock and recovered
" ' going back?' Well, I think that was ' shell shock ' I had.
" I lost control when I went into the dugout and concealed
" myself, and also for that week in which I could not control
" my tears; but after that, beyond some nightmare and dreams
" when I went down the line, after the six months down the
" line I went up the line again, and I had no difficulty whatever
" in controlling myself—not the slightest.''

Summary of Findings of the Committee as to the Nature of " Shell-Shock."

The Committee have now collated and recorded the opinion of most of the witnesses, military and medical, and we find ourselves in general agreement with their views. We trust that a perusal of the evidence will clear away many misapprehensions and make it abundantly clear what " shell shock " is and what it is not.

On all the main issues there is unanimity of opinion.

" It is demonstrated that " shell-shock " has been a gross and costly misnomer, and that the term should be eliminated from our nomenclature.

The war produced no new nervous disorders, and those which occurred had previously been recognised in civil medical practice. Owing to special conditions, however, these disorders appeared in some cases in an aggravated form, and the numbers suffering from them were very large. The cases divide themselves into three main classes :—

(1) Genuine concussion without visible wound as a result of shell explosion. All witnesses were agreed that the cases in this class were relatively few.

(2) Emotional shock, either acute in men with a neuropathic predisposition, or developing slowly as a result of prolonged strain and terrifying experience, the final breakdown being sometimes brought about by some relatively trivial cause.

(3) Nervous and mental exhaustion, the result of prolonged strain and hardship.

In many cases the three factors of commotional and emotional shock and exhaustion were combined in varying proportions.

Symptomatology and treatment will be dealt with in a subsequent section of the report.

Witnesses were agreed that any type of individual might suffer from one or other form of neurosis if exposed for a sufficient length of time to the conditions of modern warfare, and that it is extremely difficult to say beforehand what type of man is most likely to break down, the only certain test being exposure to battle conditions.

At the same time, it was admitted that there are certain individuals who are unlikely ever to become efficient fighting soldiers. No general characteristics of such individuals were given.

It is plain, however, that in the early years of the war medical examination was inadequate, and that many recruits were passed into the Army who were quite unfit to withstand the rigours of a campaign or even in many cases preliminary training. The question of the examination of recruits will be referred to later.

All the witnesses agreed that much can be done by judicious training, both of the recruit at the depot and of the soldier after he joins his unit. Broadly speaking, the more gradual his training, the better the staying power of the man. The general lines on which training should be organised will form a separate section of the report.

As effective measures of prevention the inculcation of morale and discipline stand first. A battalion whose morale is of a high standard will have little " shell shock." Included under the term " morale " are pride of regiment, belief in the cause, mutual confidence between officers and men, and the feeling that a man is part of a corporate whole.

Physical comfort, so far as circumstances allow, adequate rest and recreation are important adjuncts.

At the same time, it is evident that further study of the psychology of the soldier—" Man mastership "—is called for both by military and medical officers. Individuals who would otherwise break down may be saved by timely observation and removal to comparative safety, i.e., from the front line trenches to the transport lines, or by being given a period of rest outside a fighting area.

Having thus summarised the general trend of the evidence, we proceed to consider in detail the questions of causation, diagnosis and treatment, and prevention.

To ensure clearness we again draw attention to the interpretation we have put upon the term " shell-shock " for the purposes of our enquiry. It includes :—

        1 (a) Commotional disturbance.
           (b) and/or emotional disturbance.
        2 Mental disorders.

CAUSATION OF " SHELL-SHOCK."

No human being, however constituted, however free from inherent weakness, however highly trained to meet the stress and strain and the wear and tear of modern warfare, can resist the direct effect of the bursting of high-explosive shells.

The delicate mechanism of the Nervous System, like all the other tissues of the body, is liable to be temporarily, or more or less permanently affected, and it has frequently been observed that this affection of the Nervous System is often most severe when there is no external wound, and slight, or even absent when such wounds are present, and when there has been severe bleeding.

It was in evidence that a relatively large proportion of soldiers who were blown up, or who came into the category of commotional " shell-shock," showed symptoms of exactly the same type as those who were suffering from the emotional form. There was no evidence of organic injury of the nervous system, and the same causes which are at the root of the emotional form were, on investigation, discovered in them. There was, for instance, a family history of tuberculosis, or of nervous disease, or a personal history of previous " shell-shock," or of neurosis. In one series of cases carefully examined but limited in number such predisposing causes were found in a percentage varying from 17·4 to 35·4 in the cases of commotional " shell-shock " coming from the line. In these circumstances it was apparent that there were bodily and nervous conditions which in a longer or shorter time might have led to a breakdown and the appearance of the symptoms of emotional " shell-shock " but for the effect of the shell explosion. In a soldier, who was in fair health and condition, and who had no predisposing weakness or inheritance, the bursting shell might have had little or no effect. In the cases referred to, the explosion of a shell acted as a push would do to a man of unstable equilibrium, they lost their balance and their previously exhausted nervous system prevented them from recovering it and cast them among the number of the emotionally " shell-shocked."

Emotional " Shell-Shock."

Emotional " shell-shock " is a term which has been found of convenience. As its name implies, it is assumed that the exciting cause or causes have been of an emotional nature. Though very common on the battlefield, it may be acquired elsewhere. It was common on home service, and in its hysterical forms especially it often developed after the lapse of weeks of absence from the scenes of fighting.

Exciting Causes.

From the evidence presented to us, it appears that the purely emotional variety of shell-shock, which forms about 80 per cent. of all the cases, is brought about by a great variety and combination of causes. The exciting causes follow two main divisions. On the one hand, there is some kind of mental and physical exhaustion, of a cumulative nature, which forms a predominant feature; the exciting cause may be some unusual, definite emotional disturbance, which may have a paralysing effect on the mind or cause a dislocation of the mind, without producing any physical effect on the nervous system.

The exciting causes are therefore physical and mental, or a combination of both.

The conditions determining exhaustion include all the circumstances which, being prolonged, are productive of mental and bodily stress and strain, noise, loss of sleep, fatigue, excessive cold or heat, discomfort, insufficient and unsuitable food, the immoderate use of alcohol, the poisons of acute and chronic infectious and contagious diseases, the pain of wounds and sores, the absorption of poisonous gases, prolonged immersion in water, or exposure in the open air, and the thousand and one ills of modern trench warfare.

All soldiers on the several fronts were subjected to the exhaustive and emotional exciting causes which bring on " shell-shock," and the fact remains that " shell-shock," while common, formed only a relatively small proportion of the total war casualties. All soldiers, it was generally admitted, have fear, but in general this emotional state was under control, and the state of panic which sometimes occurred, especially in retreat, is not to be confounded with " shell-shock." Panic is only a momentary and temporary state to which human beings are liable. It is a reversion to the instincts, and may be communicated from permanently unstable minds to momentarily unbalanced minds, and the panic stricken individual in general recovers under the influence of discipline and those qualities which make for moral courage, though it was on record that in isolated cases men who at first showed evidence of cowardice, fought bravely and regained confidence in themselves when the alternative of death stared them in the face.

Predisposing Causes.

Predisposing causes are of two kinds, inherent and acquired, or a combination of both.

In the large majority of persons showing emotional " shell-shock," there was present in the family history or in the personal history, evidence of weakness, instability or defect of the nervous system. (Dr. Lewis Bruce and Professor Graham Brown). Many feeble-minded persons, especially after conscription was resorted to, passed into the army. Such feeble-minded persons were peculiarly susceptible to the incidence of emotional " shell-shock " and to the hysterical forms of it in particular. Many of these feeble-minded persons, like their fellow sufferers who showed no evidence of weak-mindedness, had a family history of insanity, or of epilepsy, or of alcoholism, or of tuberculosis.—(Dr. Roussy.)

The predisposing causes in the individual are numerous, and include such as previous mental or nervous breakdown, inebriety, the drug habit, sexual excesses ; a frequent predisposing cause during the war was concussion, which might have been sustained many years before the war.

Inherent or acquired instability may show during training, but the majority of soldiers thus predisposed by inheritance have successfully passed this ordeal. It is when the line is entered that the weakness becomes apparent. Many witnesses were of opinion that " shell-shock " was more common in soldiers who had been a short time in the line and frequently it occurred within a week or a month of entry.

The influence of predisposing conditions was specially seen in prolonged and heavy fighting when " shell-shock " cases were numerous, and increased in proportion to the severity and duration of the fighting.

Weather conditions seemed not to have the same effect as fighting. In 1915-1916 the weather was very severe in France, and the numbers of " shell-shock " patients were not obviously affected.—(Colonel Soltau.)

Among general predisposing causes were racial characteristics, education and social conditions and environments.

It was recorded that special precautions were taken to weed out from among the American troops all men who might be liable to nervous breakdown and functional nervous disorders. This was done prior to the arrival of the troops in France.

The difficulty of determining the influence of age in the causation of " shell-shock " is not only due to the absence of reliable statistics, but also to the fact that soldiers of from 18 years to 25 were more numerous than those of other ages. Certainly the incidence of " shell-shock " was very great between those ages. It must be borne in mind that the ages in question represent the developmental period when the mind has not had time to adjust itself to the new sensations and experiences of the important biological changes going on the body. Between the ages of 35 and 40 the incidence of " shell-shock " showed an increase relatively to the preceding decade.—(Professor Graham Brown.)

The nature of the soldiers' occupation in civil life appeared to have less effect than any of the causes previously referred to, and the advantages of out-of-door work were not more effectual in preventing " shell-shock " than the well-regulated life of an indoor worker, and no social class was more exempted than another.

Summary of Psychological Evidence.

Many of the witnesses maintained that the original cause of the affection was mental. Mental symptoms, according to this view, are determined by an antecedent mental injury—a fright in childhood, a reproach concerning a misdemeanour in youth or an anxiety in adult life may by psycho-analysis be traced back as the origin of symptoms and elucidate the conditions by which they have been produced.—(Dr. Head, D. Rows, Dr. Rivers.)

Evidence was given that functional nervous and mental disorders, dependent as they are on disturbances of the instinctive and emotional or affective aspects of the mind, are regarded as having their origin in a previous experience which had a strong emotional tone. The previous experience may be of an unconscious nature, and the theory is that these unconscious experiences may give rise to a mental conflict or dislocation of which the symptoms of " shell-shock " are the expression. When these unconscious experiences are brought into relation with the general body of experience which is readily accessible to consciousness and so made part of it, it ceases to act as a separate force in conflict with the general body of experience.—(Dr. W. Brown.)

Another aspect of the mental origin of " shell-shock " is the theory of repression. The patient represses unpleasant thoughts and memories and is able to suppress his painful experiences and dissociate them from the general body of consciousness. The loss of memory so common in " shell-shock " is ascribed to repressed experience, and when hypnotic influence or suggestion is used, the lost experiences are restored, and the symptoms of mental disorder disappear or are lessened.—(Dr. W. Brown.)

Painful mental experiences, such as have been referred to, are in many cases said to be " converted " and take the form of one or other of the well-recognised hysterical manifestations.

CONTRIBUTORY FACTORS IN THE PSYCHO-NEUROSES OF WAR.

Dr. Johnson defined his views in the following clear terms which may be used as a preface to the consideration of " Contributory Factors." He said :—" My opinion is that the most potent cause of all is the emotional effect produced by the bursting of high explosives acting as the immediate agent, with the stress of battle or severe mental stress acting as the accompanying latent factors. Prolonged responsibility or a ' history of fever conditions ' were secondary but less important latent factors. Long service alone, in the absence of the above factors, I would regard as a comparatively insignificant factor."

Authorities are agreed that, in the majority of cases of war neurosis, there already existed a congenital or acquired predisposition to pathological reaction in the individual concerned, and that this constitutional characteristic was of vast importance.

From the evidence given it appears equally certain that the neuroses of war may manifest themselves, provided stress be sufficiently severe and prolonged, even in those of sound nervous constitution, and it is generally accepted that under the conditions of modern warfare any individual may ultimately break down on the nervous side. The form in which this may show itself depends on his personality and temperament.

The explosion of a shell, or other incident, may or may not be the final factor causing the breakdown.

The chief contributory factors worthy of discussion may now be considered.

Responsibility.

Some by nature, education, character, and status are better qualified to hold responsibility, to be leaders of men, than others. With regard to officers during the war it greatly depended on such qualifications as to how responsibility was borne. To those suited to exercise it, responsibility, according to some, gave additional stimulus to the preservation of self-control, but to those ill-adapted, to men elevated to a rank beyond their capacity, it acted as a cause of mental unrest and contributed in no small degree to nervous breakdown.

In General Lord Horne's view, responsibility while it lasted lessened the tendency to emotional neurosis, but when it ceased liability to neurosis was increased.

Prolonged responsibility tended to cause nervous breakdown.

Again, in the case of married men, the anxiety caused them by separation from home and by possible domestic or financial worries contributed to the production of neurosis and may be given as a reason why the married were more affected than the single, as appears to have been the case.

Inaction under Fire.

As may well be imagined, a state of inaction under fire acted perniciously on the nerves of men in the trenches or troops massed together awaiting orders to attack.

Dr. Rivers in particular drew attention to it, and having, from a well-reasoned study, concluded that man's instinctive reaction to danger displays itself in " manipulative activity," pointed out the nature of the enervating conflict induced by an almost intolerable situation (see page 57).

Exhaustion, Fatigue, Sleeplessness.

Physical exhaustion alone did not act much as a contributory cause, but when combined with nervous exhaustion it played its part, and many mild cases of so-called " shell-shock " were of frequent occurrence in those who were both mentally and physically exhausted. Insufficient sleep augmented liability to nervous collapse, and tired troops were more prone to suffer if sent into action.

War Gases.

The noxious gases used in war as well as those resulting from explosions may be and often were active agents in producing neurosis. In general terms it may be said that these gases cause a harmful and depressant effect on mental function varying in degree with the particular circumstances and precise nature of the gas concerned.

War gases must be recognised as a contributory factor in the causation of nervous disorder both from the dread which they inspire and the physical effects which they may occasion.

Alcohol.

Dr. Mapother told us that alcohol did not prove to be an important factor in any large number of cases of war neurosis. Further evidence proved that it had little, if any, part in the production of war neurosis in our army. In the case of the French army, it is possible that it played a greater part than with us. Several observers, however, noted that in some cases of impending nervous breakdown excessive indulgence in alcohol manifested itself. This was considered by them as an effect of the nervous state rather than a cause, though no doubt it precipitated the ultimate collapse. On the other hand, there was a consensus of evidence in favour of the judicious use of alcohol by virtue of its soothing and secondary sedative action.

Sir F. Mott, in his "War Neuroses and Shell Shock," gives the result of a critical inquiry into the personal characteristics of 100 cases of war neurosis under his care and also of 100 wounded, but not nervously affected. In the former group—the " shell-shock " cases—there were six who had taken alcohol excessively at one time or another, and there were 48 teetotallers.

In the latter group—non-" shell-shock " cases—there were sixteen who exceeded in the use of alcohol and twenty teetotallers. Thus the use and abuse of alcohol was found to be less common in the " shell-shock " cases than in the wounded.

These figures clearly sustain the opinion that alcohol had little part, if any, in the production of war neurosis. This remark does not apply to parental alcoholism, and in Mott's investigation there was a preponderance of parental alcoholism in the " shell-shock " group in the proportion of two to one.

Syphilis.

Recent syphilis, or other venereal disease, may have acted as a contributory cause in a few instances on account of the fear, shame or anxiety engendered in the sufferer. In cases of longer standing, latent syphilis, the development of general paralysis or of meningo-vascular syphilis was not infrequent. In such circumstances an erroneous diagnosis of neurasthenia was liable to be made. Apart from erroneous diagnosis, it is not improbable that the syphilitic subject helped to swell the number of neurasthenics as a consequence of his constitutional malady. It is quite clear that syphilis was the cause of much organic nervous disease that appeared in soldiers during the war; it is not clear how far syphilis contributed to the functional nervous disorders which arose, and the fact that many cases of war neurosis had a positive Wassermann does not necessarily imply that syphilis contributed to the causation of the neurosis. It is, however, probable that it did do so to some extent at least.

Malaria, Dysentery, Influenza, Trench Fever, Epidemic Jaundice, Typhoid.

The above diseases acted as contributory causes in the aetiology of the psycho-neuroses of war, and their relative importance was determined by their prevalence and sphere of action. Dr. Graham Brown noted malaria, Dr. Hurst mentioned malaria, dysentery, infective jaundice, and much less frequently trench fever; while Dr. Johnson referred to " a history of a fever condition " as being contributory causes in such types of war neurosis as are called neurasthenia, anxiety neurosis or exhaustion psychosis.

From the above survey of the contributory factors in the aetiology of the neuroses of war, it may be seen that their action is effected either directly through the mind, or indirectly through the body as in the case of certain infections.

The Endocrine Glands and the Vegetative Nervous System in Relation to Neurosis.

There are many signs and symptoms observable in some severe " shell-shock " cases which point to an affection of the endocrine glands and vegetative nervous system. Several witnesses alluded briefly to the effects of emotional and commotional shock upon the endocrine glands. Dr. Roussy mentioned the probability of effects upon the suprarenal gland, no doubt having in mind the experiments of physiologists, upon the effects of the emotions of fear and anger on the liberation of adrenalin into the blood. Professor Graham Brown also gave statistics of cases of " shell-shock " in which there were symptoms of affection of the thyroid gland.

It is generally admitted that some or all the symptoms of Graves' Disease, viz., palpable thyroid glands, exophthalmos (protrusion of eyeballs); Von Graefe's sign (the upper eyelid lags upon the patient looking downward, and the white sclerotic is seen); fine tremors in the fingers of the outstretched hand, 9-10 per second (indistinguishable from the neurasthenic tremor): tachycardia (rapid acting heart); acrocyanosis (blueness of extremities vaso motor in origin); hyperidrosis (visible sweating) were frequently met with in severe cases of war neurasthenia. It may be observed that in many cases of neurasthenia the blood pressure was raised above normal, which may have been due to an increase of adrenalin in the blood.

Crile, in his work on Shock, asserts that there is an interrelation of function of the medullary adrenal gland, the thyroid gland and the brain. " Environmental stimuli reach the brain and cause it to liberate energy which in turn directly or indirectly activates certain other organs and tissues, among which are the thyroid and adrenal glands."

The resemblance in the facial expression between the chronic emotional activation of fear and Graves' Disease, and the frequency with which this disease is traced in civil life to an emotional origin, point to the conclusion that the effects of fear was still operating in these cases of war neurosis. This is probable, seeing that most of the cases of neurasthenia with symptoms pointing to sympathetic endocrine gland affection suffered with terrifying dreams, but as the dreams ceased to disturb, and natural sleep returned, so these symptoms of endocrine sympathetic excitation pass away.

CONCUSSION AND EMOTIONAL SHOCK.

It is desirable to see how far the evidence supports the Committee in differentiating cases designated " shell-shock " into commotional and emotional, and mixed or combined commotional and emotional forms. As a number of the witnesses applied the term "shell-shock" to cases in which there was definite evidence of exposure to the physical effects of high explosives, it is desirable to ascertain whether the term is a misnomer (as a witness stated), and whether it is possible to limit its application strictly to those cases in which there was sufficient evidence of a causal connection between the effects of the explosive force, and the symptoms resulting from the shock to the nervous system in spite of the fact that there were no external visible signs of injury.

This question is of some importance, for a man might suffer permanently from commotional "shell-shock," and yet having no visible external signs of injury, his case, we were informed by one witness, should not be recognised as a battle casualty.

The evidence forthcoming upon the following points in connection with commotional shock will now be considered :—

(1) The commotional effects dependent upon the force of the explosion, the possibilities of percussion and repercussion, the proximity of the exploding shell, and the nature of the surface upon which it bursts.

(2) Contributory effects produced by burial and gas.

(3) The possibility of concussion without evidence of visible signs of injury.

(4) The clinical signs and symptoms of commotional shock.

(5) The results of lumbar puncture and examination of cerebro-spinal fluid.

(6) Combined commotional and emotional cases.

(7) The cause of death in fatal cases.

(8) Post mortem and microscopic examination of brains in fatal cases :

(a) Cerebral commotion.

(b) Concussion or commotion with complications by gas poisoning.

(9) Opinions of French, German, and American authorities.

The bursting of a shell or the explosion of a mine may cause commotion or concussion of the central nervous system by direct aerial percussion and repercussion in closed spaces, or the aerial compression may blow the man into the air or along a road or trench, or the parapet of the trench, the roof or sides of a dug-out may be blown on to him, or a sandbag might be hurled off the parapet, hitting the man on the head or spine. Any of these results of the explosion might cause concussion without necessarily producing any injury visible upon casual observation. Most of the witnesses who had seen active service at the front, both combatant and medical, had seen men lying dead as a result of the explosion of a shell, without any visible injury; there were, however, only few of these witnesses who could give evidence which proved that death had been caused by aerial percussion.

In many of the cases it would be impossible to decide whether the case was one of concussion by forcible contact with a solid substance, or whether it was commotion due solely to aerial percussion transmitted through the skull and spine to the cerebro-spinal fluid, in which the brain and spinal cord is suspended. The tremendous forces generated by the explosion, it is presumed, are sufficient to destroy the protective mechanism which the fluid exercises under the usual conditions of jars to the body, and sudden extreme variations of atmospheric pressure. At the base of the skull, where the vital centres of the brain are situated, there is a collection of fluid which serves as a water cushion. So that if the vibrations are transmitted with sufficient intensity to this fluid, they might not only so disturb the functions of the whole brain as to produce an immediate loss of consciousness, but even cause sudden death by arrest of action of the vital cardiac and respiratory centres in the medulla oblongata.

It is the commotion of the brain, whether the man be concussed or not, which causes the symptoms, and therefore it is applicable to all cases of " shell-shock " " without-visible-injury " in its restricted application, and for this reason the term " commotion " due to explosive forces has been adopted rather than concussion. We are of opinion however from observations upon brains sent to one member of the Committee for microscopic examination, that where there has been concussion there are more likely to be gross naked-eye hæmorrhages. Three brains were examined from cases in which the history of the explosion and post mortem examination pointed to commotion due solely to transmission of the aerial force generated to the brain. The brains at the post mortem exhibited no visible changes to account for death. A careful microscopic examination, however, revealed the rupture of small vessels with hæmorrhages in many places. The existence of these ruptured vessels bears witness to the great violence of the commotion, and the fact may be usefully correlated with, and explain the presence of blood in the cerebro-spinal fluid in severe commotional cases, when this is withdrawn by lumbar puncture. Dr. Graham Brown made a systematic investigation of the cerebro-spinal fluid of all the cases admitted under his care at the Neurological Hospital, Salonika, and was able to show that if lumbar puncture is done soon after the man was blown up, the fluid invariably shows some evidence of the physical disturbance of the brain by the existence of protein, and an increase of cells (*vide infra*). Neither this change, nor even the existence of blood in the fluid are in themselves of any serious moment, but their presence is of great importance, as it affords objective evidence of the severity of the commotional shock to the central nervous system ; moreover, in a measure, the degree of the changes in the fluid accords with the severity of the symptoms at the time of its withdrawal. These changes in the fluid usually do not last more than at most a few days, nor do any of the objective clinical signs last more than a few hours to a few days as a general rule, but the emotional effects may, and frequently do, persist for a long time afterward. Other signs of true commotional shock are rupture of the tympanum, labyrinthine vertigo, and nerve deafness (*vide* Summary of Evidence).

Examination of several brains sent from France as cases of shell concussion in 1916, revealed punctiform hæmorrhages throughout the white matter. Similar punctiform hæmorrhages having been seen in carbon monoxide poisoning in civil life, we are led to believe that a number of fatal cases of shell-shock, concussion or commotion, might be due to carbon monoxide poisoning, and that those brains which showed these punctiform hæmorrhages had come from men who had been rendered unconscious by shell explosion and possibly buried, or blown into a crater or sap where this gas was present. (For full account of these investigations *vide* " War Neuroses and Shell Shock : " Mott, 1919.") Colonel Soltau in his evidence supported the opinion. He also stated he was of opinion that punctiform hæmorrhages of the brain would indicate carbon monoxide poisoning, and he informed the Committee that he had " seen " many cases of C.O. poisoning after rescue from burning dug- " outs or some of the tanks, or following machine guns in " enclosed emplacements. I have seen men die from acute C.O. " poisoning who showed hæmorrhages right through the brain." In reply to the question whether some of those cases called shell-shock might have been really due to the man being unconscious, and lying partially buried, having been poisoned by C.O. gas, he gave it as his opinion, " undoubtedly if he was lying in turned- " up soil right over a crater." He had also seen cases among mining companies, and it may be remarked that very comprehensive army regulations were issued concerning the dangers resulting from C.O. poisoning and the preventive measures necessary to avoid them. This witness stated that many more suffered with C.O. poisoning than was suspected.

Summary of Evidence of Witnesses Regarding Commotional Shock.

Most of the witnesses who had front line experience had actually seen men lying dead without visible injury, as a result of the explosion of shells or mines.

It was stated by a witness that in his opinion no man who has simply broken down mentally should be given a wound stripe, but the man with an obvious commotional shock who has been buried or blown up deserves one. He distinguished rather sharply between the two conditions.

This witness described his own symptoms of commotional " shell-shock."

" One morning during the first Battle of Ypres I was in a safe " place, and a few shells came over. I remember hearing a bang " and being knocked against a wall. The next part I heard from my corporal who said I was knocked down and ' I behaved

" "queer ' and did not seem to know where I was. I could
" not get any more out of him as to how I behaved queer. The
" first thing I remember was lying on the ground and taking
" blood off my face and looking at it and asking the corporal
" what had happened. I was deaf in one ear, but the corporal
" said, ' You are alright, sir, but the General is hit.' That
" pulled me together. Brigadier-General ———————— was
" on the ground quite close to me. I recovered at once, but
" I was still deaf and rather confused, but I knew what I was
" doing. We got the General in. He was hit in the head and
" had a nasty gash in his back. He did not worry about the
" head but about the back, and said : ' Doctor, I have always
" ' suffered from my liver, and they have got me now.' Another
" medical officer and myself dressed him up, and I was deputed
" to take him into safety. We had to walk across some fields,
" but I took him into Ypres and got rid of him. I remember
" putting him into an officers' hospital. I cannot remember
" anything that happened the day after that, although I know
" I spent the night in a field ambulance. The next morning
" they turned me out. As I say, ' shell-shock ' was not official
" then. That evening I found my battalion, but I do not
" remember anything that happened during that day. I walked
" up the Menin Road, the battalion was towards Hollebeke. I
" cannot remember seeing a soul except two Belgian civilians.
" I remember leaving the hospital, and the next thing I re-
" member I was beyond Zollebeke in a ditch. I must have been
" very frightened and sheltered from the shrapnel. Then I
" looked up and saw these two Belgians walking down the road
" and looking at the white puffs admiringly, and that shamed
" me, and I came out of the ditch and walked on. That night
" I struck a dressing station and got back to the regiment. If
" that had been 1918 instead of 1914 I should have been sent
" from the field ambulance as a ' shell-shock ' case."

Q. Your memory has never come back to you?

Witness : I have often been there since and know the place well, but my memory has not returned.

" That is my idea of commotional ' shell-shock.' If I had
" been sent down then I should have been still a ' shell-shock '
" case and drawing a pension."

Dr. J. C. Dunn : " Once I saw one man, and once two men
" together blown 15 to 20 feet in the air; once I saw a man
" blown as far along the ground (the shell burst beside him on
" a road). The last was killed, the other three were reported
" killed unwounded, but I had no chance of examining the
" bodies."

" *Q.* 27 : Two men were reclining together in a shell hole when
" a 4.2 fell between them with a bad burst. It barely dislodged
" them, singed their clothing and discoloured the cheek of each
" exposed to it. A hasty examination revealed no sign of injury,

"but both were dead (*vide* the two men and the single man
"referred to above).

"I can offer no suggestion as to the actual cause of death."

Squadron Leader W. Tyrrell, D.S.O., M.C.: "At Messines
"Ridge, 7th June, 1917, when a mine was blown under the
"German lines, debris and bodies were evulsed from a depth
"of 60 feet, depth proved by strata of soil thrown up. I visited
"it within two hours of the explosion and found dead Germans,
"three in number, lying unsoiled, unmarked—one with spec-
"tacles still on and unbroken—no visible sign or evidence of
"violence. Eyes and pupils normal, the possibility of gas was
"excluded." (It does not however follow that carbon monoxide
poisoning can be excluded.) "This is a classic instance of death
"from commotional disturbance without visible injury. I have
"seen other cases, but none so definite or so well proved as this."

One witness—a V.C.—related his own experience and that
of two other officers of long and distinguished service, who had
in consequence of shell concussion, suffered with shattered nerves.
The incident and its after effects, are worthy of record, for it
proved that a neuropotentially sound individual with distinguished service, may suffer from shattered nerves, and yet having
no wounds, his case could not, according to evidence given, be
regarded as a battle casualty, although the actual injury received
may be more severe than a wound.

He stated: "After the events I have just recorded, I tried
"to get across and I was wounded whilst I was going across. Of
"course, I do not remember it, but I was told I went sky high;
"at all events, I had something the matter with my head. I
"came back, and I was discharged from hospital and I was sent
"to Scotland. Right from the time I was discharged from
"hospital, and of course whilst I was in hospital, I had
"practically lost my memory, but things had been coming back
"to me. But I was always liable to do stupid things, and that
"never really has got right. To a great extent it depends upon
"my state of health. When I am run down and seedy, then of
"course these things occur more frequently."

Objective Signs of Commotional Shell Shock.

Ruptured tympanum was considered by most medical witnesses as evidence of commotional shock, provided that there
was no evidence of old ear disease prior to the shock. One
medical witness suffered with deafness in one ear in consequence
of proximity to an exploding shell. Dr. Gordon Wilson, a
leading authority in America on ear disease, and who served as
expert otologist to the Canadian Forces, has found that deafness
may occur as a result of shell shock concussion without rupture
of the tympanum. "Of 50 cases carefully examined 17 showed
"demonstrable signs of injury to the internal ear traceable to
"the explosive forces; that is 8·5 per cent." He has had the

opportunity of examining microscopically the internal ear of one case that died, and he has found morbid changes in the cochlea which would account for the deafness. His carefully recorded statistics are summarised : pp. 74-76, " War Neuroses and Shell Shock," Mott.

Some French authorities lay stress upon labyrinthine vertigo, but this was either not considered by witnesses as of importance in the diagnosis of commotional shock, or it was regarded as untrustworthy, without other signs of the ear being affected.

Examination of the Cerebro-Spinal Fluid and the Diagnosis of Commotional Shell Shock.

Most of the medical witnesses agreed that changes in the cerebro-spinal fluid would probably enable a differential diagnosis to be made between emotional and commotional shock. Statistical evidence, however, was lacking except in the case of Dr. Graham Brown, who from his experience came to the conclusion that 20 per cent. was too low a proportion for concussion, but he attributed this high percentage to the fact that the Doiran front favoured concussion. " At first there were no trenches, " but scrapes which the men crouched along. Later, when we " had trenches they were partly blasted in the rock. The front " was intersected by deep ravines and the lines of communication " up to the front line lay in ravines which were all well " registered by enemy artillery. The result was that the enemy " was sending over 5·9 naval high velocity and armour piercing " shells regularly. These shells were bursting in practically " confined spaces—in ravines or rocky trenches and that gives " a bigger radius in which concussion may occur." (*Vide* Appendix No. 2.)

Dr. Gordon Holmes (who had experience with the Army in the field as consultant neurologist) states :—

" We investigated shock for short periods in several centres, " and we came to the conclusion that between 4 per cent. and " 10 per cent. were actually commotional cases. In battle areas " the commotional cases exceeded perhaps 10 per cent., but in " quiet areas the proportion was very small."

Dr. W. Johnston gives 5 per cent. pure commotional, 15 per cent. mixed commotional and emotional. Lesions of central nervous system 1·5 per cent., rupture of tympanum 1 per cent.

Diagnosis of Concussion in men who became non-effective without visible wounds.

Dr. Gordon Holmes : " The diagnosis of Concussion should " be made only when the history or the clinical symptons leave " no reasonable doubt that the patient has suffered a physical " injury, either by the direct explosion of a shell, by being thrown " by it, or by being buried under the debris of a building or " dug-out."

" Attention should be paid to the following points in making
" the diagnosis of concussion :—

" The concussed man becomes immediately unconscious, or is
" at least severely dazed or stunned, and later he has usually
" complete loss of memory of the causal accident and of a period
" of time immediately after it. He is consequently unable to
" say what happened to him, how he was evacuated, etc. Men
" with functional nervous disorders frequently state, too, that
" they become unconscious after the explosion, etc., to which they
" attributed their symptoms, but by careful questioning it is
" usually found that they can recall most of their experiences.

" Various physical evidences of the direct injury are often
" associated with concussion, as rupture of the tympanic mem-
" branes, epistaxis, contusions, and more rarely signs of organic
" lesions of the central nervous system.

" The clinical symptoms vary with the severity of the con-
" dition and the date at which the patient is examined. The
" early symptoms seen as the patient is regaining consciousness
" can rarely be mistaken, but those of later periods are often
" misinterpreted. These are neither invariable or constant, but
" the most characteristic are : headache, frequently pain and
" stiffness of the neck and vertigo, mental and physical inertia,
" with drowsiness and heavy sleep which is rarely disturbed by
" dreams or nightmares, the pupils, which are more frequently
" dilated than small, are often irregular and occasionally do not
" react well to light. In the early stages the reflexes are usually
" depressed, but later generally become brisk or even
" exaggerated ; there may be fine tremors of the limbs, but the
" coarse tremulousness of the limbs and head which is so common
" in the neuroses of warfare do not develop in pure concussion."

Diagnosis of Commotional from Emotional by Dr. W. Johnston.

" (a) In early stages, evidence of organic injury to the
" central nervous system (e.g., paralysis, paresis, changed re-
" flexes; especially inequality of the pupils and alteration of
" the pupillary reflexes); hæmorrhage from nose and ear;
" rupture of the membrana tympani were also evidence of
" commotional disturbance.

" (b) In late stages, the slight damage to the nervous system
" had usually cleared up, leaving little or no trace behind.
" Patients with this form had a quicker and also a more tractable
" convalescence than the emotional type." It may be remarked
that most witnesses were of this opinion.

Gas as a factor in shell-shock.

Taking " shell-shock " to include all functional conditions
resulting from active service, as well as the true commotional
disturbances resulting from actual exposure to explosions, it may
be stated that there was a general concensus of opinion of

witnesses that functional neuroses were frequent in consequence of poison gases.

Colonel Soltau remarks, " The unknown has greater terrors " than the known. Gas mainly acts on the respiratory tract, " and the fear of suffocation causes great emotional disturbance. " It is rather akin to the fear of being buried alive." Again, the inability to know always when gas was present, together with the mental and physical exhaustion caused by prolonged wearing of a mask, were all factors which conspired together to render a man nervous and susceptible to emotional shock, altogether apart from the actual poisonous effects of the gas.

Both gas expert medical officers, Colonel Elliot and Colonel Soltau, referred to the fact that gas is a very potent cause of functional disturbances of the nervous system, and especially were they liable to arise as a result of the arsine group of arsenic compounds.

"Arsine is a concentration of one in ten to fifteen million " has a profound mental and moral effect in addition to its slight " physical effects. The physical effects are rapid and very " transient, and arsenic, as the Germans used it, caused few " fatalities. From the point of view of knocking out men " temporarily, and setting up a chain of nervous symptoms, it " was the best gas they could possibly have used."

It reduces the vitality in one in forty million concentration, so that many emotional cases may arise as a result of an infinitesimal dose. Consequently troops that have been exposed to this gas would be unable to resist bombardment, and they were more liable to be taken prisoner.

" Mustard gas (di-ethyl chlor-sulphide) was by far the most " important gas problem, and gave us between 75 per cent. and " 80 per cent. of our total gas casualties in France."

The discomfort and pain produced by the irritation of the skin and mucous membranes, the fear of choking, causing anxiety and insomnia, combined with the stress of active service, tended to nervous exhaustion, so that a number of officers and men in consequence suffered with symptoms of neurasthenia and hysteria.

The point that struck Colonel Soltau was the pronounced tendency to conversion hysteria. As a result of the irritant action of the gas upon the mucous membranes, the man suffers with laryngitis and loses his voice, there is photophobia and spasm of the eyelids in consequence of the irritation of the gas, or he vomits. All these conditions are primarily natural reactions to the irritant action of the gas, but they become perpetuated by an idea that the disability is permanent. Local treatment of the affected part only increases and supports this idea.

Professor Graham Brown put in evidence certain statistical tables compiled from data obtained in the hospital for neurological cases in the British Salonika Force. These tables, which are given in Appendix No. 2, are illustrative of the conditions as regards commotional and emotional shock in this Force; but they deal with a relatively small number of cases, and should not therefore be taken as of general application.

RESUMÉ OF OPINIONS REGARDING "SHELL-SHOCK" BY FOREIGN NEUROLOGISTS.

The discussions in France and Germany on "shell-shock," taken in their widest application, as in this country, embraced the consideration of commotion, emotion, predisposition, conscription, suggestion, exaggeration and simulation in their symptomatology and causation.

"Commotional and Emotional Factors."

Professor Octave Laurent, Surgeon of the Hospital of St. John of Brussels, was engaged for 11 months on active service in the war between Bulgaria and Turkey, and in 1914 published a work entitled "La Guerre en Bulgarie et en Turquie." On page 347 he gives a chapter upon "Accidents Nerveux produits à distance par les projectiles de guerre." In this chapter he describes a condition which he terms *commotion cérébrospinale*, or nervous injuries produced by projectiles, ball and shell, at a distance. Among the sufferers with commotion were numerous cases attributed to fatigue, simulation, and contusion. He describes cases as occurring several times at Tchatalja, in South Africa, and Matignon in Manchuria. Cases of death by inhibition have been observed with a cataleptoid attitude of the cadaver, especially in winter, and that without any vital organ appearing to have been affected by the projectile, such a termination corresponding to death at the commencement of inhalation of chloroform in which the autopsy did not reveal any distinct lesion.

Cerebrospinal commotion noted in battle and particularly in the explosion of a shell, is either accompanied or not by signs of contusion. The effects of commotion may be slight and manifested by numbness, formications and hyperaesthesia, with or without loss of consciousness, or they may be serious, provoking arrest of functions, the injured falling into a torpor, inert, as if struck by lightning, and all four limbs and the sphincters paralysed. He especially observed such cases before Adrianople; several presented retention of urine. Recovery is rapid in numbers of cases, but mental troubles may persist.

Thus in the absence of direct wound or contusion in a degree which would be adequate to account for the lesion, the whole gamut of neuropathology may be observed from simple torpor up to definite paralysis and death; however, it is often impossible to determine the part of each of the morbid factors. Agitation caused by the shell travelling at great speed, the blowing up of the body by the explosion, detonation, shock of the gases produced by the explosion, contusion by clods of earth, predisposition acquired or hereditary, terror, excitement, fatigue and privations.

The enumeration of all these factors shows that he experienced great difficulty in differentiating commotional from emotional causes in these cases.

The discussions in France and Germany have largely turned upon the respective effects of commotion and emotion; and it was generally recognised that it is extremely difficult to differentiate between pure commotional effects and the mixed form of commotion and emotion. This was emphasised particularly by Dr. G. Roussy, who gave most valuable evidence before the Committee. He states in his *précis* :—

" Under the name of ' shell-shock,' I shall include what we in France term ' commotion par vent d'obus,' that is to say, the disorders caused by the bursting of a shell or bomb at a certain distance and not determining any visible lesion or injury "; this is, indeed, the definition also reported by Sir Frederick W. Mott in his book on " War Neuroses and ' Shell-shock.' "

In France and Germany the discussion turned upon the view whether there were two forms, " The one dualist, which main- " tains that the commotional and emotional syndromes are two ' separate things well determined, having their distinct clinic " morphology, etiology, and anatomic substratum. The other, " on the contrary, unicist, which holds that in most cases these " two syndromes are indistinguishable and inseparable."

" Professeur Agregé Léri, in his book ' Commotions et " Emotions de Guerre ' defends the dualist theory. He thinks " that ' le commotionné ' is a man who immediately after " traumatism loses consciousness, being in a state of more or less " complete coma, of which he will come out sooner or later; his " condition is one of absolute physical and psychic paralysis, " often with mydriasis or bradycardia." Here, anatomic lesions " of the nervous centres, hæmorrhage or softening are excep- " tional."

" ' L'emotionné,' on the contrary, presents a very different " character. The patient has not lost consciousness, he is a " frightened man who shows all the psychic and physical signs " of fear, and may develop at any moment psychoneurotic dis- " orders. Later on, at the Clearing Hospital, at the Base " Hospital, or at the Home Hospital, that is to say as we go " further away from the moment of the bursting of the shell, the " differences become less distinct. In spite of this, the clinical " aspect of commotion and emotion remain sufficiently precise for " it to be always possible to make a differential diagnosis."

Dr. Roussy, on the contrary, maintains that the part played by emotion in determining psycho-neuropathic disorders and also commotional troubles remains preponderant.

There are certain admitted facts, which were confirmed by witnesses before the Committee to show that people were found dead in dug-outs, craters and ravines, without visible signs on the body of injury sufficient to account for symptoms of cerebral or spinal concussion. If the patient is not dead, he is rendered unconscious and his mind is a blank concerning what happened in a true case of commotion; consequently he is unable to say whether he had or had not been concussed.

Both Léri and Meige emphasise the fact that commotional symptoms are not influenced by psycho-therapy. They also point to the fact that, in cases where organic changes have occurred, the cerebro-spinal fluid withdrawn by lumbar puncture exhibits changes indicative of commotion. Léri states that the subjects of commotion are generally depressed, asthenic, aboulic, and often more or less confused mentally. They present almost constantly, even in slight cases, disturbances of voltaic vertigo. They often suffer with bleeding from the ear, or nasal or vesical hæmorrhage.

Robert Bing reviewed German opinions upon nervous accidents caused by proximity of the explosion of shells. He points out that Vogt and Gaupp, who interested themselves with " Granat Kontusion " (bomb contusion), are far from accepting the exclusive psychogenic rôle in the developument of shell shock. Gaupp insists particularly on the close relations which exist between the initial symptoms presented by patients suffering with it, and the rapid succession of conditions of atmospheric compression and decompression which takes place at the moment of the bursting of the projectile.

Aschaffenburg examined soldiers in Flanders who had been exposed to shell fire in the trenches, and who had escaped unwounded, and were comparatively well. The examination took place in most cases within twenty-four hours after leaving the trenches. Many of these showed unmistakable signs of localised organic lesions of the nervous system. A second examination a week later showed that some, but not all of these phenomena had disappeared. Here were cases, therefore, in which an organic basis was present but no traumatic neuroses had developed. Aschaffenburg gives the result of his experience in these words :—

" In assuming organic change as one of the consequences of " shell explosion, I do not thereby agree with Oppenheim that " the nervous symptoms are to be attributed to these changes. " On the contrary, it is to be noted that the most exaggerated " hysterical cases which develop after exposure to shell firing are " the ones which exhibit organic symptoms least of all."

This accords with the general opinion expressed that the cases which were assumed to be due to pure commotion affecting neuropotentially sound soldiers recovered sooner than the emotional cases.

Messieurs Mairet and Durante have performed a number of experiments to show that detonation of high explosives in proximity to animals produced minute hæmorrhages in the nervous system. They consider that this fact favours the view of a sudden rupture of the wall of small vessels by the decompression which suddenly follows on the wave of compression. These experiments were repeated by Major Crile of the American Army, and microscopic examinations were made by Professor Marinesco, which confirm the previously mentioned observations by Mairet and Durante.

Messieurs Ravaut, Guillain and Léri have published the results of examination of cerebrospinal fluid in cases exposed to shell fire, and have found an increase of albumen, the presence of blood, and lymphocytes, indicative of changes in commotion. These results agree with those of Professor Graham Brown and others.

To sum up it may be said that the evidence seems to prove that there are three types of shell-shock :—

    1. Purely commotional 5 per cent., for even Dr. Roussy admits that a few cases of such may occur.

    2. The mixed type of commotional and emotional 15 per cent.

    3. The remainder purely emotional.

It may be said that they occur in this order of frequency, and this agrees with the evidence of Dr. Johnson, who gives 5 per cent. commotional, 15 per cent. mixed commotional and emotional, and the remainder purely emotional.

" The Psychoses."

So far allusion has only been made to the psycho-neuroses, and reference will now be made to the psychoses. The general concensus of opinion by expert witnesses, who gave evidence before the Committee, was to the effect that with the exception of the temporary recoverable cases of psychoses and epilepsy, the stress and strain of war acted only as an exciting, revealing, or exaggerating cause. This was the opinion expressed by Dr. Roussy, and was the general opinion of French alienists ; particularly may we refer to the opinion expressed by Dr. Dupré.

The German psychiatrists have brought forward important evidence in support of this conclusion.

" The Psychopathic Predisposition."

Gaupp states : " The psychiatric analysis of the individual " cases points to a psychopathic basis in most of the war psycho-" neuroses and psychoses, often when the history, as recorded, " reveals nothing." Birnbaum, in his initial review of the literature on war neuroses and psychoses, came to the following conclusion :—" Soldiers developing nervous and mental disorders " show in the great majority of cases a predisposition " (by which is understood not only a congenital, but also an acquired disposition) " such as may be observed following the chronic " abuse of alcohol, and earlier head injuries with concussion."

Contrary to popular belief, there are no new types of mental disease in soldiers. There are, strictly speaking, no psychoses and no neuroses peculiar to war. The clinical pictures, symptomatology and prognosis of the psychoses are the same in soldiers as those met with in civilians, the only modification being the coloration of the hallucinations, the illusions, and the delusions by war experiences.

In the majority of the cases of psychosis the war has only revealed, excited or accelerated, and not caused the disease.

" The Psychoses in relation to Stress and Strain of War."

In respect to exhaustion from stress and strain of war being the sole cause of temporary insanity, there is a considerable difference of opinion. Bonhoeffer states that " among 10,000 " Serbs who were taken prisoners of war after suffering the most " severe exhaustion, hunger and loss of sleep, and after being " subjected to all manner of infectious illnesses, leading to " cardiac weakness, with oedema, gross wasting, great loss of " strength, and a high mortality from tuberculosis and other " infectious diseases, only five cases of psychosis developed, a " number not higher than would have been expected in peace " time amongst a similar number of civilians." From this it may be deduced, says Bonhoeffer, that the acute exhausting influences of malnutrition, lack of sleep, and excessive exhaustion do not of themselves lead to the development of psychoses; and he agrees with Aschaffenburg that exhaustion and overwork must be relegated to the background when considering the psychogenetic causes of mental diseases. Microbial toxins of infectious diseases are usually held to be one of the principal causes of exhaustion psychoses. When a man has been exposed to shell fire and he has acquired an infectious disease, the onset of an exhaustion psychosis is apt to be attributed to shell-shock.

Then with regard to emotional causes, Bonhoeffer points out that Bresler in 1914 showed that the so-called mobilisation psychoses were all either the reactions in patients who had formerly suffered with mental disease or else other forms of psychopathic reactions.

In the women who fled from Galicia and East Prussia and in the civil population of the invaded territories of Northern France no great increase of mental disease has occurred.

Neuropathic and Psychopathic Heredity.

The Predisposing Factors of War Psycho-Neuroses.

Investigations made at the Maudsley Hospital by Sir Frederick Mott, and by Captain Wolfsohn, of the American Army Medical Service, indicated that a psychopathic or neuropathic predisposition was a very important cause of war neuroses and psychoses.

Pierre Marie, Nonne, and others have come to similar conclusions.

Gaupp gave expression to a similar view : " In the psycho- " physiological make-up of the soldier is to be found a most im- " portant cause of neuroses."

The following evidence shows the importance of this predisposition, which was known in Germany before the war, as the following statement by Stier shows :—

" The manifestations seen in times of war do *not* differ from
" those seen in times of peace. For the last fifteen years I have
" been observing cases of *hysteria* in the *army*, and before the
" outbreak of war I had been able to collect more than 1,000
" cases. A comparison of my pre-war and recent experience
" shows that manifestations occurred in *practically the same pro-*
" *portions* in peace time as have appeared since the war broke
" out. *Indeed, we may state that the war has not created any-*
" *thing new in the way of manifestations ; it has merely revealed*
" *the fact that amongst a certain percentage of patients, on*
" *account of constitutional factors, an exceptionally strong*
" *tendency to react in a pathological manner to affective ex-*
" *perience exists."*

The American Army Medical Service did their best to eliminate men with neuropathic or psychopathic predispositions, and instituted a series of tests which form the subject of a large volume by Colonel R. M. Yerkes. (Psychological Examining in the United States Army, Vol. XV., National Academy of Sciences.)

Wounds and Neuroses.

There is no doubt that head and spinal injuries will cause traumatic neuroses in neuropotentially sound individuals.

The question of wounds gave rise to a discussion amongst the French neurologists, for Babinski asserted that reflex contractures and paralysis arising in consequence of a wound or traumatism, without showing characters of motor or organic diseases, are to be distinguished from functional disorders by the absolute inefficacy of physio-psychotherapy. This, however, was not the experience of Dr. Roussy and of most of the neurologists in this country and elsewhere.

M. Claude, indeed, asserted that among the large number of wounded who passed through the eighth region he had never noted these functional disorders in high-spirited officers nor in doctors. Non-commissioned officers and soldiers who showed paralysis and contractures of a particular kind were constitutional psychopaths and generally exhibited hysterical manifestations. He attributes an important rôle to the mentality of the individual in the genesis of the functional motor disorders which are not purely hysterical.

" SHELL-SHOCK WOUND."

As we have pointed out " Shell-shock " was popularly conceived to be something which developed in a soldier who had been exposed to a shell explosion in his immediate vicinity, and which gave rise to a train of symptoms of a strange and distressing kind.

In this sense shell-shock resolves itself into two categories :
(1) Concussion or commotional shock ; and (2) Emotional shock.

Whether shell-shock as thus defined should be regarded as a
battle casualty or not gave rise to no inconsiderable difficulty
during the later period of the war and the evidence placed before
us on this particular aspect of the subject was of a conflicting
character.

It was given in evidence that the victims of *concussion shock*,
following a shell burst, formed a relatively small proportion (5 to
10 per cent.)* of all the cases of shell-shock ; that the symptoms
were of a type which suggested an organic lesion of the nervous
system ; that as a rule recovery took place and that the functional
nervous symptoms, so common a sequel of emotional shock, were
not present.

There was, therefore, general agreement that the commotional
variety, if associated with a loss of consciousness, should be regarded as a casualty and the soldier given the consideration
attached to a wound.

It was stated that a number of cases, given by one witness
at about 15 per cent., showed definite evidence of a
mental wound, attributable to the intense emotional disturbance
(shock or fear) occurring at the time of a shell burst, and
followed by nervous symptoms of a functional type. The
majority of the cases, however, gave no evidence of having sustained such a trauma, although similar symptoms of emotional
upset and instability were observed in both groups. There
was, therefore, less agreement forthcoming whether the
emotional variety in which the soldier was the subject of a
" mental wound " with loss of memory should be regarded as a
battle casualty.

A greater difficulty, however, arose in cases (and they formed
a large proportion of the cases of shell-shock) in which a history
of commotional shock was given by the soldier, but of which direct
evidence was rarely forthcoming.† To this commotion he
attributed his nervous breakdown. The train of nervous or
mental sequelæ was, to his mind, definitely connected with his
experience and the natural assumption was that he had been
subjected to something which had upset his nervous equilibrium.

An analysis of the evidence on this matter will now be set
out, as it will be seen from these preliminary remarks that difficulty attends the solution of the question how far certain forms
of shell-shock should be regarded battle casualties.

---

* On the Doiran (Macedonia) front, the percentage of concussion cases was
stated to be considerably in excess of the figures from France, a circumstance
which was attributed to the rocky nature of the country.

† Independent evidence on A.F. 3436 frequently showed that the statements
made by men as to the cause of their breakdown were unreliable.

Concussion or Commotional Shock.

The immediate clinical effect upon the soldier of a cerebral commotion or concussion, due to the forces generated by the explosion of a shell or mine, is a loss of consciousness, which may last from a few minutes to several days. When the immediate effect passes away there is complete loss of memory of the causal accident and of a period immediately before and after it. This amnesia of concussion is complete and all idea of time has been wiped out for a certain period; it is an amnesia of organic nature. The soldier is consequently unable to say what has happened to him, and it is not possible to recover the memory by any therapeutic measures.

Various physical evidences of the direct injury are often associated with concussion, such as rupture of the tympanic membrane, contusion epistaxis, and, more rarely, signs of organic injury of the central nervous system.

For further evidence *see* " Commotional-shock," p. 100 *et seq*.

The symptoms vary with the severity of the condition and the date at which the patient is examined. The early symptoms seen as the patient is regaining consciousness can be rarely mistaken, but those of later periods are often misinterpreted. These are neither invariable nor constant, but the most characteristic are :—headache, frequently pain and stiffness of the neck, vertigo, mental and physical inertia with drowsiness and heavy sleep, which is rarely disturbed by nightmares ; the pupils are more frequently dilated than small, are often irregular and occasionally do not react well to light. In the early stages the reflexes are usually depressed, but later generally become brisk or even exaggerated, there may be fine tremors of the limbs, but the coarse tremulousness of the limbs and head, which is so common in the neuroses do not develop in pure concussion. The headache of concussion is usually better in the morning and early part of the day and increases from fatigue as the day advances.—(Dr. Head.)

The most important symptom in the distinction of concussion from the more common neuroses of emotional origin is the absence of emotional instability.

Minor degrees of " commotion," scarcely classifiable as concussion, were not uncommon, and we had before us several witnesses, who detailed their personal experiences of this condition. Many men have been " blown up " at one time or another during the war and have continued on duty after a temporary stunning, and in the majority no permanent effect remained, except perhaps a gap in the memory, corresponding to a temporary period of loss or impairment of consciousness associated with the cerebral commotion. It was stated by some of these witnesses that their nervous stability was in no way impaired by the experience.

Emotional Shock—" Mental Wound."

The degree of nervous and mental disturbance, associated with a shell or mine explosion, may vary from a slight or transient dizziness to a deep and lasting stupor. In the less severe forms of emotional trauma, the symptoms may be those of temporary mental confusion, which may readily pass away after a short rest. In the most severe forms, the shock may be followed by mental excitement; delirium or stupor; in some cases by automatism or " fugue."

In the severest kind of stupor, the soldier is entirely unconscious of his surroundings, he lies motionless and makes no reply to questions, his eyes show no recognition of what is before him, all the usual tests for arousing his attention fail to provoke a response. The reflexes may be normal or exaggerated, the pupil reflex may be impaired, but swallowing is effected without difficulty.

Recovery takes place either suddenly or gradually and the patient appears to be normal save for the absence of all memory of the events directly connected with the shock and for the manifestation of certain functional nervous symptoms usually of an hysterical nature, such as mutism, deaf mutism, stammering, paralysis or tremors. In the case of officers the effects are more commonly of the anxiety type, such as depression, fears, loss of confidence, lassitude, nightmares, insomnia and headache.

In contrast to the commotional cases, the " loss of memory " of the events attending the shock and the subsequent period of stupor or delirium, may be recalled by various means of which hypnosis is probably the most efficacious.

From the evidence submitted it would appear that the loss of memory is indicative of a " psychical dissociation " or "functional splitting of the personality," which the patient has sustained, and which, in the opinion of some witnesses, should be regarded as a mental wound.

Dr. Rows stated his opinion that a man, who under the influence of shell burst developed a temporary phase of mental confusion with functional amnesia had sustained a disability as real as the man wounded by a bullet. These cases, however, formed only a minority of the cases of emotional shell-shock (about 15 per cent.) and there was no single outstanding symptom which could be looked upon as characteristic of this condition.

Other witnesses (Dr. Rivers, Dr. Hurst, Dr. Rows) stated that a functional amnesia, as just described, ought not to be regarded as characteristic of mental trauma following shell burst or burial, as it might arise from some incident of warfare other than a shell explosion, and, indeed, from a mental strain dependent upon causes quite unconnected with war.

Most of the medical witnesses testified to their belief that emotional shock and its effects, whether hysterical or neurasthenic, occurred in only a minority of cases as the direct and immediate consequence of shell explosion. In the great majority of instances, the soldier had not been buried, " blown up " or in direct contact with shell bursts.

There was evidence that a considerable percentage of shell-shock cases occurred in which a commotion of minor degree from shell burst or burial was stated by the soldier to have brought about a train of functional nervous symptoms. From some figures submitted to us the number of these cases at present undergoing treatment was given as high as 35·1 per cent.

It was not at all uncommon to receive from a soldier a history that he had been " blown up " or buried and had " lost consciousness " temporarily and that he ascribed his subsequent nervous symptoms to this circumstance.

The available evidence upon this type of shell-shock was conflicting. There was a considerable body of opinion held by medical officers who had served with front line units, that the statements of men that consciousness had been lost in consequence of a shell burst or burial should be received with suspicion and " accepted only after a most searching and informed cross-" examination on every detail of the alleged incident."—(Dr. Dunn.) It was stated that to have been " buried by a shell " or " blown into the air " was one of the most common phrases upon men's lips. " The words were intended to be accepted literally " and were so accepted by those who knew no better. The fact is " they believed they were buried by a shell ; the thing becomes " real to them ; it is what they are thinking of day in and day " out and they gradually begin to believe that it is true." —(Lt. Col. Rogers.)

On the other hand there was some evidence that a minor cerebral commotion might prepare the way for the subsequent development of a neurosis ; and it was recognised also that a shell burst with cerebral commotion was in many cases merely the precipitating agency in a series of mental preoccupations and anxieties which had troubled the soldier for some time previously.

The type of psycho-neurosis thus induced differed in no respect from that which was derived from other causes amongst which might be mentioned, the anxiety attached to an unusually dangerous situation, a serious disappointment or bad news from home.

We were told also that under hypnosis it was often possible to clear up a so-called " loss of consciousness " and to show that there had been, not an amnesia of organic origin but one of a functional character.

In view of the popular conception of shell-shock as something which arose from a shell burst, it was not unnatural that if a man experienced this, he had at hand a reasonable excuse for giving way.

In view of the evidence submitted to us upon the question immediately under discussion and of the uncertainties and complications attending the mode of origin of the neuroses of war elsewhere detailed in this report, the committee make the following recommendations upon the matter of "shell-shock wound" as a battle casualty.

(a) That concussion or commotion attended by loss of conciousness and evidence of organic lesion of the central nervous system or its adjacent organs (such as rupture of membrana tympani) should be classified as a battle casualty.

(b) That no case of psycho-neurosis or of mental breakdown even when attributable to a shell explosion or the effects thereof should be classified as a battle casualty, any more than sickness or disease is so regarded.

(c) That in all doubtful cases, it is desirable to have the classification determined by a Board of expert medical officers after observation of the patient in a Neurological Hospital.

The following was the procedure adopted during the later stages of the war.

Early in 1917 all cases presenting symptoms of functional nervous disorder were sent to special hospitals as "N.Y.D." At these centres a differentiation was made by the Medical Officer-in-Charge as to whether the case was "wounded" or "sick." The diagnosis was based on evidence supplied by the regimental Medical or other responsible officer. The diagnosis of "shell-shock (wound)" was made, if there had been direct contact with the effect of explosions even although there was no visible external wound. All other cases of nervousness were classed as neurasthenia, hysteria, etc.

After June, 1917, when the special Neurological Centres had been established in each Army Area, all cases of functional nervous disorder were marked "N.Y.D.N." and transferred to the centres. Army Form W.3436 was introduced; after admission of a case into a Neurological Centre this form was sent by the officer commanding the centre to the officer commanding the man's unit for evidence as to "exceptional exposure to shell fire" or otherwise. On return of the form to the officer commanding the centre, the diagnosis was determined as to whether the man was "wounded" or "sick."

It was found that this procedure did not clear up the difficulties; although the method was logical, it turned out to be unfair and unworkable in practice.

Eventually (September, 1918) it was decided to abolish the classification of "shell-shock wound" in France, and to determine a shell-shock wound only if the disability was of so serious a nature as to necessitate transfer to England and that the decision for classification as a battle casualty should depend upon the recommendation of a Neurological Board at a special centre in the United Kingdom.

TREATMENT OF SHELL-SHOCK AND WAR NEUROSES.

A.—*In Forward Areas.*

In order to illustrate the kind of nervous disturbances to which soldiers were subject under modern conditions of warfare and to which the term " shell-shock " has been applied, an account of what has been observed during a trench raid, an attack in force or when troops were held by a " barrage " may be given.

Medical witnesses described how, after an unsuccessful trench raid, scores of young men, some of them stupid, dreamy and silent; others excited. A number also were suffering from twitching movements of the limbs, such as one sees in the emotional type of shell-shock.

In a barrage men acutely shocked may sit down violently tremulous, weeping or silent, staring or with tightly closed eyes and incapable of walking unaided. In less acute cases, as may be seen in the trenches, men crouch low in cover, starting at every gun or shell burst. Here the face may appear drawn, the voice low with perhaps some tremor of the jaw, face, fingers or limbs.

During the bursting of H.E. shells men would congregate in small groups and seek security in a trench, ditch or hole. According as an individual thought much or little of what was taking place, he carried on, interrupted, or abandoned what he was doing. The usual air was one of expectation but some groups snuggled together and affected sleep.

Symptoms of terror or shock as just described are not at all uncommon amongst soldiers in the firing line. Young and inexperienced soldiers may be seen terror-stricken with fear written on their faces, the pupils dilated and the eyes staring. The respirations and heart's action may be accelerated and the hands tremulous, blue, cold and sweating; others give the impression of having lost their self-confidence and self-control, while others again exhibit rhythmical movements of an involuntary character.

Such symptoms as these are the emotional reactions of fear. Normally they are of temporary duration, disappearing on the removal of the individual from the danger zone. Should, however, they persist after the danger has passed away or reappear under conditions similar to those which gave rise to them, a state of so-called emotional " shell-shock " has been induced.

These symptoms may be observed in numbers of men under certain conditions and may lead to much temporary disorganisation, but when once stopped, a little rest or judicious handling on the part of the officers will soon bring about reassurance.

It was a common observation that hysterical symptoms, such as paralysis, mutism and so on, were not observed in the firing line. These phenomena develop when the soldier is sent down to hospital and finds himself in a place of safety.

It was acknowledged both by regimental executive and medical officers that shell-shock was a contagious malady. Medical regimental officers of experience have told us that it was a practical impossibility in the most forward areas during active fighting to distinguish between the acute emotional disturbances due to excessive fear, and a voluntary exaggeration of the normal reactions of fear, and malingering.

Many officers refused to acknowledge the existence of shell-shock in the firing line and were profoundly sceptical of the genuineness of many cases. Owing to the large number of men who may become afflicted by it, " mass shell-shock " occurring in the firing line or in the regimental area, is primarily a medico-military matter and requires to be handled in a manner differing from the more scientifically conducted treatment, which may be adopted in individual cases in special centres outside the regimental or divisional areas.

It was pointed out, in the first place, that all cases of " shell " shock " should be viewed with suspicion and being a contagious thing no risks should be taken, however unfortunate this may be to the individual.

Secondly, men presenting the symptoms of shell-shock in a moderate degree or who may have had a slight commotion should be dealt with at the regimental aid post and retained there for 24 or 48 hours. With tact on the part of the M.O. many men, who probably were more scared than shocked, could be encouraged to carry on.

Here they can be given rest and food and a night or two of sleep. If the shock has been slight the soldier may be able to pull himself together and may readily respond to suggestions made by the medical officer. Thus many men are curable at the Aid post and return directly to duty.

Thirdly, there are other cases of a more severe and persistent character—cases showing signs of slight concussion or some degree of fatigue or exhaustion for whom a longer rest is necessary. These may be sent to the transport lines or to the divisional rest station. Every effort should be made to keep these men in the divisional area as a large number may be returned to duty within a comparatively short time.

In ordinary times, measures such as those described usually suffice, the regimental aid post and its medical officer acting as the first filter and returning all but the more serious cases to the line.

During heavy or prolonged fighting, on the other hand, large numbers of men got away and it is impossible to filter them through the regimental or divisional channels.

Regimental Medical Officers.

The question which next arises bears upon the type of man best suited for the onerous and responsible position of regimental

M.O. under modern conditions of warfare. At the commencement of the war and during its progress many medical officers went directly from civilian hospitals or practice to the regiment. Large numbers had never been in contact with soldiers and knew nothing of the duties which they had to undertake. Many went straight to the firing line and found themselves plunged at once in the turmoil and difficulties either of trench warfare or active fighting on a large scale. Notwithstanding these handicaps it may be stated that the evidence before us goes to show that many medical officers, young and inexperienced as a large number were, showed an adaptability and resourcefulness in dealing with soldiers which was entirely to their credit.

Regimental medical officers have told us that special training in nervous and mental disorders is not necessary nor desirable for those whose duties are with the regiment in the front line. " I " would rather have an experienced man about 35 years of age, " a man of the world rather than a youthful Medical Officer " with some special bee in his bonnet."—(Dr. Wilson.)

" I think the best Medical Officer for a regiment is the man " who has had sufficient all-round experience and can read the " situation aright."—(Dr. Dunn.)

" The qualifications desired in the best type of regimental " Medical Officer are intimate knowledge of human nature so as " to estimate changes in the character of the man under his care." —Squadron Leader Tyrrell.)

" He should get to know the soldier and to live with him. He " need not know much medicine—a smattering of neurology would be useful. He should not be a peace-time psychologist; " this would be a great disadvantage."—(Major Adie.)

So far as the management of shell-shock and allied conditions in the front line is concerned, and these conditions were constantly before the medical officers, there was surprising unanimity about the type of Medical Officer required for the work on the part of those who had acted in this capacity during the War.

It is very desirable however that in future men who are to act as regimental medical officers should have previous training in their duties and the experience gained in the late war might be used for guidance in the future.

It will be seen however that fuller knowledge of nervous and mental disorders is necessary for those Medical Officers who have to treat cases of the War neuroses in special hospitals.

B.—Neurological Centres in the Army Areas.

Special neurological centres were established in the Army areas in France during the winter 1916-17 in order to avoid sending large numbers of men suffering from functional nervous disorders to England, as great difficulty was experienced in returning them to their units. Moreover, the French had obtained much success by treating their cases of shell-shock in special centres in the forward areas.

Here it might be noted that in the early months of 1916 the Medical Director-General of the Navy had appointed medical officers who had previously had special experience of nervous and mental illness, to take charge of the functional ineffectives in each of the great Naval Base Hospitals.

During quiet times or in quiet areas most of the cases of shell-shock occurring at the front could be disposed of in the manner just described. During periods of active fighting, however, numbers of men suffering from shell-shock and allied conditions, exhaustion, etc., were passed on to the neurological centres which were located some 10 or 12 miles behind the front line.

These men formed a large percentage of the cases admitted to the Centres and afterwards returned to duty.

In addition numerous cases of hysteria, anxiety neuroses and mental confusion were received and submitted to treatment.

During the progress of the war, increasing experience of the treatment of hysterical and allied phenomena of shell-shock taught that these symptoms could be more effectually dealt with in France and at the earliest possible opportunity after their onset.

There was a theoretical objection to herding shell-shock patients together in special centres because of the possible baneful effect of suggestion, but in practice that had very little effect, provided the general suggestion throughout the hospital was the suggestion of getting well, or what has been termed the "atmosphere of cure." The evidence was emphatic that the recovery rate was more satisfactory than when these patients were treated in general hospitals.

It was desirable that the medical officers in these centres should have special knowledge of neurology, psychology, and psycho-therapeutic methods of treatment, and that they should have had experience also of the fighting line. But over and above this, knowledge and experience was the personality of the Medical Officer and his temperamental fitness for work of this special kind. He should possess enthusiasm, confidence, cheerfulness, and tact.

The Committee had before them a Memorandum drawn up by Dr. C. S. Myers, Consulting Psychologist to the Forces in France, upon the treatment of shell-shock. In this report, Dr. Myers pointed out that successful treatment depended upon three essentials :—

"1 Promptness of action.
"2 Suitable environment.
"3 Psychotherapeutic measures."

(1)—*Promptness of Action.*

" Where by moral suasion the regimental medical officer is " unable to effect a cure at his aid post, the patient should be " immediately evacuated direct to a special centre for cases of " transient shell-shock, under the care of an experienced medical " officer. There can be no question that this is the proper pro- " cedure, having regard to (i) the contagiousness of the affection

" within a unit, if shell-shock become recognised as an easy
" means of escape to the base ; (ii) the difficulty of determining
" to what extent the mental ' wound ' or ' trauma ' is due to
" any fault of the soldier ; (iii) the undoubted fact that the dis-
" order is very apt to become systematized, and hence more
" difficult to cure by the postponement or neglect of treatment
" which must inevitably arise if such cases are admitted through
" the usual channels to the general or surgical wards of a hospital,
" where they may be attended by medical officers who have not
" the requisite experience, interest or time to treat the affection
" properly."

(2)—*Suitable Environment.**

" The centre to which these slighter shell-shock cases are first
" sent should be as remote from the sounds of warfare as is
" compatible with the preservation of the ' atmosphere ' of the
" front. It must, therefore, be neither within easy range of
" bombardment, nor within sight of England, at a base where
" cases are being frequently transferred thither.† Tents are suit-
" able for the majority of the patients. But separate accom-
" modation is needed : (i) for the cases presenting or developing
" such serious symptoms as to demand evacuation to the base ;
" (ii) for the cases which are under suspicion of malingering, and
" (iii) for those which require disciplinary measures.

" A private room, or tent, is essential for the use of each
" medical officer, where he can examine cases individually and
" confidentially, and give them the treatment suited to their
" condition.

" At the Base, it will be often found possible to retain cases
" for a longer time than is possible in the receiving centres at the
" front, and to give them more thorough observation. They
" should be placed under the care of a Medical Officer who has
" special interest in and experience of the disorder.

" Nursing Sisters are of the greatest value, their personality,
" like that of the Medical Officers, being of paramount import-
" ance."

Isolation.—The cases in which *isolation* was necessary were not
numerous.
It was useful—
  (i) in cases of pure exhaustion occurring especiallly in older men
      without symptoms of anxiety;
  (ii) in certain cases with hysterical symptoms, where being disagreeable
      it acted as a stimulus to recovery;
  (iii) in certain cases of functional tremors;
  (iv) in cases under suspicion of malingering, or persistent exaggeration.
It was harmful in cases of anxiety neurosis, characterised by mental
depression and terrifying dreams.
  † This memorandum was written by Dr. C. S. Myers in the latter half
of the year 1916 before the Neurological Centres were fully developed in
Army Areas in France.

(3)—*Psycho-therapeutic treatment.*

" Between wilful cowardice, contributory negligence (*i.e.*, want
" of effort against loss of self-control) and total irresponsibility
" for the shock, every stage conditioning shell-shock may be
" found. It follows, then, that each case must receive individual
" attention and treatment, based on its own merits.

" Many cases, especially those complicated by neurasthenia,
" will be found to benefit by a few days' initial rest in bed, with
" careful attention to sleep, diet, and the evacuation of bowels,
" the danger, however, must not be overlooked of leaving a patient
" to brood in solitude over his worries and symptoms which are
" thus apt to become stereotyped.

" Nothing can be attempted in psycho-therapy until the
" attention, interest and confidence of the patient are obtained.
" Any attempt to treat a patient during maniacal excitement, un-
" yielding apathy or stupor, save by medicinal measures, is a
" sheer waste of time.

" The guiding principles of psycho-therapeutic treatment at the
" earliest stages should consist in the re-education of the patient
" so as to restore his memory, self-confidence, and self-control.
" For this restoration of his normal self, a judicious admixture
" of persuasion, suggestion, explanation and scolding is required.

" A genuine case which has on a previous occasion been
" treated at a receiving centre at the front should on a second
" admission be sent to the Base, if he has been previously treated
" at a Base, he should, as a rule, be sent to England upon a
" relapse."

C.—*Convalescence.*

As soon as possible every patient should be restored to an
atmosphere of increasing military discipline, gradually passing
from gentle forms of exercise to longer marches and more
strenuous drill and fatigues.

There was a difference of opinion as to whether the shell-shock
soldiers should remain under the eye of the medical officer who
had obtained his confidence from the outset, or whether he should
be mixed with the physically wounded convalescents in a general
convalescent camp.

In support of the former view is the fact that any set-back in
the direction of re-establishing self-confidence or undue neglect
or pampering which he may receive from inexpert hands invites
a relapse. If he be allowed to drift alternately between hospital
or convalescent depôt and duty in a half cured, unstable state, it
becomes increasingly difficult to cure him or he is apt to enter a
long and costly vicious circle of recurrent mental disorder.

On the other hand, we had the evidence of the Medical Officer
who was in charge of a large convalescent camp in France, to the
effect that no special arrangements were made in his camp for
the convalescence of the shell-shocked soldier. All patients, whatever their disability, were looked upon as general convalescents.

This officer maintained that if the " shell-shocks " had been treated in special divisions of the camp, the results would not have been as satisfactory as they were. In his opinion, the mixing of the shell-shock cases with other convalescents was a good measure. They were subjected to the same discipline as the other soldiers, and were given to understand that they were there to be made fit to fight again. There were no Medical Officers specially trained in the treatment of the neurological cases, and no orders were issued as regards additional rest or special attention. The decision as to whether a soldier was fit to return to his unit after the usual three or four weeks' convalescence was made by the Medical Officer in charge of the camp.

In the *Command depôts* at home also the shell-shock cases were mixed with those who had been physically wounded. This arrangement proved to be highly unsatisfactory. There was evidence that these cases received no particular attention. They loafed about and were not under proper conditions for cure. No effort was made to restore their *morale*, and there were no Medical Officers attached to the depôts, who from previous knowledge or training were capable of dealing with them by suitable methods. In consequence of the failure of the command depôts in this respect, the shell-shocked soldiers eventually were withdrawn.

The evidence on the subject of convalescence was entirely to the effect that the results obtained in France were a long way better than any obtained at home. Overseas the " atmosphere of the front " could be effectually maintained and the retarding influences of home conditions played no part.

A further explanation of this difference would appear to lie in the personality of the officer in charge, who should be a medical officer of wide knowledge and large experience.

REVIEW OF THE PSYCHO-THERAPEUTIC TREATMENT OF THE DISORDERS ARISING DURING THE WAR COMMONLY REFERRED TO AS " SHELL-SHOCK."

In the early stages of the War, just as, from the point of view of recruiting, only those individuals with marked mental or nervous disorder were considered as psychologically unfit for service, so, from the point of view of treatment of the individual who became ineffective in one course of his service, the psychological determinants were largely disregarded, save in cases of complete nervous exhaustion or gross mental breakdown. Mild mental disorders, emotional manifestations, paralyses and losses of sensory functions of non-organic origin were dealt with in either one of the following ways :—

(1) The condition was not recognised as coming within the province of the medical officer. The individual was made to take the responsibility for his functional

efficiency in the absence of any definite organic lesion, and was not released from the laid down disciplinary code which, by means of systematized inducements and punishments, maintains the efficiency of the units of the organized whole.

(2) The condition was recognised as being a matter appertaining to the medical officer, but, owing to the materialistic trend of modern scientific medicine, and to the introduction of the high explosive into warfare, it was attributed to a physical origin comparable to that inferred in cases of actual concussion of the Central Nervous system. As under the circumstances of the War, such cases of concussion were constantly occurring, and as the symptoms and signs of the two classes of disorder not uncommonly coincided, the result obtained that the whole group of disorders, both physical and psychological, were included under the diagnostic term of shell-shock, and such cases as fell under medical treatment were dealt with by physiological or physical methods on the basis of their supposedly common physical causation.

It is to be noted that method (1) is essentially a psychological form of treatment, and with troops of the quality of the Regular Army, or of the Voluntary Recruited Forces, no doubt it was the most efficient form of treatment applicable. It was in the hands of the executive officers who knew the environmental conditions, who had had experience of and who understood the mentality of the men they were dealing with, and who, no doubt, interpreted the moral code of honour under which they acted, in giving their personal opinions as to the moral responsibility of the patient, as no other body of men could.

A number of causes, however, soon began to operate to render the situation incapable of being dealt with simply by the two methods above mentioned. The rapidly growing immensity of the task and the pre-occupation of the executive officers with military matters, limited very seriously the capacity for impersonal and impartial judgments from a moral point of view, and while the stresses of the actual environment led to a more severe application of the moral code on the one hand, on the other they were producing an ever increasing number of cases of the type under review. Again, with the increasing dilution of the regular trained troops by more or less untrained men, the executive officer was being confronted with a class of man whom he did not understand. Also, the trained officer became comparatively scarce, and the interpretation of the moral code was being left more and more to the new officer who had not the experience behind him to interpret it.

The tendency then existed for, on the one hand, a certain number of executive officers to deal with cases of functional inefficiency by the application of a stringent code of disciplinary laws, while on the other a great number of the cases were left to the medical branch to be dealt with. These cases under medical hands were not differentiated to any extent from the physical casualties of battle, they were mixed with cases of illness or wounds indiscriminately, a lack of attention to the need of careful differential diagnosis between the organic and the functional disorder led to the psychological aspect of the matter being quite neglected, and universal methods adapted to the organic case were adopted.

Such methods of treatment proved, in the majority of the functional cases, of no avail, and there resulted an accumulation of unprogressing cases of " shell-shock " in the military hospitals.

From the time that the special hospitals were instituted it may be said that the psycho-therapy of these conditions began to be studied and used. Since then a great many observers have recorded their views as to the various methods by which psycho-therapy can be brought to bear on the cases, and as to the relative values of these methods. The evidence which has been heard by this Committee would indicate that there are several ways in which the patient can be approached psychologically, and that each method can attain a measure of success according to the personality of the medical officer who is undertaking the treatment. Each method, again, has its particular value in certain types of case and is very limited in others. The following are the main divisions into which psycho-therapeutic treatment falls.

1. *Persuasion.**

Here the medical officer, having assured himself that the condition is functional, persuades the patient to make the effort necessary to overcome the disability. In order to do this, he uses his authority as an officer, he brings into play all the moral suasion he can, appealing to the patient's social self-esteem to make him co-operate and put forth a real effort of will. If moral suasion fails, then recourse may be had to more forcible methods, and according to certain witnesses even threats were justified in certain cases (Major Pritchard Taylor, Dr. Dunn, Dr. Elliot, and Lieut.-Colonel Rogers).

2. *Explanation.*

In this method the causes of the origin and persistence of the symptoms are explained to the patient in reference to his own individual case. He is reassured as to the fact that he is not

---

* The term " persuasion " is here used in a wide or popular application rather than in the strict sense, according to present usage in works on Psychotherapy, in which there is the implication of a prior or concurrent factor of explanation based upon the details of the individual experiences of the patient concerned.

suffering from some terrible and lasting nervous or mental disorder, and he is shown in what direction he must turn to get rid of his troubles. This process, the inoculation of Autognosis, was of universal application and was much recommended by many witnesses of high authoritative standing.—(Dr. Head, Dr. Rivers, Dr. Myers, Dr. Brown.)

3. *Suggestion.*

In this method, the effort of the patient to overcome the symptoms is reinforced by suggestion that the symptom is not permanent, has diminished, or has disappeared, or, on the positive side, that the lost function is returning to activity. Although treated as a method by itself, suggestion obviously plays a part in all other psycho-therapeutic methods, and was largely practised in conjunction with medicinal and mechanical aids, *e.g.*, the use of hypnotics to overcome insomnia, of electrical stimulation to restore function.

The suggestions may be given under certain conditions :—
  (1) With the patient fully conscious and co-operating.
  (2) With the patient in the hypnoidal state.
  (3) With the patient in a deep hypnotic sleep.

Many witnesses recommended suggestion under the first condition, and a few, Dr. W. Brown, Dr. Rows and others, under the second and third for the revival of forgotten experiences.

4. *Analysis.*

By the method of Free Association or Reaction Time experiment, the unconscious factors behind the conscious symptoms are brought to light, the patient's mind is analysed, and by finally effecting a synthesis in which cause and effect are placed in juxtaposition in the consciousness of the patient, the symptoms are said to disappear. A full analysis in the Freudian sense (Psycho-analysis) was recommended by very few witnesses, while several witnesses spoke against its' employment (Dr. Mapother regarded it as unnecessary and impracticable, Dr. Bernard Hart as hardly applicable at all, Dr. Hurst as dangerous in setting up sexual ideas, etc.). A modified analysis, however, such as would be necessary for the thorough cross examination of the patient, and one that was not based on a purely sexual view of the mind, was recommended by the majority of the witnesses, including one of the sufferers from the condition who gave evidence, and who had derived considerable benefit from its application.

5. *Re-education.*

Having cleared away the symptoms, it was found necessary to submit the patient to a course of graduated experiences which should prepare him for taking on his duty again, and accompanying this it was necessary to implant a raised moral view very often with a widening of the intelligent conception of the military and social necessities, so that the patient should have sufficient stability and moral support to again face the stresses of his service. Most of the witnesses gave testimony to the importance of this procedure.

6. *Occupation.*

During the process of the last-mentioned course, it was generally found that it was of the utmost importance that the patient should be kept occupied consistently and not allowed to slip back into unprofitable habits by neglect or lack of mental diversion. The witnesses were agreed as to the importance of this.

All of these methods involving a direct approach of the physician to the patient are dependent upon two essential factors and a relationship between them.

(i) *The willingness of the patient to co-operate.*

This is particularly needed in the methods of analysis and explanation. With persuasion* and suggestion, if the persuasion be forcible enough, or the suggestion accompanied by painful effect, a reluctance on the part of the patient to make the necessary effort of will may be overcome, otherwise failure is certain.

(ii) *The personality of the physician.*

The physician must have confidence in his method and in his knowledge ; also he must have experience, for a line of treatment in a case diagnosed wrongly will spoil his future results, and random or ill-regulated treatment is productive of much harm. He must treat the patient and not merely the disorder, as is often the rule in ordinary physical illnesses; he must mould his treatment to suit each individual case, and he must be prepared to mete out praise or reprimand (Dr. Myers) without any bias from personal sentiment or sympathy. With all this the physician must have sufficient force to dominate the situation.

(iii) *The relationship between physician and patient.*

The doctor must get the full confidence of the patient. No half measures are possible, and there should be no possibility of the patient evading the doctor's opinion. The persistence of symptoms often resolves itself into a *tour de force* in the struggle for ascendency between the patient's selfish and social tendencies, and for the physician to be able to throw his weight into the scale on behalf of the latter, there must be no barriers of escape between the patient and himself.

---

* *Vide* footnote on page 128.

Granted the successful establishment of these three conditions, it may be said that any method adopted will meet with a measure of success; without them all methods are valueless. " *C'est la foi qui sauve ou qui guérit.*"—(Charcot.)

The evidence obtained by the Committee has shown that just as there are positive steps which should be taken to help these patients, so there are dangers which must be avoided. Chief among these is the necessity for avoiding harmful suggestion. Wrong suggestions may be made consciously by the physician through a misunderstanding of the patient, through an ignorance of the type of disorder, or through a lack of experience in Psychotherapeutic methods, and a great deal of harm may be done unconsciously. Harmful suggestions are very liable to occur during the neurological examination of a case unless the physician is on his guard, this point being emphasised by several witnesses and especially by Professor Graham Brown, who devised a method of physical examination specially contrived to divert the patient's mind from the points at issue. Nor may the physician show any surprise or undue interest in any abnormal phenomenon he may discover, everything must be taken as a matter of course.—(Professor Graham Brown.)

Apart, however, from the psychological influences brought to bear in the direct contact between doctor and patient, there is the very important element in Psycho-therapy of establishing the correct psychological atmosphere in which the patient is placed in the course of his treatment.

The atmosphere of cure.—All witnesses agree as to the supreme importance of the maintenance of the general atmosphere of cure in the hospitals where these patients are being treated ; no influence is more potent for beneficial suggestion than this. The new patient should come into contact with, and be looked after to a certain extent by the patient who has recently recovered from a similar condition. There should be no maudlin sentimentality about the hospital for functional nervous or mental disorder, there must be an air of practical cheerfulness supported by all the staff who must co-operate to produce a solid barrier against the development of any unwholesome attitudes of discontent or morbid doubting. They must construct a line of least resistance, so far as the patient is concerned, *i.e.*, that of voluntary acquiescence and cheerful co-operation towards recovery. Sympathy which is misplaced is most harmful, and the deleterious effect of indiscriminate sympathy from the general public cannot be too strongly deprecated (Miss Cockerell). Hence cases of this type should never be treated in the unofficial V.A.D. hospitals (Dr. Mapother and Dr. Hurst).

Consistency of treatment.—A line laid down by the doctor must be maintained consistently; any divergences subtract from the value of any method of treatment. The case should be in one physician's care from beginning to end as far as possible. Much harm was done by the frequent passing on of patients from hospital to hospital; in each they commenced right from the beginning over again and with a new medical man. Lines of treatment were interrupted and replaced by others, different explanations were given, different prognoses, different promises, etc., etc., until the patient lost all faith in any doctor, became hospitalized, and settled down in a chronic depression with incapacity.—(Dr. Burton Fanning, Dr. Hurst.)

Separation from the wounded or organically ill cases.—The influence on the functional case of being in contact with patients showing the signs and symptoms of real organic incapacity is a fertile source of harmful suggestion, and is to be avoided as far as possible. Many witnesses insisted upon this requirement; *see* particularly Professor Graham Brown who arranged for his cases to be isolated from the front line itself.

Disciplinary control.—In no type of case is there more need to maintain firm disciplinary control than in this. The code of inducement to, and punishment for loss of self-control cannot, of course, be enforced as in a hospital where the question of emotional instability does not arise. But rules must be laid down whereby greater liberties accrue from the exercise of normal behaviour, and medical treatment which necessarily involves restriction to bed and a resumption of an invalid's life in regard to diet, etc., inevitably follows the exhibition of symptoms arising from a recrudescence of emotional or volitional instability, and such rules must be adamant and firmly adhered to. Any patient, also, who is allowed parole, or who is placed in a position comparable to that occupied by the practically recovered convalescent from any other form of illness, must be given clearly to understand that the fact that he has suffered from " shell-shock " will not release him from any consequences of misdemeanours he may commit. Speaking generally, there should be not too many inducements to prolong the stay in hospital; particularly it should be avoided that any general impression obtain that the disorder is one for which invaliding from the service is bound to take place if the symptoms prove intractable for a sufficiently long period of time.

In making practical recommendations as to the line of psychotherapy to be adopted in dealing with these cases, it must be remembered that one form of functional disorder will not respond to the same method of treatment as another, so the recommendation should be based on a recognition of the following general types :—

Fatigue cases.
Exhaustion and Confusional states.
Conversion Hysteria.
Anxiety states.
Obsessional states.

Again, as the psycho-therapy is dependent upon the facilities which are provided for treatment, it is necessary to co-ordinate the recommendations on this aspect of the matter with the general arrangements for handling and disposing of these cases which have been suggested elsewhere. Realising that prompt application of the correct psychological influence can undoubtedly save a great number of these cases from becoming " casualties," it is recommended that treatment should begin at the Regimental Aid Post.

Here the patient will be in the hands of the Regimental Medical Officer and his assistants, who probably know the patient. After a brief period of rest, strong moral suasion and energetic persuasive methods should be adopted following an attempt to reassure the patient as to the facts of his disability. This course of action is strongly commended by witnesses who have had experience of the front line, and in the hands of competent medical officers, who need have no special knowledge but who must use their common sense, it has proved of great utility. Without, perhaps, going to the extent of regarding every case as a possible malingerer, as suggested by one witness (Major Pritchard Taylor), yet the measures taken must be determinedly stringent and forceful. (Major Adie, Lieut.-Colonel Rogers, Dr. Dunn, etc.) By this means a great majority of cases may be restored at once to duty and will be saved from a further development and fixation of their disorders. Such cases recoverable by these means would include cases of Fatigue, mild Exhaustion and mild Confusional states, early Hysterical Dissociations and Amnesias, and many of the Conversion Hysterias. The Anxiety states, the Obsessional states, and severer Exhaustion and Confusional conditions would not respond, nor would a number of the Conversion Hysterias in whom the personality was of a low grade and strongly anti-moral.

It should be noted that very little harm could be done at this stage even by misapplied forceful persuasion to a non-responsive case ; in comparison to the stress of actual battle which has caused the disability which is intractable to early treatment the most forceful methods of persuasion or suggestion are negligible as regards their capacity for producing any deleterious results.

Cases in which the condition is refractory to this early and elementary treatment, or cases which, owing to pressure of circumstance, cannot be dealt with at once, should be evacuated, sorted out at the Field Ambulance, and sent straight away to the Special Neurological Receiving Centre.

Here a determined effort can be made and sustained to deal with the more severe cases of Conversion Hysteria. Most witnesses are agreed (Dr. Rivers, Dr. Myers, Professor Roussy, etc.) that the treatment should consist of well-defined stages, and it is, therefore, recommended that the following regime should be applied :—

1. *Preparatory.*—The patient is kept in bed on invalid diet, he is seen and thoroughly examined by the medical officer, he is reassured about himself, his condition is roughly explained to

him, and he is told that his paralysis will be cured, his sight restored, or his memories reawakened, etc., very quickly and easily by the treatment which is to follow. (Professor Roussy makes the man promise to submit to any necessary treatment; Colonel Gordon Holmes would tell the man that electricity will help him along, etc.) Obviously many variants are possible here, but the aim should be to get the patient into such a proper mental attitude of thought and anticipation as will render him responsive to the next stage of treatment.

2. *Stage of Active Treatment.*—Here the patient is seen alone by the Medical Officer, and every method of persuasion and suggestion should be employed, hypnosis, electrical stimulation, forcible movements, cold douches (Professor Roussy), all being recommended as useful adjuncts to the more ordinary straightforward methods. Some witnesses (*e.g.*, Dr. Hurst) insist that the sitting should be protracted until the hysterical symptom is removed, and this would be most desirable if time and circumstance permit.

3. *Re-educative and Occupational Stage.*—In this stage the restored function in particular, and the patient generally, is submitted to re-educational exercise. Meanwhile a further analysis of the patient's mind can be carried out if necessary, combined with a general moral education so as to stabilise the " recovery " of function. The patients, when finished with as " cured," should not be permitted to get further away from the front line, but should proceed to modified duties in the area associated with the cadre to which they belong. Relapse should entail return to the same Centre of treatment.

In addition to the Conversion Hysteria cases, many of the less grave Exhaustion and Confusional states and of the milder Anxiety conditions will respond, under the conditions of the special centre, to rest, medicinal treatment, and a slight grade of analysis with reassurance and explanation. These cases can then pass on the third stage of Re-education, and can be disposed of in a similar manner to the recovered Hysterics.

The important point of the Centre should be in energetic and constant treatment and in such treatment as is calculated to produce early results. No form of protracted treatment should be attempted, and the total length of stay of patients in the centre should not exceed 2-3 weeks.

The residue of cases, consisting of Obsessional states, severe Anxiety states, Marked Mental disturbances, intractable Conversion Hysterias, and possible determined malingerers or aggravators, will then be sent on to the Base Hospital.

Special Neurological Base Hospital.

Here each individual case can be submitted to a thorough and protracted examination and treatment. No particular form of treatment can be laid down, as evidently these cases will require the utmost refinement of method specially adapted to meet the special requirements of each individual personality. The obsessional patient will need a fairly exhaustive analysis, in some cases not only of the military life, but also of pre-war and sometimes childish experiences (Dr. Head). The Mental Dissociations can be sorted out, and those of a profound variety, or those which will call for prolonged hospital environment, should be sent home to the special mental hospitals; milder varieties, and particularly the Exhaustive Confusional types, may, with advantage, be retained and treated. All cases of Mental Dullness or Deficiency should be sent home for invaliding. Intractable cases of Conversion Hysteria and possible malingering patients should be kept strictly isolated and under careful observation away from any potential suggestion from the environment. Cases of Anxiety can be given prolonged rest and thorough reassurance based on a complete investigation of the state of mind. All cases with signs of hyperthyroidism should be told that they will be invalided as a suggestion to quieten the defence mechanisms at work which maintain the disorder (Dr. Hurst).

In accordance with the severity of the conditions under treatment in the Base Hospital, so the stage of Re-education and Occupation (third stage of treatment) can be more easily graduated and more adapted to suit the requirements of the individual cases. Especially worthy of recommendation is the inculcation of the competitive spirit amongst the patients undergoing occupational therapy during the later convalescent period, and described by Major Brooke Purdon in his evidence.

There is a not inconsiderable body of opinion which believes that the value of psycho-therapeutic treatment has been much overrated. This point of view does not dispute the value of psycho-therapy in so far as it allows the physician to obtain the confidence of the patient, and thereby enables him to treat him to the best advantage and restore to the patient that confidence which he has lost.

The system of therapy advocated by this school is both physical and mental in its aims. In its physical aspects treatment is mainly directed to the restoration of the exhausted nervous and physical states of the body; to the therapeutic means at its disposal for the removal of specific and toxic products, by the use of vaccines, of hydro-therapeutic and electric treatment, and such remedies as are known by experience to have the effect of restoring the bodily organs to their normal tone. In its mental aspects it has in view the invariable subjective outlook of all persons whose mind is more or less affected, and the belief that the mental disorder of the emotionally shell-shocked patient differs in degree only from other mental disorders. With the object of replacing the pathological and subjective outlook by a normal and objective one, suitable, engrossing, and interesting occupations, especially in the open air, are provided; methodical habits, and regulated exercise studies and amusements are prescribed and supervised in the carrying out.

RETURN TO FIGHTING LINE.

The evidence of both military and medical officers showed that the neuroses cases from the point of view of further fighting value could be divided into two groups :—

(1) Officers and men who exhibited the temporary nervous effects of fatigue and exhaustion or who were victims of emotional " shell-shock " in its slighter forms.

(2) Officers and men who had permanently broken down from the strain of war or who were suffering from the more serious phenomena of " shell-shock," anxiety neuroses and psychoses.

Several medical witnesses of large experience (Dr. Holmes and Colonel Soltau) told us that soldiers who had suffered from " shell-shock " were capable of further service, and that it was an error to hold too strongly to the view that those who had so suffered were incapable of further service. In many instances the period of service in the line had been well worth while. A small percentage returned to the line and did brilliant service again.

A medical witness who had himself suffered from shell-shock (Squadron Leader Tyrrell) told us that after six months from duty he was quite well and returned to the front for a period of two and a half years, and that he knew of other similar cases.

Effective return to the line of the soldier who had broken down nervously depended upon individual temperament and the type of the neurosis. As regards the latter, cases of temporary breakdown often did quite well on returning to the line. These men were merely tired and wanted rest.

Of pilots who went home tired and who were treated in hospital a number returned and rendered efficient service.

Cases of commotional shock, if not of a severe kind, were fit to return to the line and did not of necessity show any tendency to emotional breakdown.

As regards the emotional type of " shell-shock " the majority of men returned to the line were exhaustion cases. On this point Dr. Gordon Holmes said that most of the men, if approached properly, were willing to go back and a large number were willing to return provided they were kept within the army area.

There was evidence also that a man once shocked will relapse very soon on return to the line. Men who said they were " all right again," showed the signs of strain as soon as they were back in the line and any livliness occurred (Dr. Dunn).

We had before us some figures showing the returns from the Neurological Centres which are of interest in this connection. From one centre between July and November, 1917, 80 per cent. out of 5,357 cases returned to duty (Dr. Holmes). From another centre (Dr. W. Brown) between November, 1916, and May, 1917, 85 per cent. of 1,000 cases returned to duty. From this same centre during the Cambrai fighting, November—December, 1917, 91 per cent. of 1,030 cases returned to duty.

It was admitted that there was great difficulty in ascertaining the frequency of *relapses*, in the cases which had returned to the fighting line from the centres, as owing to the movements of the divisions, men did not necessarily return to the same centre.

The only available fact as regards relapse is that few cases returned to the centres in which they were treated originally.

Dr. Gordon Holmes made the following statement on this subject :—

" Our problem was to keep the troops up to strength and a " large number of cases went back. The proportion of re- " currences among the cases sent back from centres in France, " army or base, was surprisingly small. I may give you some " figures.

" During the Passchendale fighting, No. 62 Casualty Clearing " Station and part of No. 63 were acting as a centre for these " cases in the 5th Army Area. I have records of the working " of the centre during the whole of that fighting and the number " of readmissions was under one hundred and that was during " the heaviest fighting, I suppose, that the British Army has " ever done. These figures are not so simple as they appear, as " divisions were constantly being moved from one army area " to another and it is possible that cases of recurrence occurred " after the troops had left the army area. I have other figures " of relapses during the same period. No. 3 Canadian Stationary " Hospital (acting as centre for the 3rd Army in which there " was little fighting) admitted 1,844 cases between December, " 1916, and October, 1917, and out of this number 73 were re- " garded as relapses.

" My attention was drawn to this in another manner and con- " sequently I made a further effort to determine the proportion of " actual relapses. It seemed to me that the only way was to go " through all the cases in a certain number of army centres on " one or more days. I found that in September and the " beginning of October, 1918, in three army centres there were " at that time 573 patients under treatment. Out of these cases " 57, *i.e.*, 10 per cent. of those admitted from the three armies, " claimed that they had previously had ' shell-shock.' A good " many of these cases could not be verified as having had ' shell- " ' shock ' before ; in fact the majority of these cases were men " who had been transferred to England and stated that they " suffered from ' shell-shock ' while in England. I also went " through the periods these 57 men had served with their units " after being returned as recovered from ' shell-shock.' Out of the " 57, 10 had served 10 months or more, 3 had served between " 9 and 12 months, 9 between 6 and 9 months, 10 had served

" 4 months, 3 had served 6 months, 6 had served 3 months, 9
" had served 1 month and 10 remained with their units for less
" than 1 month. In other words, 39 out of the 57 cases had
" served with their battalions for 3 months after being returned
" from ' shell-shock ' centres.''

On the question of the circulation of these cases between the
centres and the line, Dr. Holmes said : '' It has been stated that
" the men were breaking down at once and coming down and
" consequently they simply circulated between the line and the
" ' shell-shock ' centre. I do not think that is possible to avoid,
" and no blame can be attached to the M.O. who sends back a
" case which recurs once. But I recognise that it is a serious
" matter to have two or three recurrences taking place. In
" the three army centres investigated, only 16 cases claimed to
" have been down twice previously and out of these 16, 9 had
" been treated in the United Kingdom. Only 5 of these cases
" had been treated in our centres in the previous two years
" and had recurred twice under fire or other conditions.''

Soldiers should not be returned to the line under the following
conditions :—

    (1) If the symptoms of '' shell-shock '' were of such a character
        that the soldier could not be treated overseas with a
        view to subsequent useful employment.

    (2) If the breakdown were of such severity as to require
        a long period of rest and treatment at home.

    (3) If the disability were an anxiety neurosis, of severe
        type.

    (4) If the disability were a mental breakdown or psychosis
        requiring treatment in a mental hospital.

Many of these cases, however, could be usefully employed after
recovery in some form of auxiliary military duty.

COWARDICE AND SHELL-SHOCK.

Cowardice is a military crime for which the death penalty may
be exacted.

Some witnesses declined to define it and others did so with
reservation.

Major Dowson, a barrister of considerable court-martial experience said : '' Cowardice is showing signs of fear in the face
" of the enemy.'' Such a definition is not helpful to the medical
officer who may be called on to decide between cowardice and
" shell-shock.''

Cowardice, if regarded as a lack of or failure to show requisite
courage, renders discussion more feasible and assists us in compre-
hending how the brave after much stress may temporarily fail
to show their wonted courage without deserving to be called by
an opprobrious term.

Fear is the chief factor in both cowardice and emotional '' shell-
shock '' and it was for this reason that cowardice in the military
sense was made a subject of enquiry by the Committee.

Witnesses were agreed that cowardice should be regarded as a military crime to be punished when necessary by death.

Fear is an emotion common to all and evidence was given of very brave men who frankly acknowledged to it.

It is obvious then that fear alone does not constitute cowardice. Colonel Allison remarked that with second lieutenants it was their one fear, that they should show cowardice in front of their men.

Dr. Farquhar Buzzard said : " I quite see that fear passes to " cowardice. But fear is really an unconscious thing and has a " very definite physical manifestation." And again he remarked —" Cowardice is a voluntary attitude taken up by an individual ; " he adopts a certain attitude that he will not face a situation in " which he believes certain things will take place. That is " cowardice, if you like to apply the term, but the fact that my " knees shake when I am looking over the side of a building is an " absolute physical thing over which I have no control."

Prof. Roussy noted the difficulty of distinguishing between cowardice and emotional shell-shock. " Cowardice is lack of " self-control of an individual over himself. In the presence " of a situation in which there is an element of danger or in " which there is an element likely to cause fear, any man who " can control himself is a courageous man, but he who gives " way, runs away or does certain other actions not esteemed " worthy is defined as a coward."

It may then be accepted that neither feeling fear nor manifesting the physical signs of fear—pallor, shaking, tremors, quick pulse do of themselves constitute cowardice though they are more or less esesntial to it.

If the individual exercises his self-control in facing the danger he is not guilty of cowardice, if, however, being capable of doing so, he will not face the situation, he is then a coward. It is here that difficulty arises in cases of war neurosis for it becomes necessary to decide whether the individual has or has not crossed that indefinite line which divides normal emotional reaction from neurosis with impairment of volitional control.

Dr. Mapother said : " Frankly, I am not prepared to make a " decision between cowardice and shell-shock. Cowardice I take " to mean action under the influence of fear and the ordinary " type of ' shell-shock ' was, to my mind, persistent and chronic " fear."

Dr. Johnson thought that when the symptoms of fear—tremors, sweating, tachycardia—persisted or revived on slight emotional stimulation a psycho-neurosis was present.

Having regard to their terms of reference, the Committee have felt it incumbent upon them to make some inquiry into " shell-shock " in relation to courts-martial.

As regards expert medical evidence and advice in court-martial cases, the system pursued in France in the late war seems to have been a satisfactory one, namely, that when any medical question or doubt arose before or at a trial, or on subsequent review of the Proceedings, the best possible expert advice available was placed at the immediate disposal of the military authorities, either in the form of a board or otherwise. We recommend that a similar plan should be followed in future.

The subject of courts-martial held during the war received exhaustive investigation by Mr. Justice Darling's Committee immediately upon its conclusion. The report of that committee is before us, and having regard to its terms, the steps subsequently taken to carry out its recommendations, and the evidence which has been given before us, we anticipate that in any future war justice will be administered in a thoroughly satisfactory manner, if the same or a similar policy is followed.

Our conclusions are :—

That the military aspect of cowardice is justified.

That seeming cowardice may be beyond the individual's control.

That experienced and specialised medical opinion is required to decide in possible cases of war neurosis of doubtful character.

That a man who has already proved his courage should receive special consideration in case of subsequent lapse.

MALINGERING AND SHELL-SHOCK.

On this subject the ample evidence heard by the Committee revealed some difference of opinion both as to the prevalence and the practicability of detection of malingered shell-shock.

When closely considered this divergence of views is found to be to some extent more apparent than real and the bulk of evidence is not much at variance. Such discrepancy as exists is partly explicable as arising from the use of the term malingering and as to whether it is interpreted in a limited or broad sense. Again, in those who have been exposed to the stress of battle with its danger, noise, and terrors, there is frequent difficulty in deciding how much of conscious and how much of unconscious motive there may be in the actions of the possible malingerer, since in either case the fundamental instinct of self-preservation is presumably present.

The dividing line between malingering and functional neurosis may be a very fine one and many " shell-shocks " are of hysterical nature ; in most there is a halo of hysteria according to Sir F. Mott. Hysteria was called " La grande Simulatrice " by Charcot as quoted by Prof. Roussy so that simulation is common to both malingered " shell-shock " and to much genuine " shell-shock."

Further, if we bear in mind how the incidence of shell-shock varied with the morale of different units it may be comprehended how equally competent observers may have arrived at different conclusions. With these preliminary observations the deductions which the evidence appears to justify may now be formulated :—

(1) *True malingering*, meaning the action of one who deliberately attempted imposition in pretending to be suffering from " shell-shock," was of rare occurrence or, as one witness expresesd it, " absolute malingering " was very common."

(2) *Partial malingering*, exaggeration of symptoms or prolongation of a condition no longer remaining was far from uncommon and frequently arose from a desire to avoid service or for a continuation of pension. Such form of malingering was found most difficult to deal with even by specialists owing to the doubt which often existed in their minds as to the degree of intention present.

(3) *Quasi-malingering*, skrimshanking, skulking. In this group there are included those who with little or no pretence decamped from the battle as opportunity arose, pleading " shell-shock " as the excuse for their evasion. Their numbers were great. For the most part they made but feeble if any attempt at deception and ultimately by persuasion or command returned to duty.

" Shell-shock " became recognized as a handy excuse, and, indeed, a suggestion also to the many who were ready to avail themselves of any subterfuge to escape from the terrors of the front.

If this breaking away of men in small and large numbers is to be classed as malingering, then it must be allowed that malingering occurred in unprecedented proportions.

As a defence in court-martial cases " shell shock " was so frequently pleaded as to be spoken of as a " parrot cry " by a witness of much experience of courts-martial.

The Detection of Malingering.

(a) In the Front Line.

The pronounced case of acute shock cannot be doubted, and mild " shell shock." cases are best dealt with as being simple exhaustion. It is patent that an exhaustive neurological examination, even if the medical officer were capable of conducting it, is impracticable.

The medical officer, however, may discriminate, and if he knows the character and personality of the man, observes in how far his behaviour appears to be voluntary or involuntary, and makes use of such further observation as circumstances permit of, he will be assisted in deciding the false from the true.

(b) *Away from the Front Line.*

Though the clumsy malingerer may be easily detected, the able one or the mental defective may occasion considerable difficulty to the medical officer in arriving at a conclusion completely free from doubt.

In all cases of consequence the examiner should be specially versed in nervous diseases.

The presence of fine tremors, quick pulse and sweating, if persistent or readily excited by slight emotional stress, may, according to some authorities, be accepted as indicative of psycho-neurosis.

Space does not permit of considering all the details in making a differential diagnosis, but Dr. Mapother, who is quoted below, mentions many, and suggests that cases which show none of the signs of emotion impossible of simulation are very suspicious.

Reviewing the evidence, which was ample, on the subject of malingering " shell-shock " it is evident that close and often prolonged observation may be necessary, that occasionally doubt may still remain and that in all important cases the decision should be made by a specially trained physician well acquainted with functional nervous disorders.

SUMMARY of the more important evidence on which the above report on Malingering is based.

Dr. Mapother. There was not a hard and fast distinction between either of the common types of Neurosis and simulation.

The degree of awareness of intention and motive to deceive might vary even in the same cases at different times.

I think most cases of Anxiety Neurosis were wholly genuine to start with. Many remained so throughout but some were consciously protracted and exaggerated later. A few added features not to be explained as effects of fear ; more settled down to emphasis of one feature of the original symdrome.

Most cases of " Conversion Hysteria " were consciously simulating or exaggerating at first. Eventually the production of symptoms became automatic and some achieved belief in their own symptoms. None of the so-called trophic changes were proof of genuineness.

In Dr. Mapother's opinion any case showing none of those signs of emotion impossible of simulation was suspicious.

" The following were such signs of emotional disturbance as " could be accepted as excluding conscious simulation :—

" Tachycardia ; Arrhythmia ; Diffuse and forceable impulse, " etc.

" Vasemotor changes, sweating, flushing, tâche cerébrale.

" Enlargement of thyroid ;

" Fine tremor of face and tongue ;

" Fine tremor of hands of a quality only distinguishable by " experience ;

" Stammer only distinguishable by experience ;

" Increased tendon jerks only distinguishable by experience;
" Increase of supinator and triceps jerks much more import-
  " ant than of knee jerks;
" Insomnia and evidence of nightmares; ⎫ Confirmed
" Polyuria; ⎬ by
" Diarrhœa. ⎭ observation.

" Specially suspicious points were profusion and alleged in-
" tensity of subjective symptoms with absence of the above.

" Intensification of those signs of emotion produced by volun-
" tary muscles with disappearance of those impossible of
" imitation; especially condensation of the general reaction of
" fear into one such feature as stammer and an exaggeration of
" this."

  " Discrepancy of subjective symptoms with conduct;
  " Variation of symptoms when unaware of observation;
  " Variation in accordance with interests.
" Other points were :—
  " Attitude towards symptoms, e.g., emphatic repudiation of
    " mental origin;
  " Attitude towards treatment and towards recovery;
  " Attitude towards discipline and occupation;
  " Evidence of moral sense in other relations, e.g., general
    " untruthfulness, financial dishonesty, the meaner kinds
    " of sexual misdemeanour, etc."

Dr. Hurst : After much investigation of the subject I came
to the conclusion that the signs of genuine neuroses and simulation are identical, and that simulation can only be diagnosed with
certainty in the very cases in which a malingerer has been
detected *flagrante delicto*, or when he confesses that he is
shamming.

Dr. Johnson. Simulation was rare, but exaggeration of
symptoms common. In the forward areas a valuable combination
of symptoms indicating Neurosis was :—
        Fine tremors.
        Sweating.
        Tachycardia.
A full experience and knowledge of men combined with adequate
training in the subject of Psycho-neuroses forms the surest safeguard against being imposed on by the malingerer.

Dr. Gordon Holmes considered that experienced and properly
trained officers could usually detect simulation. There was
great difficulty in accurate diagnosis in those who exaggerated
or prolonged symptoms. During the battle of the Somme a
large number of men deserted from the line on the claim that
they had " shell-shock."

Dr. Farquhar Buzzard : " I think there were very few people
" I should like to say were absolutely malingering."

Dr. W. Brown stated that in 1,000 cases he had found 28
cases of serious malingering, all of whom had confessed to him.
Most was malingering loss of memory, and he considered feigned
amnesia was easily detected.

Squadron Leader Tyrrell, referring to his front line experiences, said he depended on his knowledge of the man, observation, judgment as to whether his behaviour, etc., was voluntary or involuntary, and in the exercise of common sense in distinguishing the genuine from the feigned shell-shock case.

Dr. Hampton : " Many cases were on the border line between " conscious and unconscious malingering."

Lieut-Colonel Scott Jackson : " Many cases of neurasthenia " and ' shell-shock ' were skrimshanking of the worst type."

Major Adie : " We did not see much malingering."

Dr. Wilson, in speaking of men who took advantage of an attack to get away, said : " I do not know how much malingering " there is in these cases ; it is almost impossible to tell."

Colonel Campbell considered " shell-shock " a favourite method which malingerers employed to get away from the battle front ; in a unit with poor morals this form of skrimshanking becomes contagious.

Dr. Dunn said : " In acute shock a man abandons himself to " his terror. I have not seen an attempt to simulate it, and I " cannot imagine such an attempt deceiving anyone."

Colonel Jervis considered the number of emotional breakdowns was slight as compared to the number " swinging the lead."

Colonel Soltau thought information in a suspect case could be obtained by observation during sleep and also by suddenly awakening the case. He had only detected two malingerers himself.

Major Longmore remarked that in court-martial cases " shellshock " became a parrot cry as a defence.

THE INFLUENCE OF WAR STRESS AND SHELLSHOCK IN THE PRODUCTION OF INSANITY.

Most witnesses were of opinion that the stress of war rarely produced insanity in the stable man, but that it acted, as is commonly observed with other forms of stress, as a factor upon those who by predisposition were liable to breakdown.

Many of the cases were due to exhaustion, the result of prolonged strain or infective disease, and these cleared up rapidly. A certain number belonged to the recurrent type of mental disorder, and in these cases the war conditions probably played only a small, if any, part in the cause of the attack.

The majority of the chronic cases belonged to the class known as dementia præcox. This disorder declares itself usually in the early years of adult life, consequently many of the cases might have occurred had there been no war, and the latter probably acted largely as a stress which hastened the onset of the disease. Several witnesses stated that the service patients still in asylums were for the most part suffering from dementia præcox.

It was not common for the so-called " shell-shock " patient to become insane except very temporarily. On the other hand, it was in evidence that many men who had broken down mentally were reported to relatives as suffering from " nervous breakdown." Further, as was pointed out, the legal obligations regarding insanity being in abeyance so long as the man remained in the army, as little emphasis as possible was laid upon the mental aspect. This had the advantage that many men recovered without any stigma being attached to the illness. On the other hand, in the case of those who did not recover, it became a disturbing factor to the relations when on his leaving the Army the civil law necessitated the patient's being certified as insane.

From the evidence before the Committee, they are of opinion that there is no justification for the popular belief that " shell-shock " was a direct cause of insanity, or that the service patients still in asylums were originally cases of " shell-shock " who have since become insane.

As regards the higher grades of mental defectives, it was in evidence that many had been enlisted and that some had been trained into efficient soldiers. On the other hand, there was a large group of this type of man, of whom some rapidly broke down and others failed at every class of duty except the most menial occupations in back areas.

SUMMARY OF EVIDENCE OF WITNESSES REGARDING THE INFLUENCE OF WAR STRESS AND " SHELL-SHOCK " IN THE PRODUCTION OF INSANITY.*

Dr. Bernard Hart, asked whether it was his opinion that there was a very sharp distinction between the psychosis and psycho-neurosis and that the psycho-neurosis did not pass into the psychosis, the one being almost an insurance against the other said : " The statement is largely true, but I should not be pre-
" pared, as an absolute statement of fact, to say that one never
" led to the other. I think that in most cases where it was
" thought that a psycho-neurosis passed on to a psychosis the
" condition was actually one of psychosis from the beginning,
" but in an incipient stage which may have borne a superficial
" resemblance to a psycho-neurosis. I do not think it is possible
" to make a hard-and-fast boundary between them, but I do
" think they are very distinct things."

Dr. W. Johnson said : " I saw numerous cases of acute con-
" fusional insanity, and was able to observe them usually for
" from 4 to 6 weeks. The majority showed no evidence of con-
" fusion after 12-24 hours. The remaining one-fourth recovered
" in from 10 to 12 days, with the exception of a small minority
" who still presented mental symptoms in the fourth or fifth
" week."

---

* For opinions of foreign experts, see page 113.

Dr. Mapother said : " There was much overlapping between " the contents of ' shell-shock ' and military mental hospitals. " Taking as insanity what would have been certifiable in a " civilian, I saw few cases of insanity which seemed solely due " to the stress of war or of conditions such as infection incidental " to it. Most such cases were transitory.

" There was a somewhat larger group of cases in which other " factors than those incidental to military service were present, " but in which the former factors would probably not have been " adequate to produce certifiable psychosis apart from the " abnormal stress of war.

" There was a still larger group in which war played a rela- " tively slight part—possibly ante-dating; possibly merely " colouring the psychosis—but which would in all probability " have occurred without a war. Most of the chronic cases " belonged to this class."

His impression of the service patients seen by him since the war was that most of them would have been insane had there been no war. They suffered from insanity of the ordinary type; mostly from dementia præcox.

In his experience, only cases which required certification were sent from " shell-shock " to mental hospitals.

Dr. Geoffrey Clarke stated he had no experience of cases of insanity which could be attributed solely to the stress of war or " shell-shock."

The war did give rise to temporary insanity—confusional and exhaustion states.

Dr. Stanford Reade said : " I regard ' shell-shock ' as having " little or no relation to the production of insanity, except that " the trauma, lessening inhibition, might possibly precipitate the " onset of some smouldering psychosis. In 3,000 consecutive " cases I analysed only four had any definite history of such " shock, and no causal relationship could definitely be elicited." " Stress of war " is a vague term. Mental maladaptation and various experiences and situations arising from war conditions would be the only general expression one could use. Contributory causes were, e.g., fatigue, exhaustion, syphilis, alcohol and organic disease. Some few would be due to the last-named cause only. Of the 3,000 mental cases analysed, 50 per cent. had recovered within 12 months. Of the remaining 50 per cent., some had been sent to their homes for friends to look after though not recovered, but Dr. Read was of opinion that the majority were in asylums.

Of the service patients now in asylums, he thought the majority are suffering from dementia præcox. He thought the majority would have broken down under any slight strain.

He had no knowledge that any so-called " shell-shock " case had gone to any asylum, but as regards those cases that went to " D " Block, Netley, and were sent to other war mental hos- pitals and are still in asylums, many of them when under his care were called by their relatives, quite wrongly, "shell-shock."

Dr. G. Roussy thought there have been a certain number of cases of maniac-depressive insanity, dementia præcox, and cases of mental confusion after " shell-shock," but, on the whole, they were rare.

Asked if they were aggravated or revealed rather than produced by the war, he said : " I think the war created nothing " in the way of the psychoses. It simply aggravated or revealed " these manifestations in people who were predisposed to them."

Dr. L. C. Bruce saw cases of insanity which could be attributed to the stress of war alone. Many were transitory. The majority of cases from the Western Front were exhaustion psychoses. Those from Mesopotamia and Gallipoli were due to physical illness, such as malaria, typhoid fever, dysentery.

He thought the psychoses were revealed rather than produced by the war.

He did not get many cases who, having been diagnosed neurasthenia, later developed mental symptoms.

The 15 service patients at present in his hospital were all cases of dementia præcox. None of these cases was sent in as neurasthenic.

General Paralysis of the Insane.

Although this disease only occurs in those who have been infected with syphilis and is usually regarded as being directly due to syphilis, it presented certain features which called for enquiry. Men who joined the army in apparent health were occasionally stricken by it. In many instances these men had been subjected to war strain, and many had fought in the battles of the war. The relatives of those afflicted not unnaturally attributed their condition to the war, and the illness being partly of mental character, was frequently spoken of as " shell-shock."

It would appear also that a not inconsiderable number of men who eventually developed general paralysis were officially diagnosed as neurasthenia, and that in some cases at least the real nature of the disease was not recognised at first. This might easily occur unless the medical officer had both experience and facility for complete examination.

Dr. Beaton, in the Naval Medical History of the war, in referring to general paralysis, stated " the onset of the disorder was, " as a rule, insidious ; in fact, the common presentment of the " case was that of anxiety neurosis." An examination of 100 medical history sheets of cases of general paralysis admitted to the Royal Naval Hospital, Yarmouth, during the war, showed that 25 of these had entries of neurasthenia.

Professor Graham Brown pointed out to the Committee that many men with latent syphilis exhibited signs of neurosis, and that with rest some of them seemed to recover and to break down later on. He thought that these cases may be overlooked even in special neurological hospitals, and he desired to convince the Committee that an examination of the cerebro-spinal fluid was of supreme importance.

Few, if any, of our witnesses had had sufficient opportunity of investigating the effect of war on the incidence, duration or exacerbation of general paralysis.

Dr. Mapother observed that the acceptance of the principle that General Paralysis of the Insane may be accelerated by the strain of war is quite sound and only fair to the men.

Professor Roussy informed us that in France, quite apart from the specific origin of these cases, they were regarded as aggravated by the war and pensioned accordingly.

Dr. Hurst spoke with more conviction on certain points than other witnesses allowed themselves to do, but in reviewing the evidence in general the Committee is entitled to endorse his views. He expressed himself as follows :—" There is no doubt " at all that active service had led in certain cases to a much " more rapid development of the disease than would have " occurred otherwise. In some cases the disease might have " always remained latent."

THE PREVENTION OR LESSENING OF THE INCIDENCE OF SHELL-SHOCK.

Heredity, environment, training and education in childhood are the dominant factors concerned in the evolution of the mental as of the physical personality and in consequence the pre-disposition to mental and nervous disorders of the adult is to a great extent determined before he becomes a soldier. This pre-disposition plays an immense part in the incidence of shell shock.

In this connection attention is directed to the axiom enunciated by Squadron-Leader W. A. Tyrrell, to the effect that " training " to be effective must commence much earlier than the day of " enlistment; home influence and school training must be " directed towards development of character." Similarly, Dr. T. R. Elliott stated when referring to individual susceptibility to " shell-shock " that it was not a matter of general bodily health, nor of intelligence, but of character. This aspect of the subject, however, not being within the terms of reference to the Committee will not be further considered.

The subject of prevention of mental and nervous disorders in the fighting forces in war may be conveniently dealt with under the following heads :—
    (a) The time of enlistment;
    (b) The training period;
    (c) The Active Service period;
    (d) The hospital period (diagnosis and treatment).

Of these (*a*) will be considered in the section dealing with recruiting, while (*d*) will only be now considered in so far as it is concerned with diagnosis and treatment during the period of active service.

1. *All Periods.*

The following factors are generally regarded as tending to increase the incidence and severity of mental and nervous disorders in time of War :—

(*a*) The introduction and perpetuation of the term " Shell Shock."

(*b*) The employment of such terms as N.Y.D.N. (not yet diagnosed nervous), D.A.H. (disordered action of the heart), or other designation which may become catchwords, and thereby lead to an increase in the number of nervous cases and to aggravation of slight cases of psycho-neurosis. In times of pressure a term such as N.Y.D.N. is apt to be used very loosely, and may be most harmful. Every endeavour should be made to give an ordinary clinical diagnosis, which can, if necessary, be altered later. Functional disorders of the heart are very common in the subjects of neurasthenia. The diagnosis of D.A.H. (disordered action of the heart) tended to increase anxiety and delay convalescence in recruits and in officers and men returned from the front, who while suffering from this disorder had as permanent symptoms, palpitation, pre-cordial pains and rapid action of the heart.

(*c*) All those factors by which a soldier, or even a potential soldier, is encouraged to believe that the weakening or loss of mental control provides an honourable avenue of escape from military service at whatever period of his service.

(*d*) The misconceptions prevalent among the general community, both civil and military, together with the lack of interest evinced by the medical profession before the War regarding the origin, nature, and significance of mental, and especially emotional, disorders.

(*e*) All those preventable conditions which undermine a man's mental and physical health and lower the powers of resistance, *e.g.*, bad sanitation, bad accommodation, abuse of alcohol and of drugs, venereal disease, etc.

In promoting and maintaining morale, good food, good housing, recreational relaxation and attention to the comfort and well-being of the soldier are of the greatest service.

2. *Training Period.*

There has been a general consensus of opinion amongst witnesses that the incidence of " Shell-shock " varied inversely with the morale of the troops. In defeat, in monotonous trench warfare, with its inaction and depressing circumstances, morale was reduced and neurosis increased. In pursuit, in open warfare, with scope for activity and change of scene, and in victory morale was high and " shell-shock " diminished.

Opinion is also agreed that the incidence of mental and nervous disorders is lessened by adequate and sufficiently prolonged training and that such training should aim at :—

(*a*) inculcating the highest possible standard of morale, discipline, esprit de corps, esteem of officers, and confidence both individually and collectively ; and

(*b*) ensuring and maintaining mental, physical and moral fitness and technical efficiency.

With the exception of the original Expeditionary Force and to some extent of the young troops who took the field in 1918 there is general agreement that the length of training was inadequate ; this was due to the insistent calls for troops overseas.

Stress was laid by several witnesses on the desirability of eliminating during training those individuals, who whether physically, mentally or temperamentally are unlikely to make good as fighting soldiers.

With a view to promoting and developing moral fitness, military training must include education. Further, in addition to consolidating the sense of collective responsibility and efficiency by securing the prompt and automatic obedience of orders, training must also aim at creating the spirit of individual effort. These two aspects of training may be illustrated by extracts from Colonel Campbell's evidence :—

(i) " That there is no better training than steady barrack " square drill to prepare the soldier for static fight- " ing."

(ii) " As a result of the War we study more the ethical " value of training ; we work to make the man fight " as an individual, to think and act for himself and " be resourceful."

Training must be simple, continuous and varied, and men must always be trained with one purpose, viz., to fight.

Instructors must be very carefully selected and on no account over-worked ; training is more fatiguing for the instructor than the instructed, and " the stale instructor will merely succeed in making the class as lifeless as himself." The first object of an instructor is to win the sympathy of his men : " sympathy flames into enthusiasm."

In this connection the Committee were impressed by the suggestion of Colonel Fuller, that officers should be instructed in the study of character so far as it is applicable to military life and work. They regard this as an important factor in all training which should be studied by staff and executive officers alike.

3. *Active Service Period.*

There has been a general agreement that the following factors are of chief importance in diminishing the incidence of nervous and mental disorders in the Field.

(N.B.—These are grouped approximately in order of merit.)

(*a*) Good morale.

(*b*) High standard of discipline.

(*c*) Esprit de corps.

(*d*) Good officers, especially as regards leadership and the care of their men.

(*e*) Good front line medical officers in sufficient numbers.

(*f*) Close collaboration between executive and medical officers in the front line.

(*g*) Short shifts in the line.

(*h*) Adequate rest behind the line.

(*i*) Organised recreation behind the line.

(*j*) Leave home if properly spent.

(*k*) The avoidance, where possible, of monotony (change of front, etc.).

(*l*) Early diagnosis and treatment within divisional areas.

(*m*) Retention of early cases in Army areas.

(*n*) The controlled use of rum.

(*a*), (*b*) and (*c*).—Military and medical witnesses were unanimous in insisting that good morale and all that it implies is the first essential factor in diminishing the incidence of mental disorders.

(*d*).—Every military witness laid stress on the important rôle played by officers in setting a good example, promoting confidence and enthusiasm, and in taking an active and personal interest in the welfare and comfort of those whom they command ; personality counts for much. " The men are what their officers make them." The supervision of interior economy is one of the essential duties of an officer.

(*e*), (*f*), (*l*) and (*m*).—The witnesses were unanimous in insisting on the importance of good front line medical officers, endowed with personality, possessed of a sound knowledge and experience of men and of medicine, and imbued with the importance of maintaining good morale and discipline and of promoting the mental and bodily health of all under their charge. A good medical officer can not only anticipate many cases of exhaustion neurosis in individuals, but he can feel the pulse of the unit as a whole.

All the medical witnesses who have had experience of front line service insisted on the importance of treating men who needed a rest if possible within the battalion area, or else of sending them temporarily to divisional rest camps. They also agreed that men whose condition has necessitated any prolonged treatment in hospital are as a rule useless for further front line service.

It is evident that the front line medical officers' sphere of usefulness is greatly increased by the close and intelligent co-operation of his commanding officer, and hampered in its absence. The logical corollary of this, though not specifically mentioned by any witness, is that similar collaboration between medical and executive officers is equally essential behind the line. (*Vide* also *infra*, page 153.)

In the Flying Services the medical officers' duties of antici-pating, and making early diagnosis in, cases of exhaustion neurosis were greatly facilitated by the relatively small number of individuals engaged in actual flying duties. The essential preliminary for early diagnosis is a personal acquaintance with those under his charge rather than repeated medical inspections which are only too likely to be misinterpreted. But even in the Flying Services the number of medical officers available for squadron duties during the War was nothing like sufficient, and the evidence in general suggests that for all front line forma-tions, of whatever character, where frequent and continuous changes are occurring in the personnel, more medical officers should be available than has hitherto been the case. (Squadron Leader Johnston.)

It was probably owing to the greater facilities for making early diagnosis, which existed in the Flying Services, that the evidence tends to show that returns from hospital did better in that service than they did in the trenches.

(*g*).—The policy of short shifts in the line was advocated by every witness; the extent to which it can be carried out depends on the number and quality of the troops available; the rationale underlying this policy is the facilities it affords for giving troops adequate sleep and rest and avoiding mental and physical exhaustion.

Troops engaged in a particularly dangerous sector should be relieved in turn. The knowledge that their exposure to special danger is of limited duration, that there is a time limit to their ordeal, should be recognised as of great value in sustaining the nerve of those so engaged.

The feeling of confidence which the company of others gives to those engaged in perilous service should be borne in mind and detached parties or lonely posts should receive special con-sideration in being relieved.

It is recommended also, according to evidence given, that troops should, when possible, be entered into battle gradually and not precipitated into the thick of war.

The system of short shifts was adopted in the Flying Services with good results, where circumstances rendered it more easy to carry out than in the infantry and artillery (Squadron Leader Johnston); and the evidence tends to show that its adoption more generally in the Army in 1918, at which time the military situation permitted it, was attended with beneficial results.

(*h*), (*i*), (*j*) and (*k*).—All these measures aim at counteracting the exhaustion which is inevitable on active service, and are such as would be adopted in any community where industrial fatigue might reasonably be expected.

It was pointed out by more than one witness that training behind the line might be overdone at the expense of much-needed rest.

Organised recreation behind the line was considerably developed as the War advanced; it had the advantage of promoting fitness, stimulating the spirit of competition and providing variety for both mind and body.

In promoting physical fitness and a healthy tone of mind, " tabloid sports " may be highly commended and have the dual advantage of being applicable to large bodies of men and of interesting and encouraging individual emulation even amongst the least competent.

A factor essential for the welfare of troops in rest is good food and good interior economy.

Some difference of opinion existed among the witnesses as to the value of home leave, but officers with front-line experience were practically unanimous that leave, if fairly allotted and wisely spent, was an inestimable advantage. "A man looked " forward to leave and came back refreshed in mind and body." Misplaced sympathy at home sometimes did harm.

(*n*) Front-line medical and executive officers favoured the use of rum if properly controlled; it was especially valuable in the early morning hours.

Attention is directed to the suggestion made by two medical witnesses that post-graduate classes in psychological medicine should be instituted for officers of the Royal Army Medical Corps.

Under (*b*) and (*c*) has to be considered the difficult question as to the attitude to be adopted and the steps to be taken by commanding and medical officers respectively in the case of officers and men who break down (i) gradually from wear and tear, and (ii) suddenly in the stress of battle. It is especially with regard to (ii) that a wide divergence of opinion exists, and it would appear from the evidence obtained under cross-examination that this divergence of opinion is due to ignorance as to the nature of mental disorders on the one hand, and lack of appreciation of military requirements on the other.

The Committee are of opinion that mutual understanding and close co-operation between commanding and medical officers in such cases would ensure that no injustice was done to individuals reported as inefficient in their duties, when the inefficiency was due to illness caused by strain and overwork.

Without therefore attempting to deal comprehensively with organisation and the training of combatant and medical officers, the Committee feel that the evidence received upon these matters justifies the following conclusions :—

1. Upon that part of their reference which deals with training and education, the Committee have received evidence from a large number of witnesses, extracts from which have been quoted already. There has been a general consensus of opinion, both medical and military, that in a well-trained unit, whose morale is good, there will be far less shell-shock than in a corresponding unit, ill-trained and lacking in morale. As the production of good morale is the most important object in military training, the Committee are of opinion that the best possible training should be given to every man intended to serve as a soldier, and that, by such means, and to the extent that his training is thorough and complete, he will be protected against the occurrence of '' shell-shock.'' In this connection the Committee wish to emphasise the importance of careful selection of officers both as instructors and leaders. They should be selected not only for their technical efficiency, but also for their personality and knowledge of men.

2. The Committee heard evidence from Colonel Campbell, and a scheme of training drawn up by him was put before them.* This scheme, in its general outline, received the approbation of General Goodwin. His words were:—''. . . I think his '' system is very good and very sound, but I think it wants to be '' watched carefully by medical men . . . to see that it is '' not overdone, especially in the early stages. On general lines '' I think it is quite sound and I think the men improved.'' The Committee are of opinion that some such scheme, generally adopted, and for the complete application of which adequate time is allotted, will minimise the incidence of '' shell-shock '' in any future war. From the evidence they have heard the Committee are satisfied that, owing to the circumstances of the late War in its various phases, training was at times imperfect in various aspects, and, in particular, owing to the urgent demands of the front line, it was at times so hurried as to produce only to a limited extent the morale it ought to have established in every unit and individual man.

3. In addition to, or perhaps more properly, in further elaboration of Colonel Campbell's skeleton scheme, the Committee are impressed with the necessity of training men so that so far as possible they will not be thrown off their balance by unusual stress in the performance of their duties on active service. They should be made capable of adapting themselves to sudden changes in orders, dress, duties and movement. They should be practised in carrying on duties in half or even a quarter of the usual and proper time, and should be made accustomed to strenuously attempting the impossible, as will often be their fate on active service.

---

* *See* Appendix No. 3.

4. The Committee have carefully considered the possibility and advisability of special training *ad hoc, i.e.,* some attempt (*a*) to produce the physical conditions of the front line, and (*b*) to give special instructions in " shell-shock " and how to resist it. They are of opinion, an opinion formed from the preponderant weight of evidence on this special point and from the conclusions to which they have come upon the mass of medical information put before them as to the true nature and causes of " shell-shock," that (*a*) is impracticable and that (*b*) might tend to produce the very result it is designed to prevent.

5. In relation to this matter, the Committee consider that the policy to be pursued in training should consist of instruction on the following lines, viz. :—That every man feels fear at some time and to some extent in action, and that to feel afraid is a natural thing and nothing to be ashamed of ; that no good soldier ever allows this feeling to influence him, that to give way to fear is reprehensible, and that no properly-trained soldier will have difficulty in carrying out his duty whatever the circumstances.

6. The Committee wish particularly to emphasise the importance of allowing sufficient time so that each unit may be trained fully and without hurry, and in addition to this, they consider that any system of training should be sufficiently elastic to allow the needs of the individual to be studied to a reasonable extent. They are satisfied that slow men, given extended time for training, can often be made into equally good soldiers with their quicker comrades, and that to hurry a naturally slow recruit unduly during training is specially likely to sow the seeds which may eventually mature into " shell-shock."

7. During the whole of the man's training, but especially during the earlier part of it, a careful watch ought to be kept to the utmost extent possible without letting the watch become obvious—by officers, medical and regimental, and in particular by the N.C.O.'s of the unit, in order that no abnormalities from which a medical officer might infer the presence of mental unsoundness may be overlooked ; at all stages there should be the closest possible co-operation between regimental and medical officers. No unit is likely to be well trained for active service unless there is continual inter-communication of the fullest and frankest kind between the regimental and medical officers.

8. The Committee realise that there are certain men who, while organically sound, are so constituted temperamentally that they cannot be trained into efficient fighting soldiers. Such men, can, however, be usefully employed on military duties behind the firing line in a national emergency such as the recent War. The Committee feel that if training is carried out on proper lines, the number of such men can be appreciably reduced, and any undue haste in rejection on such grounds may entail the loss of a valuable soldier.

9. The Committee heard the evidence of more than one witness as to the methods of re-training men in convalescent depots during the latter part of the War in France. The system described to them seems to be well adapted for its purpose, and under a carefully selected Commandant would be likely to produce excellent results. A convalescent camp is of little value unless an invariable atmosphere of complete cure prevails, and the Commandant must be a man of uniformly cheerful temperament, capable of inspiring the same spirit into all those under him. The minds of the patients should be diverted from their recent ailments and turned to sport and amusements, the whole outlook must be a cheery one, and everything should be organised with a view to producing high morale.

10. The Committee do not wish to leave this branch of their reference without saying that they are satisfied that to neglect morale in any of its aspects is to invite large and unnecessary casualties in battle and times of stress.

EVIDENCE OF WITNESSES CONCERNING THE PREVENTION OF "SHELL-SHOCK."

The evidence of Lieutenant-General Sir John Goodwin, K.C.B., &c., Director-General, Army Medical Service, so admirably expresses not only his own views but those of the witnesses in general that it may well be quoted in *extenso*.

Sir John Goodwin : " First of all, dealing with training, I can-
" not sufficiently emphasise the importance of gradual, sympa-
" thetic, and really efficient and thorough training. I am certain
" that troops who have been rushed through a short period of
" training would be much more liable to break down than those
" whose training had been more gradual and more thorough.

" I think I ought to say that, of course, my experience in the
" War when at the front was very fortunate, because I was with
" the original Army, the cavalry, in the first place, and then with
" the Guards Division, and I really saw very little of ' shell-shock '
" actually at the front. I am certain that well-trained and well-
" disciplined troops are less liable to suffer from these troubles,
" and by no means the least important part of a soldier's training
" is the inculcation of *esprit de corps*, loyalty, pride in himself
" and his unit, the old history of the regiment to which he
" belonged. I think that is very, very important indeed. That
" was very marked in the Guards Division. If we could have an
" ideal Army, in which every officer and man was firmly con-
" vinced and was proud of the fact that he himself was one of
" those who formed the very best company or squadron of the
" best regiment of the finest Army of the best nation on the
" earth, we should see very little of ' shell-shock.' I think pride
" and prestige have a tremendous lot to do with it. I really
" saw a very great deal of that, and it was astonishing the pride
" taken in their regiment by men in the Guards. Even a man
" who had only been for a few months in a certain regiment, it

" may have been the Grenadiers, the Scots, the Coldstreamers
" or other, was told about the old history of the regiment, and he
" was firmly determined to uphold the traditions and the honour
" of the regiment to which he belonged.   I am certain that
" troops which have been really well trained and disciplined have
" an immense advantage in every way over those who have not
" been so well trained.   I shall never forget the original Expedi-
" tionary Force in the retreat and the way they behaved.   It
" was absolutely magnificent, beyond all words.   Those men
" were utterly exhausted, wearied to the point of hardly being
" able to walk, and hardly able to keep awake.   You could not
" put a man on to a horse.   I often tried to give a man a lift on
" a horse, but he fell off from sheer exhaustion unless you held
" him on.   And yet those men were ready, and not only ready,
" but eager, to stop and fight at any moment.   They were abso-
" lutely splendid.   I can never forget them or say enough for
" them.   I must frankly say that, in my opinion, they had an
" immense advantage in that they were thoroughly well trained,
" and were proud of the units of the Army to which they
" belonged.

    " Then in the field :   In the field, of course, you must consider
" troops that have had a thorough training and discipline, and
" also newly-joined troops.   I am afraid here I am simply
" going to make a lot of statements which are probably well
" known already.   The first is that the men should be very care-
" fully looked after in every possible way.   As regards their com-
" fort : attention should be given to their cleanliness, baths, feed-
" ing, clothing, recreation, the cooking of their meals, the serv-
" ing of their meals, in fact, everything which tends to make
" men comfortable, healthy, contented and satisfied, as far as they
" can be, with their surroundings.   When troops are at rest,
" when they are brought out for these comparatively short
" periods of rest, as was done in the recent War, I think an
" immense amount can be done in the way of making that period
" a period of real rest, both physical and mental.   I do not mean
" to say that the men ought to be loafing about and doing nothing,
" but they ought to be given change of occupation, games, danc-
" ing, and everything that will cheer them up, change of exer-
" cises, change of environment and atmosphere altogether.

    " The third point that I have put down is that, if possible,
" troops should not be left too long in one sector of the line.
" While it is impossible to legislate for military exigencies, and
" military exigencies are always arising, I think that if a unit
" has had a very bad time in one particular sector, it is a mistake
" to send it back to that part of the line if it can be avoided, but,
" of course, one has got to look at that from every point of view.
" On the other hand, one particular sector of the line gets a bad
" name, for instance, the Ypres salient.   The troops naturally,
" although they did their best, did not like going there.   I do not
" want to say anything against their gallantry, they were

" splendid, but no one loves the Ypres salient. I think if troops
" are going to a sector like that, it would be almost better, after
" the unit had had a real bad doing, not to send them back there
" if it could be avoided, and that if another regiment or battalion
" were sent there, it would be more or less understood—we have
" to take our turn there, but after we have had a good bit of
" fighting we shall be taken out. But again, military exigencies
" come in. It is not always possible to do it, and I realise that.
" On one point I do feel very strongly, and that is that a man
" should not be left too long in any lonely position, or in a
" lonely nature of employment. It is very trying indeed for
" them.
" When the men are brought back from the front no pains
" should be spared to make them really comfortable. Bands
" and music I lay stress on. I think they have a very great
" effect.
" There is one point which I have left to the last, not because
" I consider it of least importance, and that is the question of
" regimental medical officers. These officers can exert an
" influence on the regiment to which they belong, or to which
" they are attached, which is of incalculable benefit. I can
" never say enough for the medical officers I had under me,
" both in the Cavalry Division and in the Guards Division. No
" words can show what I think of them, they were splendid,
" the pains and trouble they took with the men; the way they
" knew and worked with the men was simply splendid, and
" even when a young officer was put to a regiment straight away
" it was astonishing how quickly he got to know the tone of
" the regiment, and the different companies in the regiment,
" and how hard he worked for them, and the extraordinarily
" good influence he had with them."

Captain Gee, V.C., expressed himself emphatically that
frequent leave home did much to prevent nervous breakdown,
and attributed the comparative absence of " shell-shock " in his
brigade to this. He also advocated rest in cases showing initial
symptoms of nervous breakdown.

Colonel Fuller considered that if organisation, training, and
adiministration were based on a psychological foundation, " shell-
shock " and nervous strain could be combated, and considered
that in training insufficient regard was given to the psychology
of the individual. A high morale undoubtedly tended to lessen
" shell-shock." Morale depended chiefly on a sense of security
and comfort. Officers should be assiduous in their concern for
their men. Removal from the front and visits home lessen the
incidence of " shell-shock."

Dr. Mapother thought every anxiety neurosis case in its very
early stage could have been cured if taken out of the line and
sent to a rest camp.

Dr. A. F. Hurst's observations led him to conclude that infections were likely to produce neurasthenia, and to predispose
to other neuroses.

Dr. Burton-Fanning considered that faulty upbringing at home and at school was mainly responsible for nervous breakdown.

Professor G. Roussy considered that mental steadiness in the officer acted as a stimulus to the men, and that the stimulant influence of high morale of commanding officers accounted for the absence of neurosis in the " troupes d'élite " as noted by French medical officers.

He further remarked, in speaking of the French Army, " During the war, as many of our army doctors observed, the morale of troops has played a very important part in the frequency of ' shell-shock ' incidence as in the development of all so-called hysterical manifestations. Well trained troops, whose morale was well maintained by the officers, gave the minimum of neuropathic cases, on the contrary in undisciplined troops, neuropathic commotional or hysterical troubles were frequently met with and became contagious in the units."

Commander Holbrook, V.C., R.N., ascribed the comparative absence of nervous breakdown in the submarine service to physical fitness and morale of the crews. He advocated frequent leave and rest as of advantage in maintaining good nerves.

Major Longmore considered leave home of the greatest importance, and that men had been undoubtedly saved from losing their nerve through it.

Colonel Hewett held that discipline and self-discipline diminished the incidence of " shell-shock." Brief removals from the front area were salutary, but regular visits home and considerable absence increased " nerves " on return.

Major Adie tritely expressed himself in stating that there was only one word worth mentioning, and that was " Morale." If you keep up the morale there will be no " shell-shock." The medical officer should know his men, and can prevent the vast majority of nervous cases—mild " shell-shock "—from becoming " shell-shocks " by retaining them at the front, or by giving them a little rest at the front. As long as they were living with soldiers, and in the atmosphere of the front line, the tendency was to recover. They were to be looked on merely as physically exhausted. The regimental doctor should be young, something of a psychologist in knowing the soldier, and his ways. His personality and bearing were of immense importance. If not a skilled neurologist so much the better, as there would be less risk of producing the suggestion of serious nervous trouble.

General Lord Horne, placing aside commotional " shell-shock " as being in the nature of a wound and inevitable, was assured that physical fitness and morale were the surest protection against " shell-shock." Troops should be entered into battle conditions gradually. He favoured home leave as beneficial to the good soldier, and even if some indulged in dissipation its ill results were transient, and it was only the skulkers who were harmed by leave. As a Commander, he viewed with disfavour a unit in which much " shell-shock " appeared.

Colonel Jervis, excluding cases knocked out by the explosion of a shell, said that prevention was best obtained by high morale and by relief from long exposure and exhaustion. Morale was to be obtained by attention to good feeding and comfort, and by good officers. Troops should be broken to battle gradually, and in severe fighting should be given to understand that they would be relieved, so that nervous strain might be diminished.

Major Brook Purdon held that no means existed of lessening the incidence of such " shell-shock " as was due to explosion causing cerebral concussion. The emotional type might be diminished by promoting mental and physical fitness in training, good food, good housing and good education—mental, physical and moral. In the field previous training, good leadership and discipline were the points which counted. At rest " tabloid sports " promote physical fitness and assist morale. As the noise of battle and of exploding shells has a terrifying and exhausting effect, particularly on those unaccustomed to it, it would be well if it were practicable to submit recruits to some ordeal of noise.

Major Pritchard-Taylor would check the incidence of " shell-shock " by raising and maintaining morale, and considered " giving way " was a disgrace to man and unit. A man becoming shaky when noticed should be given a soft job. The front-line medical officer should be a man, rather than doctor, and as true " shell-shock " cases cannot be distinguished from the others in the turmoil of battle they are all best suspected as malingerers, and a large number will be saved.

RECRUITING.*

In order to form an estimate of the physical and mental condition of the men who formed the personnel of the fighting forces in the war, it was necessary that we should first inquire into the standards of fitness required and the methods of medical examination of recruits both before the outbreak of hostilities and throughout the War. Such an inquiry was necessary in order to enable us to determine to what extent the methods employed were calculated to ensure, and did or did not, in fact, ensure, that only those who were physically and mentally fit to undertake military training and duties were accepted for service and the unfit rejected.†

---

* The numbers in the text in this section refer to the summary of evidence quoted at the end. They have been inserted to emphasise evidence on particular points discussed.

† *Note.*—What follows is concerned almost exclusively with recruiting for the Army, since the problems in connection with the terms of reference of the Committee arose almost entirely in relation to Military (as opposed to Naval) Service. Recruiting for the Navy during the War continued as in peace with certain modifications unimportant from the point of view of this Committee.

Colliers and merchant-ships taken over by the Admiralty were in some instances worked by the crews already so engaged.

Investigation shows that the history of recruiting during the period under review divides itself into three distinct phases :—

Phase i.—Recruiting of a voluntary army during peace.
Phase ii.—Recruiting of a voluntary army during war.
Phase iii.—Recruiting of a conscript army during war.

The differences in the recruiting medical problem and in the actual results of the methods employed during these phases are so important that the sequence of events must be made clear in some detail.

I. Recruiting before the War.

Before the war we had a voluntary army, and only men between 18-30 years of age of good physique and free from any physical or mental defect were accepted for enlistment.

Men who presented any disease, or physical or mental defect were regarded as unfit for enlistment and were rejected. It was laid down further that the height, weight, and chest measurements of each recruit should accord with each other and with his age in conformity with the official table of standards.

Thus, the medical examination of recruits was in general a simple and straightforward matter, as the examiner was only required to certify that the candidate was possessed of certain physical characteristics and was free from other specified defects. Each recruit who fulfilled these required conditions was passed " fit " and accepted for service. Recruits whose condition did not conform to the required standards were regarded as " unfit " and, in general, rejected.

As, however, the candidate varied greatly in physique, mental condition and social standing, especially in certain conditions of trade and the labour market, it was frequently difficult to find sufficient " fit " men for the Army. To meet this difficulty young lads of poor upbringing and physique were often accepted in the hope that the improved conditions of life in the Army would develop them into " fit " men in a year or two. (This aspect was made very clear by Sir William Taylor in his evidence before the Inter-Departmental Committee on Physical Deterioration (1914)). Such lads were kept under close supervision by the Medical Officer during their period of training, which was modified when necessary to meet individual requirements. All recruits during their preliminary training were periodically inspected by selected Medical Officers, and those who at any time up to six months after enlistment were considered unlikely on medical grounds to become fit and efficient soldiers were discharged on the recommendation of the inspecting Medical Officer. In addition, a system existed by which a recruit could be discharged up to three months after enlistment, without reference to the Medical Authorities, as unlikely to become an efficient soldier on other than medical grounds.

In general, therefore, the Army only accepted for service the best human material, judged by a high physical standard, together with such men as were considered likely, in the more favourable circumstances of Army life, to reach the required standard of fitness.

The examination itself was carried out by Medical Officers of the Regular Forces, the Special Reserve—the Territorial Forces, under certain conditions—and by civilian practitioners specially appointed for the purpose. It is evident that their task was, in general, a simple one, which required only a straightforward physical examination and ordinary attention to the regulations for its efficient performance, viz., the selection of the " fit " and the rejection of the " unfit."

II. Recruiting of a Voluntary Army during War.

Such was the position of affairs at the outbreak of war in August, 1914. Immediately there was a tremendous rush of recruits to the Colours, and it was inevitable that they should be dealt with on the existing, almost ingenuously simple, system, which had to be expanded precipitately in order to cope with the immense requirements of the situation. The result was chaos, intensified by the fact that the regular recruiting staff was mobilised and sent overseas. Tens of thousands of recruits were besieging the recruiting offices to get into the Army; the Army was in urgent need of men, and doctors were called upon to " examine " as many as 200 recruits per diem; the whole tendency of the situation was to expedite and reduce to a minimum the medical examination(1). The medical problems involved had been visualised no more than the purely military problems. It is becoming difficult now even to remember the immensity of our unpreparedness for the war, and in no department was this unpreparedness greater than in that of recruiting. In these circumstances, thousands of men were passed " fit " into the Army every week without any medical examination worth the name. No effective means were taken to see that recruiting medical officers were in possession of, still less putting into effect, the official instructions on the subject of medical examination and standards required. Further, the system of inspection of recruits during training was quite inadequate to deal with the situation which arose. As the weeks went on, the Army itself began, as was inevitable, to realise that they were confronted with a new problem. The old simple standard by which they had selected fit recruits was no longer being applied, nor, indeed, was it applicable to the new conditions. They were being flooded with men, who, after a few weeks or months of military service, broke down and contributed an ever-growing quota to the sick returns and casualty lists.

On 20th October, 1915, the Derby Scheme came into operation; men were placed in groups according to their age and marital condition, and the various groups were called up as required.

This caused a further influx of recruits, and there was so much public criticism of the medical examination of these men that instructions were issued by the War Office for the formation of Medical Boards to replace the examination by single medical officers(2). In this connection it must be remembered that the difficulties of the War Office had been much increased by the public criticism and clamour to which their medical methods of recruiting were subjected. This criticism, though, of course, often ignorant and misplaced, was nevertheless highly troublesome and effective. The board system was therefore introduced with a view to sharing the responsibility and burden of the selection of men for military service. It was thought that the boards would act as a buffer between the Military Authorities and public criticism. Further, these boards were instructed to classify recruits by categories (the first departure from the simple classification into " fit " and " unfit " was instituted in July, 1915). Each man was placed in one of six different categories according to the type of service for which he was considered fit. and each board was expected to carry out 200 examinations a day.

III. Recruiting of a Conscript Army during War.

On January 27th, 1916, the first Military Service Act which provided for the compulsory service of unmarried men between the ages of 18 and 41 came into operation.

Further instructions with regard to the classification of recruits by categories were issued, and by May, 1916, there were actually 13 different categories in which a recruit could be placed. It was pointed out that there was a great lack of uniformity in the standards adopted by the different Medical Boards in the Commands, and further standards were issued to the Boards as a guide to classification, e.g., Category A—men able to march, to see, to shoot, hear, and stand active service conditions. The issue of such standards indicates how little the difficulties and importance of the problem presented by the medical examination and grading of recruits had been appreciated even after 21 months of war.

Meantime the provisions of the Military Service Act had been extended to married as well as unmarried men. Further efforts were made to standardise the classification of recruits and obtain uniformity in categorisation, but by the beginning of 1917 public criticism, stimulated by purposeful political methods of attack, had produced a storm of difficulty around the Medical Boards established by the War Office and its Medical Department. It was this, as much as or more than any actual failures on the part of the Boards(3), which evoked the outburst of hostile criticism which arose throughout the country in connection with the medical examination of the large number of men (about a million) called up under the Review of Exceptions Act (April. 1917). As a result the Shortt Committee was appointed to inquire into the whole matter, and in August, 1917, recommended to Parliament that the whole organisation of recruiting Medical Boards and of medical examinations and classification should be placed under civilian control. This work was accordingly handed over to the Ministry of National Service, which commenced its work on November 1st, 1917.

This Department accordingly was responsible for the medical examination and classification of recruits during the final year of the war. The essential features of its work for our present purpose were (1) the methods adopted for the examination and grading of recruits, (2) the acceptance of the principle that Medical Boards were only competent to " grade " men, *i.e.*, to sort them into one of four groups taking into consideration only their physical and mental condition.

The new Medical Boards consisted of four doctors (giving part-time service) as members and a whole-time Chairman. A certain specified part of the examination of each recruit was allotted to each member, and the final grading was the duty of the Chairman in consultation with the members. Sixty examinations a day (in five hours' work) was considered a proper output for an experienced board.

It is evident to us that this method yielded much better and more uniform results, and that, as experience was gained, the grading came to represent closely the physical and mental condition of the men examined(4). This result was also assured by the issue to the boards of clear descriptions of the physical and mental qualifications required for each grade, and also an excellent epitome indicating the usual effect upon grading of some 60 common disabilities and diseases.

It was made clear to the Medical Boards that they were concerned exclusively with the bodily and mental condition of the man, and that their function was quite distinct from that of Posting Boards whose duty it was—in the light of various considerations of which the grade was only one—to allot the men to suitable military duties. It was difficult after what had gone before to make this point clear to the public, viz., that the Ministry of National Service Boards graded the men according to their physical fitness alone, leaving the Army to choose the service suited to their fitness and other qualifications. It was still widely believed that the boards categorised men for different types of service, *e.g.*, for infantry, Army Service Corps, etc. Animated by purely political motives, many persons still took an active interest in confusing these issues, so that continued and fresh difficulties arose. Nevertheless the recognition of the essential difference between the proper functions of a Medical and Posting Board greatly simplified the problem and removed much of the misunderstanding and difficulty which had arisen in the past in consequence of the complex nature of the category —which was really a form of administrative shorthand founded on medical information—as compared with the simple nature of the grade which simply summed up the man's physical and mental condition. It was the function of a Medical Board, to " grade " recruits, of a Posting Board to " categorise " them(5).

The foregoing brief survey shows how widely the methods and circumstances of recruiting and the medical examination of recruits for the fighting forces before and during the war varied at different phases, and what modifications and adaptations were necessitated in the methods employed, as conditions changed, and experience of the difficulties accumulated.

Bearing in mind the sequence of events we have described, we proceeded to inquire to what extent the instructions issued from time to time to recruiting medical officers were calculated to ensure that due regard was paid to the mental and nervous condition of recruits, in the process of classification. Further we have endeavoured to form an estimate of the degree to which the instructions, issued from time to time throughout the successive phases of recruiting, were appropriate and of the extent to which they were in fact carried out.

At the outset we wish to say that nothing has impressed us more than the vital and essential difference between the problems presented by the examination and classification of the volunteer and the conscript.

In the problem of assessing the mental and physical fitness of the recruit for military service an all important consideration is the attitude of the candidate towards military service. In recruiting a voluntary army the candidate attempts to conceal or minimise any factor which he thinks will prejudice his chance of acceptance(6); conversely, in recruiting a conscript army he makes the most of any disqualifying defect and suggests, or even tries to prove the existence of, unexisting defects(7). The mental attitude of the recruit towards military service is therefor a cardinal factor to bear in mind in the conduct of his examination, and experience shows that no system of examination can fully overcome this difficulty; it would be greatly diminished if the examiner has before him the candidate's previous medical history(8).

Further it must be remembered that the new legislation introducing compulsory service, partly on account of its gradual development and the necessities of the position, was complicated. In addition to unwillingness on the part of the conscript to serve, in many cases he was really not quite clear whether he ought to serve or not. On this foundation there rapidly grew a large amount of legal dispute, only increased by the employment of professional advocates in the tribunals and other courts, to assist the recruit's appeal when he wished to avoid service or to obstruct the tribunal. Though we recognise that a mechanism for appeal was necessary, this condition of affairs was excessively bad and injurious to the conduct of the war by undermining the confidence of the public, and should not have been allowed to occur.

It is evident to us that the procedure embodied in the pre-war instructions to medical and recruiting officers was admirably adapted to fulfil its purpose, viz., to admit to a voluntary army in peace time only those who were physically and mentally capable of being trained into efficient regular soldiers. Indeed it could hardly be otherwise, for it had been drawn up and constantly revised in the light of many years of experience; further, as it may truly be described as the cradle of the British Regular Army, results show that it had succeeded in selecting for enlistment (apart from occasional individual errors inevitable in any system) the men who constituted an army second to none the world has known.

The history of recruiting, however, subsequent to the 4th August, 1914, demonstrates how utterly inadequate the peacetime procedure proved in the circumstances of war—circumstances in which it must be remembered that not only was the whole outlook of the population changed with dramatic suddenness, but also the scale of our preparations was rapidly increased to an extent which had never been considered within the bounds of possibility and which was consequently only gradually realised. It was inevitable that the medical problems of recruiting in such circumstances should be appreciated only as experience of the difficulties and of the failure of the peace-time procedure accumulated. During the period (18 months) in which enlistment was voluntary it is clear that there was no real check upon the enlistment of men who were unsuitable for military service owing to mental or nervous instability. With the passing of the first Military Service Act in January, 1916, the medical problems of recruiting were altered and in many respects became more difficult; it is clear to us that during 1916 and 1917 the question of the condition of the nervous system of the recruit did not receive adequate consideration either in the instructions to recruiting medical officers by the military authorities or in the minds of the officers actually engaged in the medical examination of recruits(9), though recruits with gross nervous defects, e.g., having been certified insane or with epilepsy were rejected when these defects were ascertained.

Generally, the evidence we have heard has convinced us that enough attention is not yet paid to the mental and psychological aspects of military service. The establishment and maintenance of discipline and morale as well as the cultivation of the fighting spirit and *esprit de corps* depend essentially upon an intelligent, accurate, and continuous appreciation of the mental calibre and outlook of the soldier, and the continuous adaptation and modification of his training to his psychology. This fundamental fact should find practical expression throughout the entire course of the soldier's career, and at the initial examination and assessment of the candidate no less than throughout the training of the recruit and the handling of the trained soldier.

Advantage would have accrued if the authorities had considered, and made use sooner of, the medical recruiting methods in countries where conscript armies had previously existed, for instance in France. In France, long before the war, recruiting medical examinations had been carried out on something like the board system, so that responsibility was shared and a consensus of medical opinion obtained. In addition, the system, being well understood and more or less under public observation, no longer gave rise to the prejudices, suspicions and misunderstandings which arose in this country. Should the necessity arise in future, boards should be established without delay, and the public informed of the conditions of examinations at the earliest opportunity.

During the final year of the war, when the overtaxed War Office was relieved of recruiting and the medical difficulties were more thoroughly appreciated in the light of three years' experience, we are satisfied that the administration was placed upon a much sounder basis(10). This conclusion is borne out not only by the evidence we have heard, but by the Report upon the Medical Department of the Ministry of National Service, and that upon the physical examination of men of military age by the same Ministry.

The recognition of the proper function of a Medical Board (already alluded to) marked a great advance. The procedure by which a specified part of the medical examination of each recruit was allotted to each of four examiners, and the final grading determined by the Chairman was admirably adopted to ensure that the examination was complete and nothing was missed. The proper arrangement of accommodation for boards and the issue of instructions limiting the number of recruits called up for examination in a day were important aids to general efficiency. Finally, the instructions issued to Medical Boards indicate clearly that the medical problems had been thoroughly grasped and their solution in practice well thought out. The Committee wish to direct particular attention to the following extracts from the Instructions issued for the guidance of Medical Boards.

" In grading, attention will be paid to :—
" (a) The man's previous health ; for this purpose it will sometimes be necessary to supplement his account of himself by reference to his usual medical attendant.
" (b) His actual physical and mental condition ; of this the Board will form its own opinion.
" (c) The work he is doing ; for information regarding this it will be necessary in some cases to refer to the man's employer."

" Examiner No. 1 will test the vision and hearing and nerve reflexes, especially the reaction of the pupils and the knee jerks, and will examine the eyes, ears, teeth, throat, and thyroid gland. He will also ask each recruit for any medical certificate which he may have brought; these will be examined and passed with the man's documents to the other members of the Board.''

'' Examiner No. 4 will investigate the mental condition and previous health of each man, making special enquiry for a history of rheumatic fever, tuberculosis, fits, or asylum treatment.''

'' Each Board should have a well-worked-out system for obtaining consultant advice adapted to its own conditions.''

'' Medical certificates from general practitioners or consultants, and any other documents bearing on his case that a man may bring, will receive full consideration and be examined by every member of the Board.''

'' An average degree of mental capacity is assumed for Grades I, II, and III. Imbeciles and those who exhibit a considerable degree of defective mental development will be placed in Grade IV. In doubtful cases a report from the man's employer will often give valuable assistance to the Board; enquiry should also be made as to the standard he attained at school and his wage-earning capacity.''

'' *Epilepsy (Grand and Petit Mal)*—all cases of true epilepsy in which the diagnosis has been established, and all cases in which there is definite evdence that the man has had epileptic fits during the preceding seven years, should be rejected. Convincing documentary evidence will be necessary and certificates should always state whether the certifier has seen an attack or its immediate results, and whether he knows of other cases of epilepsy in the family.''

'' The presence of symptoms of instability of the nervous system, *e.g.*, greatly exaggerated knee jerk, mental deterioration, widely dilated pupils or tremor, should be regarded as sufficient corroborative evidence for purposes of rejection.''

'' If a man states that he is the subject of this disease, but no attacks have occurred for 7 years and there are no marked symptoms of instability of the nervous system, he may, if otherwise fit, be placed in Grades II or III. No man with a well-authenticated history of Epilepsy at any period of his life should be placed higher than Grade II.''

'' In all cases where the diagnosis of Epilepsy rests upon unsupported statement and in which no corroborative evidence is forthcoming, it should be assumed that a condition of true Epilepsy does not exist, and the man will be graded in accordance with his degree of general physical fitness.''

'' *Mental Diseases and Defects.*—Attention has already, under the head of ' General Conditions and Physique,' been drawn to the fact that an average degree of mental capacity is required of of all recruits for Grades I, II or III. Men who have at any period of their lives been inmates of asylums as persons certified to be of unsound mind, and those who at the time of examination show symptoms of mental disease, should be rejected.''

'' Whenever mental disease is suspected, the recruit should be examined for symptoms of nervous instability (*see* Epilepsy).''

" *Neurasthenia.*—In the case of many men who complain of this condition, it is slight in degree, and should not be considered as a bar to Grade I. Severer cases should be graded or rejected on the evidence of nervous instability tendered and found (*see* Epilepsy)."

" All men with an Argyll-Robertson pupil (loss of the reflex contraction of the pupil to light while it remans upon convergence and accommodation) should be rejected ; in case of doubt, the man should be referred for examination by the ophthalmic surgeon."

" In addition to the causes of rejection already mentioned, men suffering from tabes, general paralysis and all organic diseases of the central nervous system, however early the disease may be, should be placed in Grade IV."

These extracts suffice to show that the importance of ascertaining, and giving due weight to, the mental and nervous condition of recruits was thoroughly realised, during the final year of the war, and appropriate instructions to secure this end issued.

During the first three years of the war, however, it is evident to us that the importance and complexities of this particular aspect of the recruiting problem were not grasped, nor did the procedure in force at successive stages of these years result in any real discrimination between those recruits who were, and those who were not of normal nervous stability. As a result, a great number of men who were ill-suited to stand the strain of military service, whether by temperament or their past or present condition of mental or nervous health, were admitted into the army ; there is no doubt that such men contributed a very high proportion of the cases of hysteria and traumatic neurosis commonly called " shell-shock "(11).

It seems probable to us that had a more prolonged period of graduated training been possible a certain percentage (probably not large) of such men could have been developed into efficient soldiers, certainly for the non-combatant arms, but it is extremely doubtful how far the necessary time and attention, which would have been required for this purpose, would have been worth while. Further, experience shows that once a man is accepted for service it is in practice impossible to ensure that he will not be employed in the firing line ; in periods of emergency military exigencies over-ride every other consideration. We are of opinion that the army would have been better off without them.

On the problem of the method which should be pursued in order to pick out such men when they come forward as recruits, we have heard various opinions from many witnesses. It is our considered view that properly trained recruiting medical officers with appropriate instructions should not find in general any insuperable difficulty (12) in this, especially if they have before them a written medical history of the recruit (13) and appropriate consultant advice for cases of special difficulty (14). They should also be able to recommend special observation during training for selected cases (15).

We do not regard the specific efficiency tests (such as Binet) as suitable for the purposes of general recruiting (16), nor do we think that consultant advice need be provided except in such cases in which it is specifically asked for, and the circumstances are such that it is practicable to provide it.

All recruits throughout their preliminary training should be under continuous medical observation. Medical officers in charge of recruits during this period should be made acquainted with such "Behaviour Characteristics" as were used in the training of recruits in the American Navy (17), and should instruct the N.C.O.'s to bring to their notice any recruits who exhibit such abnormalities of conduct (18).

The two reports of the Medical Department of the Ministry of National Service already referred to, form an important chapter in the history of recruiting in this country, and among much valuable information emphasize one vital lesson to be derived from our experiences during the war—to this lesson we have already referred, but it is a factor of such overwhelming importance that we make no apology for again drawing attention to the essential difference between the examination and classification of the volunteer and the conscript, viz., the mental attitude of both medical officer and recruit are diametrically different in the two cases, a psychological fact which has most important practical bearings, notably in the estimation of the condition of the recruit's nervous system.

In view of this consideration, and the probability that in any future war with a Great Power there will be a repetition of the same three phases of recruiting which we experienced during 1914-1918, we recommend that—

Phase I.

1. Where a candidate for entry into any of His Majesty's Naval or Military or Air Force Services is required to certify in writing that he has not to the best of his belief suffered from certain specific conditions, "Insanity" and "Nervous Breakdown" shall be included.

2. Where a candidate is called upon to reply verbally to questions as to his previous health, "Insanity" and "Nervous Breakdown" shall be included in the question.

3. A proved history of certified insanity or epilepsy shall entail rejection (19).

4. The following directions be included in the instructions issued to medical officers who are employed in the examination of candidates for H.M. Naval, Military and Air Force Services (20).

"In examining a candidate the Medical Officer will "observe the demeanour of the candidate and the degree of "intelligence with which he responds to questions and

" directions. He will ask him a few simple questions about
" his childhood, family, occupations, etc., and from the
" replies should be able to form an estimate of the mental
" capacity, power of attention, memory, emotivity and
" general mental calibre of the candidate."

" Further information may be gained by observing the
" facial expression and conformation of the skull, nose, jaws,
" palate and pinna (Hydrocephalus, Microcephalus, evidence
" of injury or other physical stigmata may be noted). Every
" examination will include Romberg's test observation of the
" pupils as to (1) regularity of outline; (2) size and equality;
" (3) reaction to light. The patellar reflexes will be tested—
" others if necessary. The presence of tachycardia, tremor,
" or sweating if persistent—constitutes a serious disability.
" Candidates who present well-marked signs of nervous in-
" stability or serious mental defect should be rejected. In
" estimating the degree of mental or nervous disability pre-
" sented by a candidate the medical officer will consider to
" what extent the condition is likely to be a bar to effective
" military service, rejecting the unfit, obtaining a colleague's
" or specialist's opinion in dubious cases, and recommending
" special observation during training for those whom he
" accepts in spite of a minor degree of mental or nervous
" defect.

" A note will be made on the mental and nervous stability
" of each candidate on the Medical History Sheet."

The above directions should be embodied in the medical instructions for recruiting and available in pamphlet form for issue
to all Medical Officers engaged in recruiting duties, adequate steps
should be taken to see that they are in their possession, and that
the Medical Officers concerned have made themselves thoroughly
acquainted therewith (21).

5. Only " fit " men as judged by the pre-war standard for
the Regular Army should be enlisted in the Regular Army. If
it is desirable to accept men falling into Grades II or III of the
Ministry of National Service for the Militia and Territorial Army
they should be re-graded (with those accepted as Grade I) every
year.

6. All Regular Special Reserve and Territorial Medical Officers
should undergo a prescribed course of instruction in the methods
of examination of recruits, and the physical and mental standards
required. Special officers should be earmarked in each district
for these duties on mobilization. In addition a selection should
be made from those who served with H.M. Forces or were employed as civilians on the examination of recruits during 1914-
1918, and a separate list (to be revised every two years), kept of
these selected names.

Phase II.

7. *On Mobilization* instructions should be issued that only
Grade I men of the Militia and Territorial Army are to be employed on front-line duties with fighting units.

8. The recruiting machinery should be at once expanded (in accordance with pre-arranged plans) in order to meet the expected rush of recruits, the peace time recruiting staff being retained in these duties.

9. This expansion should include calling up the Special Officers earmarked for recruiting duties (*see* 6).

10. The experience of 1914-15 shows that in the enthusiasm and upheaval, which follows immediately upon the outbreak of war, the routine regulations of peace are ignored, and methodical system is replaced by chaotic confusion. This is a factor of prime importance. Explicit instructions should therefore be issued that

> I. The routine medical examination of each recruit is to be fully and carefully carried out. The number of men examined by each medical officer should be determined by this consideration alone; in general, the number should not exceed four, or at the most five, in an hour.
>
> II. The medical history sheets are to be completed as in peace.
>
> III. A return is to be rendered daily of the number of candidates examined by each medical officer.

The carrying out of these instructions should be ensured by frequent visits of inspection by superior officers.

11. As soon as appropriate arrangements can be made, the medical examination of candidates should be handed over to boards in place of single medical officers.

These arrangements should embody the principles described in the Report of the Ministry of National Service. These boards should grade the men according to the standards of bodily and mental fitness therein defined.

The allocation of recruits to suitable military units should be the function of posting boards, who should be advised by special medical officers as to the duties which men in the various grades can perform (22).

It is assumed that in the first instance the military authorities would desire to enlist only " fit," *i.e.*, Grade I men. Candidates in lower grades could therefore be relegated to the reserve, pending further developments. If lower grade men are accepted, their training should be modified to suit their capabilities, and should ordinarily be longer.

Phase III.

Whenever military service is made compulsory the procedure employed by the Ministry of National Service (described in their Report) for the medical examination and grading of recruits should be put into operation.

The essential features, in our opinion, are :—

> (i) The sectional method of examination whereby a specified part of the examination of each recruit is allotted to

each of four members of the board and the final grading determined by the Chairman.

(ii) The issue of definitions of the physical and mental qualifications for each grade, and of directions on the usual effects of common diseases and disabilities to chairmen and members of boards (23).

(iii) The provision of consultant advice for difficult and doubtful cases.

(iv) The provision of appeal boards with due safeguards.

(v) Recruits should be encouraged to bring certificates from their own doctors, and other documentary evidence of their previous health for the information of boards. These should include all available medical records.

(vi) The number of recruits examined per day by a board should be specified in instructions and not exceeded.*

(vii) The work of the boards should be under constant supervision and inspection to ensure uniformity of practice and grading.

(viii) Special attention should be paid to the correct completion of medical history sheets, and the accurate rendering of records and returns.

(ix) The public should be informed early of the medical conditions of the examination, and responsible persons

---

* It is believed that it is desirable for military reasons to call up for training in the first instance only the fittest part of the male population. (The eugenic aspects of such policy is a different matter.) If this is the case experience in the late war shows that this would be best accomplished by calling up recruits by age groups; among other reasons for this is the progressive fall in the percentage of fit men from 18 years of age onwards. This is well shown by the following figures showing the percentage of Grade I men among 71,382 men examined in the West Midland region, between November, 1917, and April, 1918. This group is selected as an example since it represents a mixed population of city workers, artisans, industrial and agricultural workers

Age.				Percentage of Grade I.	Age.				Percentage of Grade I.
18	...	...	...	71·7	25	...	...	...	44·2
19	...	...	...	67·6	26	...	...	...	42·9
20	...	...	...	60·0	27	...	...	...	38·9
21	...	...	...	56·7	28	...	...	...	36·2
22	...	...	...	52·1	29	...	...	...	36·1
23	...	...	...	49·6	30	...	...	...	33·7
24	...	...	...	50·3					

It will be observed that the percentage of Grade I falls 10 per cent. between 18 and 21, another 10 per cent. by 24, and again by 27, and has fallen more than 50 per cent. by 31. The progressive fall is maintained after 30—the percentage at 35 being 28·6 and at 40, 13·9.

The number of recruits who should be examined per day by a Board will clearly vary according to the fitness of the men, since with a high percentage of fit men there is a low percentage of men whose examination entails careful examination of defects and vice versa.

should be allowed to see the method of the examination, so that there may be no mystery or suspicion about it. The public should be convinced, as far as is possible, of the fairness of the medical tests and examinations.

In conclusion, we are of opinion that the adoption of the measures we have recommended would result in the admission into the fighting services of a much smaller percentage of recruits mentally and nervously unsuitable for military service than was the case in 1914-1918; such men are unlikely to become efficient soldiers, and likely under the strain of war to become the subjects of the different types of hysteria and traumatic neurosis commonly called " shell-shock." The occurrence of these conditions militates against the efficiency of the Army, swells the sick returns, increases the amount of hospital accommodation and transport required, and absorbs the time and attention of medical personnel. Eventually a large number of men are returned to civil life, a burden to themselves and the country, requiring prolonged and costly treatment, necessitating a greatly increased pensions list, and extremely difficult to re-establish in civil life (24).

As far as it is possible to foresee the conditions of any future war on a large scale, it seems probable that the circumstances are likely to make even greater demands upon the mental and nervous resources of the personnel of the fighting services than the events of 1914-1918. If this should prove to be the case, appropriate measures designed to admit into the services only those who are possessed of at least an average degree of mental and nervous health and stability will be a factor of prime importance in the successful conduct of the war.

SUMMARY OF EVIDENCE OF WITNESSES REGARDING RECRUITING.

(1) (a) *Sir James Galloway* : When the war commenced volunteering was still the rule. There was a tremendous rush of men to the colours, and the methods which were still in vogue, including examination by one medical man, broke down on account of the amount of work. The medical men could not examine the large number of recruits coming in, with the result that large numbers entered the service with what must have been a very superficial examination. A medical man was stated to be able to examine 200 to 300 recruits a day for service, and I think that alone explains the nature of the examination which was carried out in many cases.

(1) (b) *Lieut.-Colonel Clay* : As soon as war was declared the machinery which was in existence for recruiting practically became non-existent, because the machinery was carried on by officers, N.C.O.s and men who were immediately mobilised and went into their regiments and left the recruiting organisation in a state of chaos.

Certain officers who were ear-marked to take over recruiting offices were brought together, and got together and created recruiting machinery to deal with the vast number of men who responded to Lord Kitchener's call. After the recruiting campaign the whole of the country was simply seething with recruits. They were medically examined—I say it without fear of contradiction—in a most haphazard manner; 20 per cent. to 30 per cent. of the men were never medically examined at all. Their attestations were made out, and they were fallen in in parties and drafted to regiments of what was commonly known as Kitchener's Army. The system was this : 600, 700 or 1,000 men went to the depot. The recruiting officer went outside and fell in the party and called the roll, and the party was put under the command of an officer, an N.C.O., or a civil policeman, whoever was handy, and marched off to go to, say, the 9th Surreys at Shoreham. Bill Jones in the back row said, '' I don't want to go to Shoreham.'' Other men said the same, and before the party had marched off 20 to 30 had changed places with other men who had not been medically examined. The party marched to Shoreham with their documents, and they were handed over.

It was at this period that I was brought in by Major-General Adye to put things right. It was realised that in the Eastern Command alone 49,000 men were serving without attestation. The only way we could trace these men's attestations was through their enlistment, so we got clerks in the different offices to work double time, engaged numbers of clerks to work during the night to work on the men, because it had not been realised that the men would join up who did not care whether they had been attested or not. Consequently when we checked with pay records we were in a position to find which men had not attested. Thousands of men were never medically examined, and consequently we had to get an Army Order published that all men for whom attestations were not forthcoming were to be re-attested. That was the position which carried us on over Christmas until February, 1915. I spent weeks in going round the depots in the Eastern Command, and I collected over 30,000 attestations which were lying on shelves and had not been sent in. That is exactly how in the early days men not physically fit for the Army, and who would not have gone into the Army had they received a proper medical examination, went in without one.

It must be remembered, too, that we had civil practitioners. I know of one doctor who medically examined 400 men per day for ten days, and he did not work 24 hours in the day. That was the same right the way through the country in 1914 and early in 1915 up to the time of the Derby Scheme.

Things had got more sorted out by September, 1915, and we did not get that big rush until July. Then machinery was working better, but even then civil practitioners got 2s. 6d. for every man examined, and the consequence was they examined as many men as they possibly could in the day.

(2) *Sir James Galloway*: It was seen by Sir Alfred Keogh, then Director-General A.M.S., that this condition of affairs could not go on, and he it was who established the system of examination by medical boards, for two reasons, first of all, to obtain a better medical opinion than could be given by any one medical man—a consensus of the opinions of two, three, four or five medical men; and also to avoid the difficulties which would arise when the men began to appeal against the medical findings. That is to say, one of the important functions which the Medical Boards fulfilled was to act as a defensive agent for the Government and for the War Office.

(3) *Sir James Galloway*: The Medical Boards at first varied greatly in efficiency, but the quality of their work constantly improved; the men who were selected developed the particular qualities necessary to make a satisfactory medical examination and to understand what physical fitness means. Such medical men were gradually placed on the Boards and others eliminated, and the quality of the Boards improved continuously during 1917.

(4) *Sir James Galloway*: I had the position of Chief Commissioner of the Ministry, and was in charge of the whole system of medical recruiting work. I had excellent assistants, and the result was that these Boards still increased in efficiency, and I may say that the medical opinions given by these Boards came to be truly reliable and valuable medical opinion.

You will see, therefore, how matters developed. In the first instance the men taken into the Army were volunteers not concerned to make much of their physical defects; they came in willingly. In process of time this attitude of mind changed, and there was a tendency to criticise the findings of the Medical Boards, and this mental attitude spread almost, I may say, like an epidemic disease to large sections of the community, and it became a difficult matter to make the decisions of the Medical Boards acceptable to large numbers of those called up for service.

Naturally enough decisions did become more accurate; we did determine more satisfactorily the physical and mental fitness of recruits coming forward.

The Ministry of National Service drew up regulations as to the methods of medical examination and mentioned specially the defects which affected the grading of recruits. Reference was made to the question of the mental fitness of the recruits. The question of the mental aspect became more and more a prominent feature in the work of the Boards.

(5) (a) *Sir James Galloway*: I would like to make clear this further point to the Committee as it involved a change so far as the medical work of the Boards was concerned. When these Civilian Medical Boards under the Ministry of National Service were established, for the reasons to which I have referred, the system of grading was entirely changed. Up to the 1st November, 1917, the men who came up for examination as recruits

were classified according to the military categories. This became so difficult on account of the great and increasing variety of the duties required to be performed in the Army and so many mistakes were possible that it was decided that under the action of compulsory military service the man should be classified simply in physical grades. These grades 1, 2, 3, and 4 which became very well known in the last years of the war had nothing whatever to do with the fitness of the man to perform any special military duty, but they expressed as nearly as could be ascertained the opinions of medical men as to his physical, and to a certain extent also, his mental fitness. Whether the man so graded was fit for any type of military service was not the concern of those Medical Boards, that was purely a military affair and had to be decided after the man passed into the Army. We had to examine many men who never came into the Army. They might be retained in civilian life for various reasons, but when the man was called up for service and placed in the Army he was re-examined and categorised according to the idea formed of his fitness for any special department of military duty, e.g. :— the Cavalry, Machine Gun Corps, Infantry and so forth. I wish it to be clearly understood that we made this complete change in the aspect of the problem which we put before the medical members of the Boards acting as examiners.

(5) (b) *Sir James Galloway* : In 1917 a man passing into the service might have to serve in something like 64 different types of service and we felt that it was not possible for the Medical Boards to classify a man and place him in one of those 64 possible categories of service in which he would subsequently serve. Even the most experienced of military medical men could not do so. The only way in which it could be definitely found out was by trial.

(6) *Dr. Spencer Hurlbutt* : With regard to the volunteers, they did not volunteer any statement for the most part. I should think almost invariably they did not. With regard to the conscripts, yes.

(7) *Q.* . You sifted the evidence you could get as far as it was possible to do so?

Dr. Spencer Hurlbutt : Yes.

Q. . Are you suggesting that this letter which you have handed to me is a sample of the sort of letter you received?

Dr. Spencer Hurlbutt : Yes.

Q. . Perhaps the Committee would like to hear it—
Dear Sir,

Pardon me for writing you these few lines as I can't speak because I stammer a great deal and you won't be able to understand me fully as my heart hurts me if I talk.

These is my points :—

1. I am very short winded and when walking five minutes there's pains in my left side shocking which causes me to stop walking.

2. A few years ago I suffered with pneumonia, bronchitis and pleurisy combined in one and my doctor gave me up as a bad job which left me with a complaint in chest and lungs shocking.

3. Discharges from left ear continually running, which causes me to be a bit deaf on my left ear.

4. Suffered with right leg all my life, and can't hardly walk on account of being weak on my left. The London Hospital wanted to take it off for me.

5. I suffer with fainting fits and weak nerves. Please take notice of me as I am certain I shan't be able to stand the army. I will be dead before I'll reach my station.

Please oblige,
R. H.

(8) (a) *Sir James Galloway* : I feel strongly, especially with reference to the mental capacity of the candidate that the only way, beyond the chance given by observing such a gross defect as epilepsy—the only real way is to know the man's mental history for some time.

Q. . Further in your answer you say : " In a great many " cases suitable records of this nature exist." What have you in mind?

Sir James Galloway : Records of the whole population. Hundreds of thousands of the population have been examined from time to time, for insurance, for entrance to schools, for entrance to large firms and in hospitals and I had in mind that if any collation of such evidence were possible we should have already existing in the country much of the knowledge required to deal with an emergency such as we have passed through. With reference to National Health Insurance there already existed records of information which were not at our service.

(8) (b) *Dr. J. I. C. Dunn* : School medical inspection records and national health insurance records might be made available. No recruit should be accepted or rejected on these documents, but they could constitute part of the evidence determining acceptance or rejection.

(8) (c) *Sir James Galloway* : The last sentence of this paragraph I think is very important.

My own experience with regard to mental weakness or deficiency is that the important information that should be obtained is not so much a certificate from a medical man of his opinion, as by the opportunity of observing the recruit for some time, or failing that, reliable information as to the medical history of the men in the past. This information obtained from a continuous record of observation, is a thing which would be of most value, with the exception of definite evidence of such a gross defect as the occurrence of a fit of epilepsy and the statement by a medical man that he had observed such a fit; the evidence as to the recruit's mental condition was often vague and we had to depend on the judgment of the medical men actually dealing with the recruit at the time.

(9) (a) Q. . When you first started recruiting, did not you have regulations for the Army Medical Service which gave very full instructions in Appendix 16?

Dr. Burton Fanning : I am sorry, sir, I do not remember them.

Q. . Were you doing recruiting in a regular recruiting depôt?
Dr. Burton Fanning : Yes.

Q. . Then I think there would be a book of this sort with the regulations giving full details based on the experience of probably 100 years.

Dr. Burton Fanning : I am afraid I do not remember anything about them.

9. (b) Q. . Can you tell us the approximate date of the first instructions you received with regard to the examination of the mental or nervous conditions of recruits coming before you?

Dr. Spencer Hurlbutt : I recollect none before November, 1917.

Q. Did you ever see any instructions with regard to the examination of recruits before those issued in November, 1917?

Dr. Spencer Hurlbutt : No.

Q. But before November, 1917, you as the examiner exercised your own discretion in general as to whether you accepted or rejected the man?

Dr. Spencer Hurlbutt : Yes.

Up to the time when the Ministry of National Service Instructions came out I have no recollection of receiving any instructions with regard to the special examination of recruits as to mental and nervous stability. Subsequent to the Ministry of National Service instructions coming out in November, 1917, the examiner was instructed to examine the recruit with regard to the reaction of the pupils, knee jerks, &c., and to make enquiry into the personal history and record of mental condition. That is all I can recollect.

(10) (a) Q. . What is your view as to what extent, if any, the question whether each recruit suffered from nervous instability or not was constantly in the minds of the Board in grading him?

Dr. Spencer Hurlbutt : I think it was in a great measure. A nerve condition hardly ever stood alone. That is my difficulty in answering this question. Other points had to be considered.

Q. . But do you think in looking back that it occupied a correct fraction of the picture, so to speak, in grading the man. ?

Dr. Spencer Hurlbutt : Oh yes, quite. That is, from 1917 onwards.

Q. . And before that time?

Dr. Spencer Hurlbutt: Before that time it was a negligible quantity.

Q. . You mean it was not taken into account?

Dr. Spencer Hurlbutt: It was not taken into account as it should have been.

Q. . You would, therefore, infer that before 1917 a large number of nervously unsuitable men were taken into the army, but after November, 1917, they were properly graded, and the severe cases not taken into the army?

Dr. Spencer Hurlbutt: That is my view.

(10) (*b*) *Q.* . At what period in the war in your experience did it become recognised that the question of the examination of the recruit as to his mental and nervous stability was necessary?

Lieut.-Colonel H. Clay: In October, 1917, we had in every area in the country properly constituted Medical Boards. Previous to that they had been Boards in name, but each officer did so many men himself. In October, 1917, proper medical boards were formed.

(10) (*a*) *Q.* . In the ordinary examination of the recruit, did you examine his pupils.

Dr. Spencer Hurlbutt: I do not think it was done except in cases of defective sight in the early stages. After November, 1917, the reaction of the pupil was considered.

(11) (*a*) *Sir James Galloway* : With reference to the possibility of the use in military service of unstable mental men, my opinion is that those who are epileptic or who have been definitely insane are not fit for any form of military service. Some of them might be useful in sedentary military work under observation, but it would not be worth while for the country to take them under any conditions which can be foreseen. Short of these conditions, I can conceive a nervously unstable man doing on occasion brilliant military service. Probably such a period of brilliant service might be succeeded by a period of depression, of uselessness, or even of danger. Such men are likely to obtain admission to military service if they desire.

Under the conditions I have tried to outline, it will be understood that large masses of the male population entered the Army with very little medical discrimination. Under ordinary conditions many of these would in process of time prove to be unfit from the nervous and mental point of view. They have proved to be similarly unfit under war conditions, possibly in larger numbers than under peace conditions. These may account for the larger numbers remaining under treatment of the so-called " shell-shock " or neurasthenic type of patient.

11 (*b*) *Dr. Burton Fanning*. I am strongly of opinion that the nervously unstable man cannot as a rule be made an efficient soldier. I know of a few men who recognised that they were of nervous temperament and who had sufficient force of

character to go through with service in spite of what it cost them; eventually some of these found the strain of front line work beyond endurance. But the vast majority of neurotics had no intention of "sticking it," whatever might be their sensations, and mostly thought that even preparation for warfare was beyond them. Most of their service was spent in hospital or in pretending to do useless jobs.

I think it was chiefly the patients' attitude of mind. They had never taken exercise; they had not been prepared for muscular exercise; they had always lived a sedentary life; they knew they would not stand the long marches, and they never intended to.

I can only say that an enormous proportion amongst the men who broke down obviously had been neurotics previously.

All I can say to that is that what I am basing my opinion on is that I took all these fellows' histories, and they all satisfied me that they had been neurotic for years, if not from boyhood.

(11) (c) *Dr. Burton Fanning*: Threequarters of the medical cases were Home Service men; of these one-third had functional nerve disorder.

Q. . Newly enlisted men?

Dr. Burton Fanning: Yes. We got more and more cases as they were more and more conscripted.

Q. But conscription did not come at that time.

Dr. Burton Fanning: After 1916.

Q. You did get these conditions prevailing in men who were Voluntary Army men?

Dr. Burton Fanning: To a much less extent. I was at Cambridge on and off from 1915 to 1917, when I went to France, and all that time the number of these functional cases was getting more and more. In 1916, out of 2,240 medical in-patients 640 were from overseas and presented few cases of neurasthenia—1,600 were from Home Forces, and 509 were suffering from neurasthenia.

(12) (a) *Dr. Burton Fanning*: I think the nervous condition can be satisfactorily examined at an ordinary recruit's attendance —but it must be by a doctor alive to the importance of functional nervous disorders, experienced in their diagnosis.

(12) (b) *Sir James Galloway*: I believe the basis of what we want is that these men should know neurology as the basis of their work quite apart from what is known as psychological medicine. That is really the most important foundation so far as any work of this kind is concerned. I believe myself that the other part of it, *viz.*, the psychological part, is not a matter which can be acquired in a short time, but requires a man of judgment and large experience to give any opinion as to the real psychological value of a person, whereas the actual decision of whether he is suffering or not from a definite neurosis is a quality which may be more easily acquired as it fits in with his general medical training.

(12) (c) *Sir James Galloway* : The main thing, undoubtedly, is that these candidates should be examined from the physical point of view, and in that I include the neurological point of view. The full examination of every man from the point of view of his mental condition I think would be an entirely impossible thing, but in any case in which the question does arise he should be specially examined.

(13) *Sir James Galloway* : In peace time the nervous and mental condition of the candidate can be fairly well investigated at the time of his physical examination. This can be done by the medical examiner, especially if he has received training in psychological medicine. The evidence of medical certificates in this respect is usually of little value except when a valid medical certificate states such a definite fact as an attack of true epilepsy. Outside the possibilities of direct medical examination at the time, the most trustworthy evidence obtainable is by knowing the past history of the mental condition of a candidate. In a great many cases suitable records of this nature exist. If these records could be collated the difficulties of estimating the mental quality of a candidate would be greatly diminished.

(14) *Sir James Galloway* : We always tried to retain on the list with reference to these particular questions, general physicians with the widest outlook on affairs rather than the specialist.

(15) *Sir James Galloway* : I believe that the most suitable plan for classification of men for service is by the process of grading according to their physical and mental condition. The apportionment of these men for military duty can only be undertaken properly when they are in the Army and their peculiar adaptabilities are discovered. The varieties of service are now so great that the best use to which a man can be put in the Army can be found out after he has been watched by skilled observers for a certain time. The grading of which I speak is on purely physical and mental lines, and should have nothing to do with military duty.

(16) (a) Q. . Given all the leisure necessary, but without the medical history of the recruit, is it possible to make a useful estimate of his mental stability?

Sir James Galloway : I have been reading of the exceedingly elaborate methods put into operation by our colleagues in the United States, which I followed with a good deal of interest as I knew some of their medical officers engaged in this work when they were observing our methods on this side. From experience of what did happen to the American troops, I do not think it did much good. I do not think their casualties so far as " Shell-shock " was concerned were much minimised by this elaborate examination.

(16) (b) *Dr. J. I. C. Dunn* : On the practical utility of physical tests of nervous stability I am profoundly sceptical except, perhaps, for some particular services. The diagnosis of a diffident manner " active knee jerks," " tremor," would on the one hand exclude from the line many an invaluable officer and N.C.O. ; on the other hand give unlimited scope to the " medical officer specially trained . . ." and to the cunning shirker. I have known men who winced or collapsed at a distant shell-burst pass the R.A.F. test, and not be found out (or fired out) for a year.

A Binet test is worthless in the hands of those who would use it, and unnecessary to the few who can use it intelligently.

(17) *Behaviour Characteristics*, used in the training of recruits in the U.S. Navy during the war.

(1) Resentfulness to discipline or inability to be disciplined.
(2) Unusual stupidity or awkwardness in drills or exercises.
(3) Inability to transmit orders correctly.
(4) Personal uncleanliness.
(5) Criminal tendencies.
(6) Abnormal sex practices and tendencies, including masturbation.
(7) Filthy language and defacement of property.
(8) Distinct femine types.
(9) Bed-wetters.
(10) Subjects of continual ridicule or teasing.
(11) Queer or peculiar behaviour.
(12) All recruits who show persistently, the following charac-teristics :—Tearfulness, irritability, seclusiveness, sulkiness, depression, shyness, timidity, anti-social attitude, over-boisterousness, suspicion, dulness, sleeplessness, sleepwalking.
(13) Chronic homesickness.

(18) (a) Q. . There is just one question which I should like to ask you. You say in your précis that it would be impossible for an adequate examination to be carried out at the time of recruit-ing, and yet you draw attention to the paragraph of the regula-tions regarding mental capacity and say that great care is to be taken in ascertaining the mental capacity of the recruit. You are aiming by that paragraph as far as possible towards the ideal of having the man examined by a mental expert, which is an ideal but it is an impracticable idea. That is my way of looking at it. You are telling the man to do his best, but you are not expecting him to be a trained psychologist. Accepting that, I quite agree with that and I think we all do, would it be practicable to arrange that during his early period of training the recruit should be care-fully watched?

Lieut.-General Sir John Goodwin : But he is surely.

Q. . He is watched by whom?

Lieut.-General Sir John Goodwin : By the medical officers in charge of his regiment or depôt, and also by the Medical Inspector of Recruits.

Q. . Do you think that is the way best suited for observing early divergencies from the normal in the ordinary life of the recruit?

Lieut.-General Sir John Goodwin : I think so, and of course his company officer who sees him every day and all day would at once inform the medical officer of the regiment that Private so-and-so has been rather queer lately.

Q. . As a rule I found, in my experience, that it was not the medical officer who first noticed any divergency in the conduct of the recruit, because in the presence of the medical officer or of any officer the recruit's attitude changes at once?

Lieut.-General Sir John Goodwin : I quite agree with you.

Q. . It is either a member of the Service of the same ranks who knows him intimately as a friend, or the subordinate officer who is pretty close to him, who would be in a position to detect slight irregularities.

Lieut.-General Sir John Goodwin : Yes, but now you are coming to the very, very important point of the backbone of the British Army which Kipling talks about, *the non-commissioned ranks*. Those are the men, of course, who are the first to notice anything, the Colour-Sergeant, the Corporal in his room, the Sergeant in his Company, those are the men, and they would at once go to the Company officer or, as I know very well from experience, to the medical officer and say : " Beg pardon, sir, I do not like the look of Private so-and-so, lately he has been funny in his manner. His room-mates have told me so and so."

Q. . These are the people to whom one can look really?

Lieut.-General Sir John Goodwin : Yes.

(18) (*b*) *Q.* . How long does a recruit remain in the depôt now?

Lieut.-Colonel Sylvester Bradley : It was twenty weeks, but a few weeks ago it was altered to 12 weeks again. The recruit's whole time is taken up, and any kind of experimental work is very difficult.

Q. . During the time he is in the depôt, the medical officer does not attempt to test the recruit?

Lieut.-Colonel Sylvester Bradley : Not for his mental capacity at all.

Q. . And is nothing more definite done when he gets to his unit?

Lieut.-Colonel Sylvester Bradley : No, unless the man is brought up. The man would not be notified until the Sergeant-Instructor brings him up before the Commanding Officer and says he cannot do anything with him; that he is always dirty or absent without leave, and always getting jugged for something or other.

Q. . Do you yourself think it would be possible to have anything in the way of some continuous medical examination of the recruit from the time of his enlistment?

Lieut.-Colonel Sylvester Bradley : I am convinced of it.

Q. . By what system?

Lieut.-Colonel Sylvester Bradley : The system wants working out. First of all, get an efficient medical officer at your depôt. I do not know whether one ought to go into these details at this meeting. At the present time the medical officers at our depôts are nearly all retired officers of the Corps. You very seldom get a regular officer. To ask a retired full Colonel, who retired some 10-11 years ago to suddenly introduce mental tests into his work is not very reasonable. He is not assisted by any instructions, but left to his own devices. I think the retired full Colonel is rather incapable of being instructed by his juniors.

Q. . Perhaps the instructions could be put into regulations for which he would have more respect?

Lieut.-Colonel Sylvester Bradley : Provided one had keen regular officers, trained in their work, at the depôts, I think very much more could be done, but also it ought to be done in conjunction with the educational branch and the combatant branch. You see all these recruits go to school. You have your educational instructors; they have a certain knowledge of the men. The classification which the educationalist makes never comes before the medical officer at all.

Q. . Could he get it if he wanted it?

Lieut.-Colonel Sylvester Bradley : He could, but unless it is all part of the routine of the depôt, I am afraid even the keen medical officer would find great difficulty in carrying it out, unless it was part of the routine so that he could go to the combatant officer and the combatant officers would call upon him to examine recruits as to their mental capacity. At the present time the number of recruits being rejected before training is treble what it was before the war, and every recruit rejected at his training is a dead loss to the State of £50 on an average. The State loses between £100,000 and £200,000 annually solely on account of recruits being rejected before training.

(18) (c) *Q.* , I think myself that one has to get rid of the unstable recruit as soon as possible, and that it must be done during the period of training, and I think one's efforts should be concentrated on that rather than on any attempt to get at him at the time of recruiting.

Lieut.-Colonel Sylvester Bradley : That is what has been done in the American Army. They have stopped trying to do tests on enlistment, and they are now performed early in the training.

Q. . Well now, my feeling is that the medical officer does not come so much into it. Take the case of a mild mental defect; he would not see that at all; it would only appear and strike the people who were in close contact with the recruit?

Lieut.-Colonel Sylvester Bradley : Quite.

Q. . What sort of indications would you feel that they should look for?

Lieut.-Colonel Sylvester Bradley : I do not know that they should look for them. It is a very difficult question. Sometimes an instructor takes a dislike to a man for a personal reason and he brings the man up before the Company Officer or to the Commanding Officer and says this man is no use to me; I can't do anything with him on parade and I think he is " gone " in the head. And then the man goes to the medical officer. That is what is done as a rule, or they may try to get rid of him in some other way. But they generally push him to the medical officer as they prefer to let the medical people have the responsibility of getting rid of him.

Q. . One of the methods adopted in the American Navy was to get out a series of what they called behaviour characteristics and if a man exhibited any of those characteristics then the Petty Officer or the Instructor would bring him to the notice of the medical officers. Such characteristics would be the difficulty in submitting himself to discipline or incapacity for discipline, solitariness, diffidence in mixing with other men or taking part in recreations. Do you think if one drew the attention of non-commissioned officers to these points that it would be of any value?

Lieut.-Colonel Sylvester Bradley : I think it would, provided you are going to have a test to put the man through. You don't want to induce the non-commissioned officers to bring more men up unless you have a test to put them through.

(19) (a) *Q.* . Do you consider that a man who has been insane can be trained into an efficient soldier?

Lieut.-General Sir John Goodwin : I do not consider it possible, Sir, unless perhaps in a very exceptional case, and, in any case, I would never recommend it. I do not think it should be attempted.

If he is known to be insane, or if a man is found to be insane while he is in the Service he is invalided out and not permitted to re-enlist.

Q. . So that whatever the form of insanity the man had suffered from he would be considered unfit for admission to Military Forces, and the reasons for that?

Lieut.-General Sir John Goodwin : That he is not likely to become an efficient soldier for general service, that even if he is fit for service in peace time he would probably break down under the stress of war and might become a danger not only to himself but to others for whose lives he was responsible.

Q. . So that you are prepared to uphold the present regime that under no circumstances should a man who has once suffered from insanity of any sort be admitted into the Army?

Lieut.-General Sir John Goodwin : Quite so.

Q. . With regard to epilepsy, you would not admit an epileptic into the Army?

Lieut.-General Sir John Goodwin : No, Sir.

Q. . You were very emphatic earlier that anyone who has been known to be insane would be excluded from the Army. I would just like to know—without unnecessarily questioning that opinion—whether that conclusion has been formed as the result of extensive experience of the disadvantage and danger of accepting persons who have been insane, or whether it is on the question of general principle?

Lieut.-General Sir John Goodwin : On both. I think it is wrong in principle and wrong from my own personal experience. I do not think that any man who has been insane should be enlisted into the Army and if he has once been insane he should be forthwith discharged from the Army. I feel that a man who has been insane is liable to give way again and it is not as if his giving way only affects himself. He may be a sentry, he may be a guard, he may be doing very important work and the lives of hundreds, if not thousands of men of the Army may depend upon him.

Q. . I rather take it you mean where the insanity has been of a proved character by certification or other means?

Lieut.-General Sir John Goodwin : Yes.

Q. . Because otherwise, in the case of conscription, the man who did not wish to serve would plead previous insanity.

Lieut.-General Sir John Goodwin : I mean the insane man, the epileptic man ; the man who has had epileptic convulsions or the man who has been insane.

Q. . At any time even if it is years ago?

Lieut.-General Sir John Goodwin : Even if it were ten years before. If he had been insane I would not have him in the Army.

(19) (*b*) *Q.* . What about the men who have been, for instance, in asylums?

Lieut.-Colonel Sylvester Bradley : I would not have anything to do with those.

Q. . Then you would not take anybody who had been in an asylum?

Lieut.-Colonel Sylvester Bradley : That is, as I say, my personal opinion ; it is not backed by any scientific knowledge.

Q. . On the assumption that he might become insane again?

Lieut.-Colonel Sylvester Bradley : He might, yes ; there is the possibility.

(19) (*c*) *Q.* . You would prefer to retain the present conditions as laid down in King's Regulations, that the man who has been in an asylum should not be admitted into the Army?

Major Brooke Purdon : If I were offered my choice, certainly.

(19) (*d*) *Q.* . Do you approve of a general rule that all cases that have been in an asylum should be excluded from the Army?

Dr. L. C. Bruce : I would not have them in a regiment at any cost ; they are no use.

Q. . Even when the disease is a good distance back?

Dr. L. C. Bruce : Even when the disease is a good distance back. In my opinion the man who has been in any asylum is a damaged article.

(20) *Q.* . It seems to me, that what happens in the Army is precisely similar to what happens in the Navy—that no attention whatever is given to the mental state of the candidate.

Lieut.-Colonel Sylvester Bradley : Quite so as far as tests are concerned.

Q. . It seems to me that if attention were given to it, good might result?

Lieut.-Colonel Sylvester Bradley : I think so undoubtedly. I certainly think we ought to attempt it.

(21) *Q.* . In your answer to question 6 you say that you do not remember receiving any instructions. Are you referring to the time when the Army was responsible for the examination of recruits?

Dr. Burton Fanning : As I have told you, my examination of recruits experience was so choppy. I did it for a few months and then left off.

Q. . The Army was responsible for the examination of recruits up to November 1st, 1917, and after that the Ministry of National Service was responsible. Was your experience wholly before that?

Dr. Burton Fanning : And after. I came back from France at the end of 1917 and took up recruit work again.

Q. . Why didn't you see any instructions under the Ministry of National Service?

Dr. Burton Fanning : I do not remember having any. I remember a book, but I am not sure that I ever read it.

Q. . Then you remember receiving the instructions but you also remember you did not read them?

Dr. Burton Fanning : Was not that the Chairman's job?

Q. . I have no doubt it was.

Dr. Burton Fanning : I am sure I never read the book. I remember seeing the Chairman referring to it.

Q. . You did not read the instructions which you received?

Dr. Burton Fanning : No, I did not.

(22) *Lieut.-General Sir John Goodwin* : Well, then, in war time I have noted here that the system adopted by the Ministry of National Service was satisfactory. It is very difficult, indeed I think myself that is is impossible to decide at the recruit's examination as to which branch of the service he is best fitted for. That can only be done after he has completed a certain portion of his training. I have often known men, on being recruited, say they wished to go into the cavalry. In a few months' time they had changed. They had seen what the training of the infantry was and had felt that their line in life was in the infantry. I do not think at the recruit's examination, in most cases, it is possible to decide which branch of the Army he is best fitted for.

(23) *Colonel J. F. C. Fuller* : You see, Sir, really these notes are made up for a big European war where one nation is pitted against another nation. The present position is rather different. The whole of the men who voluntarily enlist in our volunteer Army do so because they are either unemployed or practically unemployable, and the whole Army is based on the assumption that about 30,000 men a year will be unable to find work in civil life.

Q. I was talking of mobilization for war?

Colonel J. F. C. Fuller : I suggest taking in practically everybody.

Q. If there is no occupation for them they tend to go sick and you may have to keep them in other ways. Would you suggest any way of taking them in in relays—this man I will take later if I must take him in?

Colonel J. F. C. Fuller : I think what one found out during the war was that we took in to start with a very high category of men and got them killed off and when towards the end of the war we wanted good fellows, then we got a very low category. I think it was very wicked in the war to see the number of highly skilled mechanics shoved into the trenches and shot down, in thousands. If the ordinary stupid man gets shot, it does not make very much difference.

Q. The difficulty is to get them classified in such a way to begin with ; you have no scheme of classification?

Colonel J. F. C. Fuller : No, except that I think we ought to place the whole of recruiting on a modern and scientific footing and not on a footing invented by Frederick William or somebody who measured Grenadiers by the yard.

(24) Two and a half years after the Armistice approximately 65,000 ex-Service men were drawing disability pensions for " neurasthenia " and of these 9,000 were undergoing hospital treatment for their condition.

Special Instruction in the Psycho-Neuroses for R.A.M.C. Officers.

We are strongly of opinion that the treatment of the psychoneuroses can only be satisfactorily undertaken by those medical officers who have received special training in the subject. The length of time necessary for such a training is naturally dependent upon the attainments and previous knowledge of the individual officer. It was found that three-month courses of instruction were sufficient to give a useful practical acquaintance with the subject, but a considerably longer period of study is clearly desirable, and should presumably be practicable when the urgent conditions of war are not actually present.

An adequate course should include instruction in

(1) Psychology ;
(2) Neurology ;

(3) Psychiatry;

(4) Psychopathology, including the nature and treatment of the various types of psychoneurosis, and the doctrines and relationships of the various schools of thought.

(5) Clinical instruction.

It would seem to be very desirable that a limited number of R.A.M.C. officers should undergo a complete course of instruction of this type so that suitable centres of treatment can be rapidly organised on the outbreak of war.

SUMMARY OF RECOMMENDATIONS.

General.

1. The term shell-shock should be eliminated from official nomenclature, the disorders hitherto included under this heading being designated by the recognised medical terms for such conditions. Abbreviations such as N.Y.D. Nervous or Mental, or N.Y.D.N., D.A.H., etc., should be avoided, as they are liable to become catchwords, and so react unfavourably on the patients themselves and on others.

Classification of Casualties.

1. Concussion or commotion attended by loss of consciousness and evidence of organic lesion of the central nervous system or its adjacent organs (such as rupture of the membrana tympani) should be classified as a battle casualty.

2. No case of psycho-neurosis or of mental breakdown, even when attributed to a shell explosion or the effects thereof, should be classified as a battle casualty any more than sickness or disease is so regarded.

3. In all doubtful cases it is desirable to have the classification determined by a Board of expert Medical Officers after observation in a neurological hospital.

Prevention.

(A) *Training.*—1. Every possible means should be taken to promote morale, esprit de corps and a high standard of discipline.

2. Training should be sufficiently prolonged to ensure that the soldier is not only physically fit and efficient, but also that he has had time to acquire such a standard of morale as will enable him to put the welfare of his unit before his own personal safety.

3. Close observation should be made by officers, both regimental and medical, and by non-commissioned officers of the unit on individuals during the whole of their training, so that abnormalities from which mental or nervous instability may be inferred may not be overlooked. For this purpose there should be the frankest co-operation between regimental and medical officers.

4. The study of character, so far as it is applicable to military life, is recommended for all officers with a view to teaching Man-Mastership.

5. Special instruction should be given to Royal Army Medical Corps officers in the psycho-neurosis and psychoses as they occur in war, and selected officers should be encouraged to specialise in the study of these disorders.

(B) *On Active Service.*—1. The practice of withdrawal of officers and men showing incipient signs of nervous breakdown or over-fatigue for rest either in the battalion or divisional area should be officially recognised and systematised.

2. So far as the military situation permits, tours of duty in the front line in stationary warfare should be short, especially in bad sectors. Adequate rest and organised recreation should be provided for units when out of the line.

3. Monotony should be avoided by changing units, as circumstances permit, between fronts and sectors.

Leave home should be encouraged.

4. The promotion of all measures making for good sanitation and the physical comfort of the men, both in the line and also in rest billets and base depots, should receive constant attention.

5. Rest of mind and body is essential in all cases showing signs of incipient nervous breakdown, and when possible it should be given under conditions of security and comfort and freedom from all military duties.

6. The fullest use should be made of Convalescent Depots for re-training and hardening men discharged from hospital. These units should invariably be pervaded by an atmosphere of complete cure.

The above recommendations, suitably modified to meet particular circumstances, should be applied to the other fighting services.

Treatment.

(A) *In Forward Areas.*—No soldier should be allowed to think that loss of nervous or mental control provides an honourable avenue of escape from the battlefield, and every endeavour should be made to prevent slight cases leaving the battalion or divisional area, where treatment should be confined to provision of rest and comfort for those who need it and to heartening them for return to the front line.

(B) *In Neurological Centres.*—When cases are sufficiently severe to necessitate more scientific and elaborate treatment they should be sent to special Neurological Centres as near the front as possible, to be under the care of an expert in nervous disorders. No such case should, however, be so labelled on evacuation as to fix the idea of nervous breakdown in the patient's mind.

(C) *In Base Hospitals.*—When evacuation to the base is necessary, cases should be treated in a separate hospital or in separate sections of a hospital, and not with the ordinary sick and wounded patients. Only in exceptional circumstances should cases be sent to the United Kingdom, as, for instance, men likely to be unfit for further service of any kind with the forces in the field. This policy should be widely known throughout the Force

Forms of Treatment.

The establishment of an atmosphere of cure is the basis of all successful treatment, the personality of the physician is, therefore, of the greatest importance. While recognising that each individual case of war neurosis must be treated on its merits, the Committee are of opinion that good results will be obtained in the majority by the simplest forms of psycho-therapy, i.e., explanation, persuasion and suggestion, aided by such physical methods as baths, electricity and massage. Rest of mind and body is essential in all cases.

The Committee are of opinion that the production of the hypnoidal state and deep hypnotic sleep, while beneficial as a means of conveying suggestions or eliciting forgotten experiences are useful in selected cases, but in the majority they are unnecessary and may even aggravate the symptoms for a time.

They do not recommend psycho-analysis in the Freudian sense.

In the state of convalescence, re-education and suitable occupation of an interesting nature are of great importance. If the patient is unfit for further military service, it is considered that every endeavour should be made to obtain for him suitable employment on his return to active life.

Return to the Fighting Line.

Soldiers should not be returned to the fighting line under the following conditions :—

(1) If the symptoms of neurosis are of such a character that the soldier cannot be treated overseas with a view to subsequent useful employment.

(2) If the breakdown is of such severity as to necessitate a long period of rest and treatment in the United Kingdom.

(3) If the disability is anxiety neurosis of a severe type.

(4) If the disability is a mental breakdown or psychosis requiring treatment in a mental hospital.

It is, however, considered that many of such cases could, after recovery, be usefully employed in some form of auxiliary military duty.

Cowardice, Desertion and Neurosis.

In many cases it is extremely difficult to distinguish cowardice from neurosis since in both fear is the chief causal factor. The Committee recommend that the system pursued in France in the late war, of obtaining the best possible expert advice when any medical question or doubt arose, before or at trials for serious military offences, or on subsequent review of the proceedings of the Court, should be followed in the future.

Recruiting.

1. Every effort should be made at the time of enlistment to ascertain the nervous and mental conditions of candidates both from their previous histories and from their present condition.

2. Only " fit " men as judged by the pre-war standards for the regular Army should be enlisted into the regular Army. If it is desirable to accept men falling into Grade II or III of the Ministry of National Service for the Militia or Territorial Army, they should be re-graded (with those accepted for Grade I) every year.

3. All Regular, Special Reserve and Territorial Force Medical Officers should undergo a prescribed course of instruction in the methods of examination of recruits and the physical and mental standards required. Special officers should be earmarked in each district for these duties on mobilization. In addition, a selection should be made from those who served with His Majesty's Forces or were employed as civilians on the examination of recruits during 1914-18, and a separate list kept of those selected.

4. On mobilization the recruiting machinery should be expanded on the lines indicated above, and measures should be taken to see that recruits receive an adequate medical examination. As soon as possible Medical Boards should take the place of single recruiting medical officers.

5. The allocation of recruits to suitable military units should be the function of Posting Boards advised by special medical officers.

6. If military service is made compulsory the procedure employed by the Ministry of National Service for the medical examination and grading of recruits should be put into operation.

In conclusion the Committee desire to record their sorrow at the loss they sustained by the death of their friend and colleague, Dr. H. W. Kaye, of the Medical Directorate of the Ministry of Pensions. Throughout their long deliberations, he gave them his generous and whole-hearted support; and his experience in regard to matters important to the enquiry was always influenced by the kindly interest he felt for those who had suffered in mind or in body as a consequence of the War. They feel that by his untimely death a valuable life has been lost to the service of the country.

'The Committee are also desirous of placing upon record their high appreciation of the services of their Secretary, Major W. R. Galwey, O.B.E., M.C., R.A.M.C. His work in arranging for the attendance of witnesses, in collating and abstracting documents, and in co-ordinating the experience and recommendations of expert witnesses with the requirements of army organisation has materially aided the Committee. He has proved himself in every way an able and experienced Secretary.

The Committee feel that it is a matter for great satisfaction that they are able to present an unanimous report.

SOUTHBOROUGH, *Chairman.*

THOMAS BEATON.

JAMES L. BIRLEY.

C. HUBERT BOND.

MAURICE CRAIG.

MARTIN FLACK.

HAMILTON C. MARR.

EDWARD MEAGHER. *Members.*

GILBERT MELLOR.

FREDERICK MOTT.

A. DICKSON STIRLING.

W. ALDREN TURNER.

STEPHEN WALSH.

WALTER WARING.

22nd June, 1922.

APPENDIX No. 1.

QUESTIONS FOR THE GUIDANCE OF WITNESSES GIVING EVIDENCE BEFORE THE WAR OFFICE COMMITTEE OF ENQUIRY ON " SHELL-SHOCK."

1. Did you have time and opportunity for investigating the mental and nervous stability of the candidates for the Service? If so, on what observations did you base your conclusions?

2. Was it your experience that the candidate for the Service who had been the subject of mental or nervous disorder stated that fact at the time of examination, and if so, what steps did you take to investigate such statements before passing or rejecting him?

3. What is your opinion as to the practicability of making an adequate examination of the nervous and mental condition of the candidate at the time of his physical examination? If practicable, what form should it take?

4. Would you recommend any other measure in order to ascertain the nervous and mental condition of candidates?

5. Had you adequate opportunity for observing the mental and nervous state of recruits?

6. What instructions did you receive with regard to estimating the nervous and mental stability of recruits? How far was such estimation practicable? On what observations did you base the conclusions you reached? Were you able to give effect to these conclusions with a view to recruits being suitably drafted?

7. What procedure was adopted when a recruit was considered nervously or mentally unfit for any particular arm of the Service or for retention in the Service?

8. How in your opinion should recruits be classified for modern warfare having due regard to their physical, mental and nervous condition?

9. Is it your experience that certain individuals can never be made efficient members of a modern fighting service? If so, to what type of individual does this apply?

10. Do you consider that a nervously unstable man can be trained into an efficient soldier?

11. Do you consider that a man who has been insane can be trained into an efficient soldier?

(a) If so, do you recommend that this should be done?

(b) Do you consider that he is exceptionally liable to shell-shock?

12. Do you consider that a mental defective can be trained into an efficient soldier?

(a) If so, do you recommend that this should be done?

(b) Do you consider that he is exceptionally liable to shell-shock?

13. What do you understand by the term " Shell-shock "?

14. Have you any opinion as to the type, temperament, and intelligence of men most likely to be affected by shell-shock? Was there any general characteristic common to the individuals so affected?

15. Under what conditions have you seen shell-shock and mental breakdown arise:—

    (1) In barracks and during training?

    (2) After severe physical stress—

        (a) marching?

        (b) exposure?

    (3) After severe mental stress?

    (4) After or associated with fever—dysentery, malaria, etc.?

    (5) Associated with venereal disease?

    (6) Associated with alcohol?

    (7) From bursting of high explosives—

        (a) shells?

        (b) bombs?

        (c) torpedoes?

    (8) From the effects of poison gas?

    (9) From stress of battle?

    (10) From prolonged responsibility?

    (11) From long service alone?

    (12) From any other cause?

Having regard to the above which condition or group of conditions is in your opinion the most potent cause of shell-shock and mental breakdown?

16. Was the incidence of shell-shock greater amongst troops who were fresh in the line or in those who had been in the line some time?

Was it more common during or immediately following an engagement, or when troops were in reserve?

17. In what ways does shell-shock manifest itself:—

    (a) In depôts or barracks?

    (b) In the field?

18. Which do you consider more common:—

    (a) Shell-shock due to commotional disturbance?

    (b) Shell-shock due to emotional disturbance?

From your experience can you say that there are any tests by which one can distinguish neurosis from commotional and emotional causes—

    (a) in the early stages?

    (b) in the later stages?

19. (a) Do you consider that responsibility increased or lessened the incidence of shell-shock?

    (b) Do you consider that shell-shock is more likely to arise in married or single men?

    (c) Was the incidence in any way related to age?

20. Have you any suggestions to offer towards lessening or preventing its incidence:—

    (a) in training?

    (b) in the field?

21. Upon what conditions do you consider the morale of troops depends?

    (a) Does good morale in troops tend to lessen the incidence of shell-shock?

    (b) Does shell-shock tend to undermine the morale of troops?

    (c) Have you any evidence to offer to show that shell-shock became contagious in a unit?

22. Do you consider that the incidence of shell-shock is increased or lessened by : —

    (a) Frequent removal from front areas?

    (b) Regular visits home?

23. Do you consider that any steps could be taken in the training of the soldier to minimise or prevent the effects of emotional disturbance due to explosives or stress in active service? If so, at what stage of training is the special training or treatment to be applied?

24. Did you observe any signs which would be of value in discriminating between genuine neurosis and simulation?

25. Have you actually seen cases of commotional shell-shock such as have been reported to occur from the bursting of high explosive shells, or from explosions in mines, dug-outs, etc.? It would be helpful if you could describe the symptoms of such cases.

26. Have you had any experience of lumbar puncture and the finding of blood in the cerebro-spinal fluid or bleeding from the ear with rupture of the tympanum or labyrinthine vertigo in cases of commotional shock?

27. Have you seen death occur from shell-shock without visible injuries to account for it? Was it possible that carbon-monoxide gas was the cause of death?

28. What mode of treatment did you find most valuable in cases of " shell-shock," " Conversion Hysteria " and " Neurasthenia " respectively—

    (a) in forward areas?

    (b) in back areas?

    (c) in home areas?

Have you any views as to the relative merits of—

    (a) Physical methods?

    (b) Suggestion?

    (c) Hypnotism?

    (d) Therapeutic conversations?

    (e) Psycho-analysis?

    (f) Isolation?

    (g) Re-education and occupation?

29. What is your experience of the treatment of shell-shock patients—

    (a) in special hospitals?

    (b) along with the physically wounded?

Has your experience been favourable towards the treatment of war neurosis being in the hands of medical officers specially trained in neurology, psychology and psycho-therapy?

30. Do you consider that a soldier who has once suffered from shell-shock is capable of further active service? Have you experience of such cases returning to the line, and if so what was the result?

31. Have you observed cases of insanity which you can attribute solely to the stress of war or shell-shock? Are such cases transitory in your experience or may they become chronic?

32. Have you observed cases of an emotive state in the form of irresistible fear of danger, associated with crises of terror and anxiety at the front, leading up to desertion from post of duty or to reckless behaviour?

33. Have you observed cases of dementia præcox which prior to diagnosis of the mental disease had a history of having been frequently punished or " crimed " for minor delinquencies?

34. Have you any information regarding the influence of alcohol in relation to—

    (a) Shell-shock and war neurosis?

    (b) Irresponsibility and neglect of duty?

    (c) Crime and suicide?

35. Have you any evidence as to the part played by mental failure as a cause of—

(a) drunkenness?
(b) desertion?
(c) minor crimes or other forms of abnormal conduct?

36. Have you any experience of courts-martial for cowardice and other military crimes?

37. Have you observed cases of true epilepsy result directly from shell concussion apart from visible head injury?

38. Have you experience of emotional shock similar to shell-shock arising during peace either at home or abroad? If so, under what conditions?

APPENDIX No. 2.

NUMBERS OF PATIENTS TREATED IN THE NEUROLOGICAL DEPARTMENT, BRITISH SALONICA FORCE.

TABLE 1.

ALL CASES.

Rank.			Number.
Officers ...	...	...	112
Other Ranks	...	...	812
Total	...	...	924

TABLE 2.

CLASSES OF DIAGNOSIS (" OTHER RANKS " ONLY, AND ONLY FOR FIRST 750 DISCHARGES FROM THE DEPARTMENT).

Diagnosis.	Number.	Percentage
A.—"Concussion", from line... ...	81	10·8
B.—"Nervous breakdown" from line...	95	12·6
C.—"Neurosis," from base hospitals...	469	62·5
D.—Organic nervous disease	105	14·0
Total	750	99·9
Of these, insane ...	40	
mental defect	16	

TABLE 3.

OFFICERS—PROPORTION OF " CONCUSSION " AND " NERVOUS BREAKDOWN " CASES ADMITTED DIRECT FROM THE LINE.

Diagnosis.	Number.	Percentage.
A.—"Concussion"	6	17·1
B.—"Nervous breakdown"	29	82·9
Total	35	100·0

TABLE 4.

ALL CASES ADMITTED FROM LINE—OFFICERS AND OTHER RANKS.

Diagnosis.				Number.	Percentage.
A.—"Concussion"	...	...	...	87	41·2
B.—"Nervous breakdown"	...	...		124	58·7
Total	...	...	...	211	99·9

TABLE 5.

COMPARISON OF PHYSICAL SIGNS IN CASES ADMITTED FROM THE LINE.

This Table indicates definite pathological changes in the cerebro-spinal fluid of concussion cases.

Cerebro-spinal Fluid.

Condition Tested.	Time after explosion or shock.	State of Fluid in Classes.	
		"Concussion" cases.	"Nervous breakdown."
Pressure	Early stages ...	Markedly raised ...	Slightly raised.
	Later stages ...	Increase is progressively less.	
Number of lymphocytes.	Less than 24 hours	Increased in 87 per cent. cases (8 fluids).	No increase (4 fluids).
	24–48 hours ...	Increased in 14 per cent. cases (23 fluids).	No increase (8 fluids).
	48 hours and more	Increase is rare (25 fluids).	No increase (14 fluids).
Albumen and globulins.	Less than 24 hours (excess "marked").	Increased in 40 per cent. cases.	No increase.
	24–48 hours ("marked" or "moderate").	Increased in 65 per cent. cases.	No increase.
	48–72 hours ...	Increased in 64 per cent. cases.	"Slight" excess (rare).
	72 hours and more (excess "slight").	Increased in 22 per cent. cases.	No increase.
Number of cases in which records of lumbar puncture extant.		56	26

Note.—The incidence of increased number of lymphocytes appears to be raised in the earliest cases, and thereafter gradually to fall; that of increased albumen and globulins seems to rise to a maximum in the second and third period of 24 hours after the explosion, but the *degree* of increase falls steadily from the earliest period.

TABLE 6.

COMPARISON OF PHYSICAL SIGNS IN CASES ADMITTED FROM THE LINE.

This Table shows that the Tendon reflexes in concussion cases, are more *depressed* in the first 24 hours after an explosion, and more *exaggerated* in the 4th period of 48 hours, thereafter again receding to normal excitability.

Reflexes.

Reflex.	Hours after Explosion.	Percentage of Cases in Classes.					
		"Concussion" (78 cases).			"Nervous breakdown" (94 cases).		
		Excitability.			Excitability.		
		In-creased.	Normal.	De-creased.	In-creased.	Normal.	De-creased.
Abdominal Tendon ...		8 18	78 58	14 24	— 8	— 85	4 7
Number of cases.							
8... ...	24 and less...	—	62·5	37·5	—	—	—
25... ...	24–48 ...	8	52	40	—	—	—
23... ...	48–72 ...	22	52	26	—	—	—
10... ...	72–96 ...	40	60	—	—	—	—
12... ...	96 and more	25	75	—	—	—	—

TABLE 7.

This Table shows a much greater incidence of derangement of co-ordination (the first four defects) and of true nystagmus in concussion than in nervous breakdown cases. The occurrence of these defects seems to point to a cerebellar derangement in consequence of the concussion.

Co-ordination.

Defect.	Percentage of cases in classes.	
	"Concussion" (78 cases).	"Nervous breakdown" (94 cases).
Deviation in pointing	41	9
Dysdiadochokinesis	29	9
Dysmetria	18	3
Asynergia	11	5
Nystagmoid, jerking, eyes	25	22
True nystagmus, eyes	5	0
Tremor	78	84

TABLE 8.

COMPARISON OF PHYSICAL SIGNS IN CASES ADMITTED FROM THE LINE.

This Table does not point to any great difference between the two classes—save perhaps in the matter of ocular convergence.

Signs of Hyperthyroidism.

	Percentage of cases with the sign in the left-hand column, in classes.	
Sign.	" Concussion " (78 cases).	" Nervous breakdown " (94 cases).
Dilatation of pupils	19	20
Defective convergence, eyes	32	25
v. Graefe's sign	12	15
Widening palpebral fissure	1	4
Exopthalmos	0	3
Thyroid gland enlarged	4	3

TABLE 9.

COMPARISON OF AVERAGE AGE, CIVIL STATE, AND RANK IN CASES (" OTHER RANKS ") ADMITTED DIRECT FROM THE LINE.

This Table shows some interesting differences between the two classes.

	Average of percentage in classes.	
Peculiarity.	" Concussion " (78 cases).	" Nervous breakdown " (94 cases).
Average age, in years	26·3	28·6
Percentage of married men in class ...	30·7	37·8
Percentage of N.C.Os. above L/Cpl. in rank	12·8	7·5
Percentage of L/Cpls. in class... ...	7·6	6·3

Note.—A. The nervous breakdown case is (on an average) older than the concussion case. If concussion is " accidental " this difference points to the greater liability of older men to break down.

B. In the same way, married men would appear to be more liable to break down. But this may mean merely that the older man is more likely to be married (or, conversely, that the married man is older on an average). The Table does not really indicate which factor (age or married state) influences breakdown. Both factors may do so.

C. The *smaller* percentage of the higher ranks of N.C.O.s in the nervous breakdown class suggests that responsible position (which may be lost by breakdown) acts against the occurrence of breakdown.

D. But where the position is under any circumstances easily lost and regained (L/Cpls.), it has apparently little effect one way or the other, although it may have a slight influence.

E. These figures for rank are all the more striking when it is remembered that N.C.O.s of higher rank are usually *older* than the average soldier.

TABLE 10.

EXAMINATION OF "NORMAL" SOLDIERS IN THE LINE (147 INDIVIDUALS) AND OF SOLDIERS ABOUT TO COME UNDER FIRE FOR THE FIRST TIME (58 INDIVIDUALS).

This Table shows differences between men under fire and men about to come under fire.

Sign.	Percentage of men who shewed the sign in the left-hand column, in— Platoons.	New draft.
Tremor	55	40
v. Graefe, a, "present"	9	3
v. Graefe, b, "marked"	4	0
Thyroid enlarged (slightly) ...	16	7
Exophthalmos	14	?
Palpitation...	10	19
Nightmares ("shells")	5	17
Broken sleep	11	31
Talking, etc., in sleep	11	?
Sores ("I.C.T.")*	42	
Average age (years) ...	26	28

TABLE 11.

"NORMAL" SOLDIERS UNDER FIRE (142 INDIVIDUALS).

Sign.	Percentage of men in the platoons who shewed the sign in the left-hand column : the men taken in age groups. Years—					
	19–20.	20–23.	23–26.	26–31.	31–36.	36.
Tremor	45	40.	56	58	80	64
v. Graefe (a and b)	18	16	6	—	16	27
Thyroid enlarged (slightly) ...	18	26	23	5	5	4
Exophthalmos	18	12	6	30	16	18
Palpitation	9	5	15	12	10	18
Nightmares ("shells")	—	2	3	8	10	27
Broken sleep...	9	7	6	5	21	18
Talking and shouting in sleep ...	9	5	9	21	16	18
Sores (I.C.T.)*	36	37	44	46	47	54
Number in group	11	43	34	24	19	11

(TABLE 10) *Note.*—The men actually under fire show a markedly greater incidence of positive signs associated with hyperthyroidism. The men about to come under fire for the first time show markedly greater incidence of palpitation, nightmare, and broken sleep.

(TABLE 11) *Note.*—Soldiers under fire only. The incidence of Tremor, palpitation, sores, nightmare, talking in sleep (and perhaps broken sleep also), all rise with increasing age. That of Thyroid enlargement falls. Those of v. Graefe's sign and Exophthalmos fall and then rise again, there apparently being two maxima.

This Table *suggests* that the positive signs of v. Graefe Thyroid enlargement and Exophthalmos are closely connected in one group; and that the Tremor, palpitation and dreaming, etc., are connected in another group; and, further, that the two groups are to a certain extent independent.

---

* Inflammation Connective Tissue.

APPENDIX No. 3.

PRINCIPLES OF TRAINING.

A.—Concentration of mind.
B.—Training to be natural.
C.—Training to be continuous.
D.—Selection, care, etc., instructors.

A.—Concentration of Mind.

1. *Intensity of Purpose.*

Victory is gained by the army with the greatest intensity of purpose. Intensity of purpose is a form of will-power. Will-power is the driving force, the determination to get there. Will-power is also the controlling force which keeps men calm and collected when shells are bursting. The will-power—the driving and controlling force—of an army depends upon the will-power of the individuals of which that army is composed.

Will-power can be developed, just as muscular strength can be increased. Every time a muscle is exercised it is strengthened; every time an effort of will is made the will-power is increased.

2. *Development of will-power.*

In men of action, the movement of the muscles reflects the character of the brain. Quick decided movements indicate an alert controlling brain. Slack movements indicate a slack brain, lack of will-power, no driving force. Rapid and vigorous muscular action is the response to quick and complete concentration of mind. Concentration of mind requires an effort of will. Mind, will, muscles, all alike are developed by exercise, so that every effort of will makes for increased will-power, just as every concentration of mind makes for increased brain-power.

3. *Effect of Concentration.*

The effect of mental concentration is not usually fully realised. A few seconds of concentration make a lasting impression on the brain. If you want to get up early in the morning what do you do? Think hard about it—concentrate upon it—before going to sleep with the result that you wake up early. This happens after concentrating only once and for a few seconds. If you concentrate every night for a few weeks you will form the habit of waking early every morning. So it is with training. Make men concentrate upon it and maintain that concentration. By so during their will-power will be increased. Their brains, accustomed during training to concentrate instantly and thoroughly, through sheer force of habit, will do the same during the mental and physical disturbance of battle. No training can be of lasting value which is performed carelessly and which lacks the necessary mental concentration. Will, decision, and the power of concentration are among the essential characteristics of leadership. Without them a man is mentally flabby, undecided, incapable of assimilating and imparting knowledge, and utterly useless as an instructor or leader, however subordinate.

4. *Action of brain upon muscles.*

The muscles are directed and controlled by the brain. The brain is the C.O., and the muscles the men under him. If a General wants a unit to carry out a movement, he orders it through the C.O. He would never ignore the C.O. and direct the men himself. If he did, it would mean that his army could work only when he was present and able to direct. He must train his C.O.s to direct, and upon their training will depend the interpretation and execution of his orders. So it is with the squad. The instructor is the General; the brains of his squad are his C.O.s. If an instructor does not compel each man in the squad to use his brain he will be in the same position as the General who decided to do without his Commanding Officers. While the instructor is present, the men of his squad will follow his direction. But he has failed to develop their brains, their initiative, their will-power, their faculty for mental grasp and concentration. When the time comes that they must think and act for themselves, their brains are undeveloped, their muscles will be without a Commanding Officer, and they will be almost entirely useless.

5. *Mental Effort harder than Physical.*

It is harder to make a mental effort than it is to make a physical effort. The great task in getting out of bed is not the physical action of rising, but the mental effort of making up one's mind to do so. The instructor, therefore, must expect a heavy strain upon his will-power and nervous energy, especially with a new class, when he endeavours to make each man put his whole mind into his work, use his own will-power, and not merely work mechanically and without concentration. The class must be trained to make the mental effort, to compel the C.O. (their own brains) to direct their men (their own physical activities) and not leave them to rely upon the personal direction of their General (the instructor).

6. *Influence of perception.*

The mind is influenced in some degree by everything it perceives. A squad, in time, will reflect the character of its instructor, in much the same way as the physical movements of a man reflect the character of his brain. If the instructor is slow of thought, undecided, lacking in driving power, he will convert a good squad into a bad one. If he is quick, alert, virile, full of tact and of compelling energy, he may raise a poor squad almost to his own level. "An army of stags led by a lion is better than an army of lions led by a stag." It is the power of personality of the instructor which builds the character of his squad, which develops their will power, which are projected from him into them, and which compel them to concentrate all their mental energy upon their work.

7. *Method of Inducing Concentration.*

To induce men to concentrate their minds upon their work, first win their sympathy by studying their temperament and their moods, and by catching and holding their interests. Be solicitous for their welfare. Make them like you and make them like their work. Then they will pull with you and not against you. Sympathy flames into enthusiasm. The enthusiasm of a class will react upon the instructor and endow him with increased power.

Let the men understand and see what they are doing. Give them a goal to strive for and an object to keep in view. Let them see for themselves the result of their efforts.

8. *Necessity for Variety.*

Introduce variety into their work. Rest is change of occupation. The brain cannot concentrate for any length of time upon one particular subject any more than one particular set of muscles can be exercised indefinitely. The strain is too severe. Fatigue follows, and with fatigue comes lassitude and loss of interest. The P.T. Tables are arranged so that no one set of muscles shall be subjected to prolonged and persistent strain. The sequence of exercises changes the strain from group to group, prevents local fatigue and stimulates the whole physical frame. Mental exercises must be arranged with the same idea of relief. It is monotony which dulls and tires the brain. It is change of work, of subject, by which the brain is rested and stimulated.

9. *Methods in detail of obtaining Concentration.*

What to do.	How to do it.	What not to do.
1. Gain the sympathy of the class.	1. Study temperament, mood, conditions of life &c. of members of the class. 2. Learn to know each individual's characteristics. 3. Ascertain previous occupations, training &c. 4. Study comfort, provide suitable clothing, work indoors in bad weather.	1. Treat all men as " sealed pattern goods " with one form of training for all. 2. Set slow exercises in cold and windy weather. 3. Carry out training in deep mud, wet weather, &c. 4. Work in tight clothing.
2. Interest the class ...	1. Give simple reasons for the training. 2. Introduce anecdotes and humour. 3. Explain by illustration. 4. Encourage. 5. Arrange short crisp spells of work. 6. Keep away counter attractions. 7. Hold competitions.	1. Talk too much. 2. Rag or bully. 3. Ridicule by cheap or offensive wit. 4. Expect perfection at once. 5. Find fault too frequently. 6. Worry over unnecessary detail. 7. Spend too much time on one subject.
3. Class must concentrate on work—make mental effort.	1. Cut down detail to minimum. 2. Use question and answer. 3. Explain by illustration—work eye and brain. 4. Stir up passions, patriotism, hatred, &c. 5. Work with teeth clenched and muscles contracted. 6. By controlled charges. 7. By " Master and Pupil ". 8. By quickening exercises and movements. 9. Vary words of command. 10. Hold competitions.	1. Repeat details too often. 2. Handle men and put them into positions. 3. Keep class too long at one practice.
4. Work with an objective.	1. Train with a definite purpose. 2. Arrange training so that men can see and correct their faults. 3. Let them see result of their efforts by means of targets, discs, parry-stick, &c. 4. *Work by result and not by time.* 5. Hold competitions.	1. Work to kill time. 2. Work only by word of command. 3. Leave results to the imagination, i.e. have imaginary targets, &c.

What to do.	How to do it.	What not to do.
5. Variety.	1. Change words of command.	1. Give long-winded detail in unchanging monotone.
	2. Move yourself ; put action and acticity into your explanations.	2. Keep to sterotype assault courses and practices.
	3. Change scenery.	
	4. Vary practices.	3. Give lifeless illustrations.
	5. Vary ground.	
	6. Vary work.	

B.—TRAINING TO BE NATURAL.

1. *Fighting limited by the human element.*

Warfare is based upon and limited by the human factor, by the bodies and brains of men. Its results depend upon the manner in which their bodies endure the hardships of war and the exertion of battle, and upon the manner in which their minds bear the strain of war and make the superhuman effort which battle demands. Body and mind, therefore, must be trained to withstand and accustom themselves to the conditions which war and battle produce.

In battle a man has to think and act for himself—to think without other guidance than his own, to act on instantaneous appreciation of a situation. He must be trained to use eye, brain, and muscle in concert. In battle a man gets "rattled," but discipline and self-control will steady him. Discipline is the outcome of the training of the mind; self-control is the product of will-power.

2. *Training must conform to War.*

In games we train by practising the game itself. In training for war it is not possible to practise war; but the conditions attending training—the atmosphere, the environment of training—must be natural, must approach as nearly as possible to the actual conditions of war. Remember, it is training that must conform to battle; battle will not conform to training. While training must be made to conform to battle, at the same time tactical principles must be studied and strictly adhered to.

3. *Purpose of War.*

Create the atmosphere of war by instilling into men a knowledge of the purpose and the goal of war. The purpose of war is to kill, the object of killing—the goal of war—is victory. War is a killing match. Every Bosche killed is a point scored. The army which scores the most points wins the match. Peace implies for one side, victory; for the other, defeat. The task in hand is to kill another million Bosches. That is a tangible goal; that is victory; that is peace. Every Bosche brings peace a minute nearer.

4. *Man fights as he trains.*

A man will fight as he trains. If he trains without a purpose, he will fight without a purpose, and he will get out of the battle at the first possible opportunity. If he trains with the purpose of killing, he will fight in battle with the determination to kill.

5. *Development of endurance and self-control.*

During training, the more often and more nearly that a soldier can be worked to the abnormal physical and mental state, produced by the stress of battle, the better his powers of endurance and self-control will be developed. Self-control cannot be developed in the absence of emotions needing control. Endurance cannot be practised when there is nothing to endure. Endurance is a product of will-power combined with physical fitness; so men must be made as physically fit as possible, trained to physical fitness as they are trained in games.

6. *Man power and killing power.*

Killing power, not man power, wins a war. A man merely dressed in uniform and hurried into battle decreases rather than increases the power of an army. Every weapon is made for one purpose—to kill. He does not know his weapon; he is incapable; he has no confidence in himself. His incapacity and distrust are contagious. He lowers the morale of others wherever he goes. If he does not get killed or wounded, he goes sick. He lessens the man power as well as the killing power, for other men have to look after him. Before he can be of use he has to acquire killing power, to be trained in the use of his weapon, to gain self-control and the power of endurance. Man power is only converted into killing power by training.

7. *Method in detail of training on Natural Lines.*

What to do.	How to do it.	What not to do.
1. Impart discipline and self-control.	1. Have clothes, kit, apparatus, etc. put away tidily.	1. Tolerate sloppy drill movements.
	2. Have mental effort with every movement, drill or otherwise.	2. Allow pointing at imaginary targets.
	3. Make class " see red."	3. Allow wild charges.
	4. By pointing at fixed marks, discs, etc.	4. Make charging distance too long.
	5. By controlled charges.	5. Allow blind and rapid firing.
	6. By fire control after charging.	
	7. By cool, deliberate firing after charges.	
	8. Vary position of dummies, targets, etc.	
	9. Vary range and targets.	
2. Train eye and brain.	1. Give reasons for orders.	1. Work by word of command, and train by ear.
	2. Teach by illustration.	
	3. Ask questions.	
	4. Practise Master and Pupil.	2. Repeat detail when once it is understood.
	5. Aim at some definite object.	3. Ignore the principle of variety.
	6. Vary schemes.	4. Allow pointing etc. at no named target.
	7. Give quickening practices and exercises.	
3. Produce physical fitness.	1. By controlled charges and movement.	1. Train without movement.
	2. By quickening practices.	2. Countenance lack of vigour and dash in work.
	3. By " Mad Minute."	
	4. By vigour in pointing and parrying.	
4. Introduce natural conditions	1. Stir up desire to kill.	1. Make stereotyped assault courses.
	2. Use bullet and bayonet after charge.	2. Allow training to become spiritless and mechanical.
	3. Keep assault course natural, with trenches dug-outs, houses, street-fighting, and "night and day."	3. Concentrate solely on the bayonet.
	4. Make dummies life-like.	
	5. Train with gas masks, helmets, etc.	
	6. Combine all arms in assault scheme.	

What to do.	How to do it.	What not to do.
5. Practise tactical principles.	1. With control. 2. With movement and protection. 3. With mutual support. 4. Have assault schemes with practice in special uses of various weapons employed.	1. Allow wild uncontrolled charges. 2. Go over assault Courses with no definite scheme.

C.—CONTINUITY IN TRAINING.

1. *Creation of Morale.*

Training must be continuous. The more a man is trained the more skilful he becomes; the more skilful he becomes, the more his confidence increases. If a man knows he can do a thing well, he develops confidence in himself. If he knows that his comrades are equally skilful, he gains confidence in them. His confidence is multiplied. Confidence is both contagious and inspiring.

What is morale? Morale is confidence in one's self and confidence in one's comrades. It is collective confidence, the spirit of a good team at football. Morale can be, and has to be, created. It is the product of continuous and enthusiastic training.

2. *Product of continuous training.*

The more a man trains his eye and brain and muscle, the better they work together, until in time they combine spontaneously, by reflex action, or what is commonly called second nature. A man's brain should be so trained that in battle it is impelled to do the correct thing naturally, almost automatically and without effort. This stage is reached only by careful and continuous training.

3. *Simplicity in training.*

Training, in order to be continuous, must be simple. The methods of instruction must be simple, and little or no apparatus needed, so that the training may be carried on anywhere and by anybody. Training which can be carried out alone by highly trained specialists is doomed in war time. Training which required a quantity of elaborate apparatus is doomed also. Training which can be carried out only in watertight compartments and cannot be combined with its kindred branches of training is unnatural and signs its own death warrant.

4. *Unity in training.*

Success in battle depends upon how much and how well one type of weapon helps another, on mutual support, on "good team work." So it must be in training. One branch of training must work with and help the others, not work against them or run them down.

5. *Keynote of all training.*

The greatest force in an army is the private soldier. Get him to train himself and you have solved the whole problem of training. The keynote of all training, therefore, should be simplicity, so that a man may train himself. A man fights as he trains, if he trains by himself, he will fight by himself. Make training so simple that during some portion of the training hour men can be paired off, on the master and pupil system, to train each other.

6. *Spirit of training.*

Induce men, by every means possible, to train each other, not only during parade hours, but out of parade hours, as well. Create the voluntary spirit, the spirit of individual effort, and you will kindle an unconquerable spirit throughout the Army. Ten minutes' voluntary training during a man's leisure time is worth ten hours' compulsory training during work hours. The value of training lies not in the amount done but in the spirit in which it is done.

7. *Detailed methods of ensuring continuity of training.*

What to do.	How to do it.	What not to do.
1. Ensure simplicity ...	1. Teach simple methods of attack and defence. 2. Train by eye and brain. 3. Improvise Courses, targets, dummies, &c. 4. Carry out short practices at any time and place. 5. Train in any confined space during bad weather.	1. Employ elaborate K.O. methods. 2. Give elaborate detail. 3. Use unnatural words of command.
2. Enable all officers and N.C.Os. to train men under them.	1. Employ simple methods. 2. Hold competitions.	1. Leave training to specialists.
3. Get men to train each other.	1. Use simple methods. 2. Make men like the training. 3. By competitions. 4. By master and pupil. 5. By setting aside portion of parade hours during which men can train each other. 6. Make men understand that they themselves are the most important factor in training.	1. Make parade times too long. 2. Use unnatural words of command. 3. Look upon training solely as specialists' work.
4. Combined with other training.	1. Combine bayonet and bullet practices. 2. Combine bayonet and bomb practices. 3. Use bayonet training to assist in training men for firing.	1. Exploit the bayonet at the expense of other arms.
5. Arrange competitions.	1. By individual competitions with training stick. 2. By individual competitions on assault and tin ring courses. 3. By team competitions. 4. By A.R.A. competitions.	1. Make competition too elaborate.

D.—Selection, Care and Reinvigoration of Instructors.

1. *Selection of Instructors.*

The greatest care and discrimination must be exercised in creating and selecting an instructor, for upon the instructor depends the final efficiency of the classes he may teach. Consciously or unconsciously, he will project his own characteristics, his own personality, into the class. A " dud " will turn out " duds," a " live wire " will turn out " live wires." For our games we carefully select the best possible men to act as coaches and trainers. How much more important is it to select only the best when appointing instructors for training in warfare? We must select the best for it as they alone who will create and develop the power which will win the war.

2. Qualities of Instructors.

To be successful, an instructor must :—
1. Have a thorough practical knowledge of his subject.
2. Be endowed with imagination.
3. Be broad-minded and enthusiastic.
4. Be adaptable and open-minded with regard to methods.
5. Be full of nervous energy.
6. Have a knowledge of, and sympathy with, human nature.
7. Have a pleasing and winning personality.

3. Nervous Expenditure of Instructor.

The work of influencing and enthusing a class places a great nervous strain upon the instructor. It requires a big mental effort and great mental concentration to catch and hold the interest of each man in a class, and an even bigger expenditure of nervous energy to make all respond to the stimulus of instruction, and evince enthusiasm for the subject taught. An instructor, therefore, is continually expending nervous force, and is getting practically nothing back in return.

4. Limitations of Nervous Expenditure.

Enthusiasm may be sustained by encouragement from superiors and by the reflected enthusiasm of a class; but if the best is to be obtained from an instructor he must be given time and opportunity to make good the wastage brought about by periods of intense and concentrated physical and mental effort.

If he is to work with his class at " live wire " pitch, he must not be kept at that pitch perpetually. The strain upon brain and nerve must be watched and considered, and opportunity afforded to slacken the strain, and to renew the nervous energy which has been expended. Once an instructor loses his vital driving force—his compelling power, and gets " below par," it is difficult to revitalize him and to restore his personal magnetism.

5. Necessity for Renewal.

Among the earliest lessons an instructor learns is the necessity to study his class as individuals, and to treat his students with consideration. The good instructor—the real instructor—does study his men, and never dreams of overworking them or of making them stale. If it is essential that the class should not be overtired, it is even more imperative that the instructor should retain or renew his freshness. For not only must the stale instructor eventually reach the breaking point, but before he arrives at that stage he will have bored more than one class with his futile efforts to call up reserve energy which he has already expended, and will have succeeded in making them almost as lifeless as himself.

6. Symptoms of Over-work.

Overwork affects both mind and body. Its effects are seen first in lack of vitality and want of interest, which develop later into positive dislike for the training; or in nervous exhaustion, the symptoms of which frequently are intense irritability, lack of self control, lethargy of action, incapacity for sustained thought, and repugnance to companionship. Instructors of nervous temperament who are compelled by this very temperament to put abnormal energy into their work may be permanently impaired by overwork and its consequence. Cases are known in which instructors of this type have been rendered temporarily insane by inconsiderate treatment and because timely opportunity for recuperation has not been afforded.

7. Consideration for Instructor.

In framing a syllabus the first consideration should be given to the instructor, for it is upon him that the greatest strain must fall. If only from the necessity to economise man power he must not be allowed to expend himself recklessly. Each hour during a day and each day during a course must be carefully considered and allotted. Variety in plenty and proper periods of rest must be arranged in the daily routine, and regular holidays and breaks provided during the course. For, while it is possible to put on pressure for a short spell, that pressure cannot be maintained during a whole course. Remember that you cannot run three miles at hundred yards' pace. Frequent short spells of rest are better than a longer rest after a sustained effort of work.

8. Recuperative Course.

After each course of three weeks, there should follow a recuperative course for instructors of from five to seven days. It should be utilised as a rest for the brain and for the methodical restoration of the nervous tissue. Rest does not imply idleness; quite the opposite, for the best rest and the best restorative are change of occupation and change of environment. Environment and occupation can both be diametrically changed under a scheme of training which is the direct antithesis of the training that the instructor has taught and practised during the ordinary course.

9. Change of Occupation.

He has been a teacher; make him a pupil. He has been teaching destruction, the practise of war, the art of killing. Reverse the procedure. Let him practise construction, and the arts of peace. Let him practise building, carpentering, gardening, stock raising. Give him an allotment. Set him to work among the farm stock and poultry. Awaken and stimulate his interest in this work. He may at first be adverse from the new employment and the new environment, for a feature of nervous exhaustion is the persistence .with which its victim insists upon attempting to " carry on."

10. Awakening new interests.

By example and interest his officers may induce him to transfer his interest to these more peaceful pursuits. By awakening the competitive spirit—offering small prizes for best carpentry, best allotment, best stock, best produce—the interest may be sustained. The instructor is a citizen as well as a soldier. By showing the benefit which a knowledge of these avocations will confer when the war is ended and the various land settlement schemes are in practice, he may be induced to retain his interest even during the course which follows. By so doing he may evolve for himself many recreative periods during the ordinary course, and thereby lessen the nervous exhaustion of that and subsequent courses.

11. Restoration of Nervous Energy.

Working during the recuperative course at these more peaceful pursuits. the instructor, either by environment or by force of association, will recall home and pleasant surroundings, will gradually forget the problems and the pressure which have contributed to his exhaustion, and unconsciously will imbibe new mental strength and new nervous energy.

The process may be materially assisted by the provision of lectures upon matters of interest, by concerts and musical entertainments, by dances, by cinematographs and by any other means that will divert the mind from the work it has been concentrating upon, and allow it to think and reason upon other subjects whose oppositeness affords the variety and relief which are needed.

12. *Value of Recuperative Course.*

Properly arranged and properly organized recuperative courses will serve to revitalize the instructor and will send him back to his ordinary duties, with brain rested and nerve restored, "full of beans," and once more up to the "live wire" standard.

APPENDIX No. 4.

WITNESSES WHO GAVE EVIDENCE BEFORE THE COMMITTEE.

1. Gordon Holmes, Esq., C.M.G., C.B.E., B.A., M.D., F.R.C.P.
   Late Consultant Neurologist, British Armies in France.
   Physician, National Hospital for Paralysis and Epilepsy.
2. Lieut.-Colonel H. Clay, C.B.E., D.C.M.
   Chief Recruiting Staff Officer, London District.
3. Surgeon Commander J. Boyan, R.N., M.R.C.S., L.R.C.P.
   Naval Recruiting Depot.
4. William Brown, Esq., M.A., M.D.
   Late Neurologist, 4th and 5th Armies, France.
   Reader in Psychology, Oxford University.
5. General Sir H. S. Jeudwine, K.C.B.
   Late General Officer Commanding 55th Division, France.
6. Sir James Galloway, K.B.E., C.B., M.A., LL.D., F.R.C.P.
   Late Chief Commissioner Medical Services, Ministry of National Service.
   Late Consulting Physician, 1st and 2nd Armies, France.
   Senior Physician, Charing Cross Hospital.
7. Brevet Colonel J. L. G. Burnett, C.M.G., D.S.O.
   1st Gordon Highlanders.
8. Lieut.-Colonel A. A. Goschen, D.S.O.
   Royal Artillery.
9. G. Scott-Jackson, Esq., C.B.E., D.S.O., M.D.
   Late Officer Commanding Territorial Force Battalion, Northumberland Fusiliers.
10. Brevet Colonel G. C. Stubbs, D.S.O.
    1st Suffolk Regiment.
11. Brevet Lieut.-Colonel Viscount Gort, V.C., D.S.O., M.V.O., M.C.
    Grenadier Guards.
12. Major-General Sir A. W. L. Bayly, K.C.B., K.C.M.G., C.S.I., D.S.O.
    Late Inspector of temporary non-effectives.
13. Lieut.-Colonel J. S. Y. Rogers, C.B.E., D.S.O., M.D., C.M.
    Royal Army Medical Corps (Territorial Force).
    Late Regimental Medical Officer, 4th Battalion, Black Watch.
14. Henry Head, Esq., M.D., F.R.C.P., F.R.S.
    Consultant Physician, London Hospital, late Neurologist Royal Air Force Hospital, Hampstead.
15. R. G. Rows, Esq., C.B.E., M.D., D.Sc.
    Director of Section for Mental Illnesses, Neurological Hospital, Tooting.
16. Professor T. R. Elliott, C.B.E., D.S.O., M.A.. M.D., F.R.S.
    Late Consultant Physician, British Armies in France.
    Professor of Medicine, University College, London.

17. Colonel A. B. Soltau, C.M.G., C.B.E., M.D., F.R.C.S., M.R.C.P.
    Army Medical Service, Territorial Force.
    Late Consultant Physician for Gas Cases, British Armies in
        France.
    Consultant Physician for Gas Cases, Ministry of Pensions.
18. E. Farquhar Buzzard, Esq., M.A., M.D., F.R.C.P.
    Physician, St. Thomas' Hospital.
19. C. M. Wilson, Esq., M.D., M.R.C.P.
    Physician, St. Mary's Hospital.
    Late Regimental Medical Officer.
20. J. I. C. Dunn, Esq., D.S.O., M.C., D.C.M., M.D., D.P.H.
    Served in ranks during South African War and as Regimental
        Medical Officer in the Great War.
21. Squadron Leader W. Tyrrell, D.S.O., M.C.
    Medical Service, Royal Air Force.
22. F. A. Hampton, Esq., M.C., M.B.
    Physician to Hospital for Epileptics, Maida Vale.
    Late Regimental and Royal Air Force Medical Officer.
23. W. H. R. Rivers, Esq., M.A., M.D., F.R.C.P., LL.D.
    Praelector in Natural Science, St. John's College, Cambridge.
    Late Consultant in Psychological Medicine, Royal Air Force.
24. Captain F. E. Hotblack, D.S.O., M.C.
    Tank Corps. Staff College, Camberley.
25. Bernard Hart, Esq., M.D.
    Physician, Mental Diseases, University College Hospital.
26. Spencer Hurlbutt, Esq., M.R.C.S., L.R.C.P.
    Late Recruiting Medical Officer and Deputy Commissioner of
        Medical Services, Ministry of Natural Science.
27. W. Johnson, Esq., M.C., M.D., M.R.C.P.
    Physician, Royal Southern Hospital, Liverpool.
    Late Neurologist with British Armies in France.
28. Lieut.-Colonel R. B. Campbell, D.S.O.
    Inspector of Physical Training, Aldershot Command.
29. Professor Graham Brown, D.Sc., M.D.
    Professor of Physiology, University of South Wales.
    Late Neurologist, British Salonica Force.
30. Captain R. Gee, V.C., M.C., M.P.
    Late Royal Fusiliers.
31. Major Dowson, O.B.E.
    Barrister-at-Law.
32. Colonel Fuller, D.S.O.
    Deputy Director of Staff Duties (Training).
    Late General Staff Officer, Tank Corps.
33. E. Mapother, Esq., M.D., F.R.C.S., M.R.C.P.
    Medical Superintendent, Maudsley Neurological Hospital.
34. A. F. Hurst, Esq., M.D., F.R.C.P.
    Physician, Nervous Diseases, Guys' Hospital.
    Late Officer-in-Charge, Neurological Hospital, Seale Hayne.
35. F. Burton Fanning, Esq., M.D., F.R.C.P.
36. Geoffrey Clarke, Esq., M.D.
    Medical Superintendent, County of London Mental Hospital,
        Bexley.
37. C. Stanford Read, Esq., M.D.
    Late Officer-in-Charge, " D " Block, Royal Victoria Hospital,
        Netley, and Neurological and Mental Specialist, Ministry
        of Pensions.
38. Professor G. Roussy.
    Faculté de Médicine de Paris.
    Late Consultant in Neurology to the French Army.
39. Lieut.-Colonel J. Allison, M.B., D.P.H.
    Royal Army Medical Corps, Territorial Force.

40. Commander N. D. Holbrook, V.C., Royal Navy.
    Late Submarine Commander.
41. Major P. E. Longmore, 1st Battalion, Hertfordshire Regiment.
    Barrister-at-Law.
42. Lieut.-Colonel E. Hewlett, C.M.G., D.S.O.
    Late Inspector of Infantry Training.
43. Major W. J. Adie, M.D., M.R.C.P., Royal Army Medical Corps (S.R.).
    Physician, Great Northern Central Hospital.
    Medical Registrar, Charing Cross Hospital.
    Neurologist, Ministry of Pensions.
44. General Lord Horne, G.C.B., K.C.M.G.
    General Officer Commanding, Eastern Command.
    Late General Officer Commanding, 1st Army in France.
45. Lieut.-Colonel E. C. S. Jervis, D.S.O.
    Late 5th Lancers and Machine Gun Corps.
46. Major-General Sir B. E. W. Childs, K.C.M.G., K.B.E., C.B.
    Late Deputy Adjutant-General and Director of Personal Services,
        War Office.
47. Miss Cockerell, R.R.C.
    Late Matron, Maudsley Neurological Hospital.
48. Major W. Brook Purdon, D.S.O., M.C., M.B.
    Royal Army Medical Corps.
49. Lieut.-Colonel C. R. Sylvester-Bradley, M.R.C.S., L.R.C.P.
    Royal Army Medical Corps.
    Medical Inspector of Recruits, Eastern Command.
50. L. C. Bruce, Esq., M.C., M.D., F.R.C.P.
    Medical Superintendent, Perth District Asylum.
    Late Lieut.-Colonel Royal Army Medical Corps.
51. Major Pritchard Taylor, D.S.O., M.C., M.B.
    Royal Army Medical Corps.
52. Air Vice-Marshal Sir J. M. Salmond, K.C.M.G., C.B., D.S.O.
    Royal Air Force.
53. Squadron Leader E. H. Johnston, O.B.E.
    Royal Air Force.
54. Squadron Leader E. W. Craig, M.B.
    Royal Air Force, Medical Service.
55. Lieut.-General Sir T. H. J. C. Goodwin, K.C.B., C.M.G., D.S.O.,
    F.R.C.S.
    Director-General, Army Medical Service.
56. Mr. A. J. Bradbeer ⎞
57. Mr. Chas. Willis ⎟ Patients under the care of Ministry of
58. Mr. H. Callister ⎟ Pensions who suffered from war
59. Mr. G. T. Griggs ⎠ neurosis.

APPENDIX No. 5.

BIBLIOGRAPHY OF FOREIGN LITERATURE TO WHICH REFERENCE IS MADE IN THE RESUMÉ OF OPINIONS OF FOREIGN NEUROLOGISTS.

Aschaffenburg. Quoted by Bonhoeffer, *vide infra.*
Babinski. Revue Neurologique, November-December, 1916. Neurologie
    de Guerre.
Babinsky et J. Froment Hysterie-Pithiatisme. Collection Horizon.
Bing, Robert. Opinions Allemandes sur les Accidents Nerveux déterminés
    par l'Explosions du Projectile à proximité. Schweizer Arch. f. Neurol.
    u. Psychiat. Bändl. Heft. 2.

Bonhoeffer. Die Dienstbeschädigungsfrage in der Psychopathologie. *Die Militärärztliche Sachsverstandigentätigkeit auf dem Gebiete des Ersatzwesens und der Militärischen Versorgung.* Erste Teil, Jena. Fischer, 1917.

Claude, H. Revue Neurologique, November-December, 1916. Neurologie de Guerre.

Claude, H. Dide et Lejonne. Psychoses Hystéro-émotives de Guerre. Paris Medical, 7th October, 1916.

Crile, G. W. The Kinetic Drive. Wesley Carpenter Lecture. New York Academy of Medicine, 1915.

Dupré, M. E. Psychoses de Guerre. Revue Neurologique, November-December, 1916. Neurologie de Guerre.

Gaupp, R. Die Dienstbrauchbarkeit der Epileptiker und Psychopathen. *Die Militärärztliche Sachsverständigentätigkeit auf dem Gebiete des Ersatzwesens und der Militärischen Versorgung.* Erste Teil, Jena. Fischer, 1917.

Gaupp, R. Neuroses following injuries in Warfare. Zeitschrift für die gesamte Neurologie und Psych. Orig. 34, 1916.

Laurent, Octave. La Guerre en Bulgarie et en Turquie. Paris, 1914.

Léri André. Revue Neurologique, November-December, 1916. Neurologie de Guerre.

Léri André. Commotions et Émotions de Guerre.

Mairet et Durante. Commotional Syndrome-Presse Médicale, June 15th, 1917.

Meige, Henri. Revue Neurologique, November-December, 1916. Neurologie de Guerre.

Piérre Marie. Revue Neurologique, November-December, 1916. Neurologie de Guerre.

Roussy Gustave et L'Hermitte. Psycho-Névroses de Guerre. Collection Horizon.

Stier, E. Dienstbeschädigung und Rentenversorgung bie Psychopathen. *Die Militärärztliche Sachsverständigentatigkeit auf dem Gebiete des Ersatzwesens und der Militärischen Versorgung.* Erste Teil, Jena. Fischer, 1917.

Wolfsohn, Captain J. W., M.R.C., U.S. Army. The Predisposing Factors of War Neurosis. Lancet, 3rd February, 1918.

Yerkes, Colonel R. M. Psychological Examining in the United States Army, Vol. XV., National Academy of Medicine.

Printed in Great Britain
by Amazon